AN IMPERFECT OCCUPATION

THE HISTORY OF MILITARY OCCUPATION

Edited by John Laband and Ian F W Beckett

AN IMPERFECT OCCUPATION

Enduring the South African War

JOHN BOJE

University of Illinois Press
URBANA, CHICAGO, AND SPRINGFIELD

Manufactured in the United States of America
C 5 4 3 2 1
∞ This book is printed on acid-free paper.

Some of the material used in this book has been used previously in three articles coauthored with Fransjohan Pretorius. The articles are "Of Gold and Iron: Boer Collaboration in the Winburg District," *South African Historical Journal* 63, no. 2 (2011): 277–94; "'Kent gij dat volk': The Anglo-Boer War and Afrikaner Identity in Postmodern Perspective," *Historia* 56, no. 2 (2011): 59–72; and "Black Resistance in the Free State during the Anglo-Boer War," *Historia* 58, no. 1 (2013): 1–17.

Library of Congress Cataloging-in-Publication Data
Boje, John.
An imperfect occupation : enduring the
South African war / John Boje.
pages cm. — (The history of military occupation)
ISBN 978-0-252-03956-0 (hardcover : alk. paper) —
ISBN 978-0-252-09765-2 (e-book)
1. South African War, 1899-1902,—Occupied territories. 2. Civil-military relations—South Africa—Winburg. 3. Civilians in war—South Africa—Winburg. 4. Winburg (South Africa)—History. I. Title. II. Series: History of military occupation.
DT1896.B66 2015
968.0481—dc23 2015013223

Contents

Preface

THIS IS A BOOK ABOUT THE Winburg district in the erstwhile Orange Free State at the time of the South African War (1899–1902) and how its residents experienced the tightening grip of British military occupation.

Why Winburg?

On a visit to Winburg some ten years ago, the unofficial guide, Stoffel van der Linde, showed me a metal post outside the municipal offices and said that it marked the central point of the Free State.[1] I doubt it somehow, but that post may serve as a metaphor for the centrality of Winburg in the history of the Free State, of its typicality as a microcosm of rural towns and districts throughout the Free State, and of its uniqueness in certain respects. It was here that more than a thousand Voortrekker wagons, bringing white settlers into the interior, concentrated in 1837. Winburg was the first town proclaimed in the Free State. It was the center of resistance during an earlier period of British rule, the Orange River Sovereignty (1845–54), and its famous sons included generals Koos de la Rey and A. P. Cronjé, as well as President M. T. Steyn. As a fairly cosmopolitan town, where English was widely spoken, amid a conservative, almost exclusively Afrikaans-speaking countryside, the town and district were typical of the Free State as a whole. Yet that solitary post may also speak of Winburg's uniqueness, for the Orange River Colony Volunteers, a Boer formation of the British army, flourished here, as did Bergh's Scouts, a black corps under Boer officers fighting on the side of the British.

Actually, my acquaintance with Winburg goes much further back. My four grandparents all came from the Winburg district and they had very different stories to tell—or, more commonly, not to tell—about enduring the South African War. My paternal grandfather, we used to say when we were children,

The ex-Tommy and his Boer bride: Charles Thorold and Louise Josephine Boje.

spent the war hiding under his bed. Where we got this story from I don't know, but he came from the Cape Colony and had to be careful. Colonials who involved themselves on the Boer side were guilty of treason and some were even executed. His wife spent time in the Winburg concentration camp, where she lost a son, my uncle Lukas, whom I never knew, and adopted an orphan girl, my aunt Joey, who later married a former British soldier. My maternal grandfather fought in the Winburg commando until the fall of Bloemfontein, when he opted out of the war. Afterward he was a POW in Simonstown, in contrast to his elder brother, who, according to his own account, gave the British a hard time on the battlefield and later gave his wife a hard time by refusing to return from exile in Bermuda, because that would entail acknowledging Edward VII as his lawful sovereign. For her part, my maternal grandmother spent many months on the open veld evading capture and internment. So at a time when the establishment discourse was of a homogenous nation fighting heroically to the bitter end, I enjoyed bewildered childhood intimations of a divisive, nasty, multifaceted war.

What I have set out to do in the following pages is to get away from the "grand narratives" so that the real voices of ordinary people might be heard, ordinary people like my grandparents, but also the disregarded black people of the Winburg district, articulating their varied responses to the complexities of living with invasion, gradual subjugation, and lingering occupation.

Many people have helped me in a variety of ways, in particular Anthony, Edward, and Ashley Boje; Roy and John Devenish; Pam Gebhard; Ingrid Booysen; Etna Labuschagne; and Peter Morey. I am grateful to them and to Albert Grundlingh, who allowed me access to his B.A. Hons. mini-dissertation on Senekal, and to Ami Maree for the wonderful scoop of her great-grandfather's Winburg concentration camp diary.

It has been a great pleasure working with the staff of the University of Illinois Press, who have been unfailingly friendly and generous in all of their dealings with me. Particular thanks are due to Jill R. Hughes, a most meticulous and insightful copyeditor.

An Imperfect Occupation is based on a doctoral thesis, "Winburg's War: An Appraisal of the Anglo-Boer War of 1899–1902 as It Was Experienced by the People of a Free State District," submitted to the University of Pretoria in 2009. It gives me joy to dedicate the final product to Fransjohan Pretorius, my mentor, and to Elizabeth, my love.

Introduction

ON THE EVE OF THE South African War of 1899–1902, Winburg, located approximately sixty-five miles northeast of Bloemfontein, was the chief town of a large district, bounded by the districts of Bloemfontein, Thaba Nchu, and Ladybrand to the south; Ficksburg and Bethlehem to the east; Lindley and Kroonstad to the north; and Hoopstad and Boshof to the west. The Winburg district comprised five wards: Winburg, Vetrivier, Zandrivier, Taaiboschspruit, and Onder-Wittebergen. It included two towns, Winburg and Senekal, and the villages of Ventersburg and Smaldeel. The key administrative officials in the wards were the field cornets, who served as intermediaries between the government and the citizenry. Their office included a multitude of functions, both civil and military. They were justices of the peace, road supervisors, stock inspectors, proclaimers of the law, and military officers, all rolled into one. By the end of the nineteenth century there was a considerable measure of job diversification, but field cornets continued to operate across a wide spectrum of responsibilities. With respect to their civil functions, the field cornets of the Winburg district were responsible to the *landdrost* (magistrate/district commissioner) or to the assistant landdrost in Senekal; in their military role they answered to the district commandant, Marthinus Prinsloo.[1]

In the Winburg district there were six field cornets, one for the chief town and one for each of the five wards. In the run-up to the war, Antonie Vlotman was the field cornet for Winburg town, but he resigned on 3 October 1899 on the grounds of ill health, saying he was exhausted after three days of commandeering (calling up men for military service). He was replaced by Adriaan Swanepoel.[2] The ward field cornets were Helgaardt Theunissen (Winburg ward), Willem Pretorius (Vetrivier), Sarel van Zyl (Zandrivier), Cornelis Oosthuizen

(Taaiboschspruit), and Jan Schutte (Onder-Wittebergen, later Senekal ward). It is typical of conservative leadership patterns at this stage that at the outbreak of war Schutte had already served as field cornet for thirty-four years.[3]

According to the 1856 census, the Winburg district had a total population of 6,617, of whom no fewer than 4,136 were white; by 1880 the population had grown to 15,858, of whom only 6,590 were white; and in 1890 black Africans further outnumbered whites, who now made up only 7,662 of the overall population of 16,685.[4] The marked increase in the black population could probably be attributed to the broken clans, dispersed by internecine warfare and by Boer conquest, gradually returning to their previous homes.

Farming in the District

The word "Boer" means farmer, and with very few exceptions the people of the Winburg district were involved in agriculture. Donald Denoon remarked with some asperity that most of the white population regarded themselves "as land-owners rather than land-users, and cattle-owners rather than cattle-breeders," and it was said of the early farmers in the Zandrivier ward that, apart from hunting, they spent their time either counting their cattle or looking for them.[5] Yet there was concern to improve the quality of livestock, and by 1880 Winburg was one of the most productive agricultural regions in the Free State. An agricultural society was established there as early as 1857, followed by a wool improvement society in 1884.[6]

The Onder-Wittebergen ward was particularly suited to the production of high-grade wool. In the decade 1880 to 1889 wool production increased from 1,301 to 2,517 bales. This increase is associated with a growing acceptance of sheep dipping (to protect them against parasites and to promote the healing of skin irritations). After 1890, when inexpensive fencing material became available, enclosure of fields promoted effective commercial farming. The corralling of stock at night became unnecessary, so healthy and contaminated animals were no longer crowded together and a farmer's livestock could be separated from that of his neighbor. Fewer cowherds and shepherds were needed and stock theft was reduced. Furthermore, "camps" (paddocks) kept animals away from crops and from fields where grazing was being established, so fodder could be produced and over-grazing eliminated. Mattheus Wessels pioneered barbed-wire fencing in the area, at a cost of five pounds per roll. At the time of the war, John Leech had about nine miles of fencing dividing his farm into paddocks.[7] Progressive farmers imported stud bulls, rams, and stallions from overseas, and at the outbreak of war Stephanus Jacobs's thoroughbred stock was worth more than seventeen thousand pounds.[8]

At first cattle farming was directed to the provision of draft animals, but the needs of the burgeoning Witwatersrand resulted in increased emphasis on slaughter stock. Small wonder, then, that the number of cattle in the Onder-Wittebergen ward leaped from 18,030 in 1880 to 29,584 in 1889.[9] The development of the Witwatersrand goldfields after 1886 stimulated crop production to an even greater extent. Wool and hides were export products and therefore unaffected by the demands of the local market, while milk and meat required the costly infrastructure of dairies and refrigeration. The arable eastern part of the district, particularly the fertile Caledon valley, lent itself to cultivation. Furthermore, the expanded workforce that plowing, sowing, harvesting, and threshing necessitated was more readily available in consolidated black settlements in the east of the country.[10]

Social Changes

Productive expansion in the 1880s and 1890s had important social consequences. Modernized agriculture necessitated a readily accessible and effectively controlled workforce. Ordinance 7 of 1881 limited farmers to five black family heads per farm.[11] However, large landowners could accommodate black settlements on their property and opposed the agitation for anti-squatting legislation that would put an end to blacks' self-sufficiency while distributing their labor more equitably. Such legislation was never vigorously implemented, not only because the state lacked the muscle to do so but also because the officials themselves were members of the wealthier landed class.[12] A progressive farmer, Frans Schimper, called for the establishment of strictly controlled reserves, forced labor (an expedient repeatedly rejected by the Volksraad, the Free State parliament), punitive taxes for the unemployed, and the distribution of labor by commandants and police.[13]

The second and related development is that there was little scope for *bywoners* (landless white farmers, sharecroppers) on farms under cultivation.[14] Commercial farmers preferred to use blacks, who cost them less, had experience in the cultivation of corn (maize, locally known as mealies), and could contribute teams of oxen for plowing, as well as the labor of their wives and children for seasonal work. The growing importance of black peasant production is evident from the fact that not long after the war, 165 out of 1,260 farms in the Winburg district were under the charge of blacks.[15]

The absence of suitable rail connections put a premium on wagon transportation. In April 1889, approximately 650 wagons a week passed through Senekal on the main road from the Caledon valley to the Rand. For this purpose, too, wealthy farm owners availed themselves of black entrepreneurship in preference to the long tradition of employing poor whites to drive the wagons. In 1896, 75 percent of the wagons that left James Robertson's mill near Wepener were driven by blacks.[16] Not only did this practice excite populist resentment of prosperous blacks, but it also gave rise to conflict between undercapitalized small farmers and progressive farmers with many acres under cultivation, as well as between farmers in the west and those in the more fertile east of the Winburg district. Furthermore, the displacement of bywoners affected the organic solidarity of Boer society.

Drought, locusts, and a virulent cattle disease, the *rinderpest* epidemic of 1896, drove many farmers off the land to seek jobs in the gold mines and on the railways, but conditions improved once more in the run-up to the war. In 1899 there was an abundant harvest. "It is pitiful," Elsa Leviseur wrote in her diary, "that there are no men left on the farms to gather in the harvest. Our poor country! There is always something the matter: either drought or rinderpest or locusts and now that worst of plagues, the Rooinek."[17]

The Cosmopolitan Towns

Winburg was a cosmopolitan town, predominantly Afrikaans-speaking but with a substantial number of English speakers. It is difficult to say what proportion of the townspeople was English speaking, because the division tended to be blurred: some Afrikaners habitually spoke English, and some English speakers called themselves Afrikaners. The prevalence of English surnames may be an indicator of intermarriage rather than a guide to separate identities. A sampling of English surnames in the Winburg records in combination with Afrikaans first names includes Bell (Frederik Johannes), Bolton (Thomas Frederik Johannes), Brown (Jacobus), Buck (Cornelius Johannes), Burchell (Lourens Jacobus), and Burnett (Frederik Willem). Even English surnames in combination with English first names can be misleading. George William Cooper, for example, was an Afrikaans-speaking landdrost of Senekal, and James Collins, landdrost of Bloemfontein and later of Winburg, is described as a member of "an illustrious Afrikaans family."[18] However, if this criterion—English surname and first names—is applied to the 1899 voters roll for the town, no fewer than 38 of the 93 voters (roughly 41 percent) would appear to have been English-speaking. It could be objected that the voters roll is unrepresentative, as English merchants are more likely to appear on it than impoverished, newly urbanized Afrikaners, but the occurrence of English surnames on the commandeering list for Winburg town yields a very similar result: 69 out of 162 names, or 42.5 percent.[19]

From the beginning of the 1870s, Free State towns established "locations" (black townships). Winburg's location was situated about half a mile southwest of the town, still today the "location" of the Makeleketla township. To live in these locations, black people had to be in the employ of whites. They could also live on their employers' premises but were subject to a 9 P.M. curfew. According to the 1880 census, there were 315 blacks living in Winburg town; by 1904 the number was 1,759.[20]

From 1862 onward, residents of the Onder-Wittebergen ward agitated for the establishment of a town in their ward. In 1887 the Volksraad at last agreed to the proclamation of Senekal with the proviso that a separate district would never be established.[21] The town achieved a higher status with the appointment of an assistant landdrost, who had jurisdiction over the approximately three hundred farms of the ward. The wish for a separate district continued to be denied on the grounds of cost. However, during the war the Senekallers soon operated as an independent commando, and after the conclusion of peace Senekal did become a separate district.

According to the census conducted in 1890, Senekal was then a town of forty-nine houses with 263 white and 253 black residents.[22] Like Winburg, Senekal had a substantial English-speaking population; of the 64 people on the voters roll, 28 (approximately 44 percent) either had English surnames and first names or were members of the Jewish community.[23]

Black men had to register their presence in the location, and if they were unemployed their services could be commandeered for unpaid civic duties for two days at a time;[24] in times of war they were drafted for longer periods without pay. Underlying these regulations was the assumption that whites were entitled to black labor. This is neatly illustrated by the polysemic use of the word "maid" (in Afrikaans usage, a disparaging word for a black woman; in English, a servant) in an item in the *Friend* in which the paper's Senekal correspondent protested, "It is a patent fact that the inhabitants of our *dorp* [village] cannot obtain maids to look after their children or assist in their house . . . although there are upwards of seventy young black maids in the location."[25]

On the eve of the war, Ventersburg consisted of thirty scattered houses, a smith's shop, a mill, two churches, two hotels, and a telegraph office. The railway line to the north bypassed Ventersburg, so a railway stop called Ventersburg Road, eleven miles from the village, was opened in February 1892. Smaldeel, which was originally called Winburg Road and renamed Theunissen in 1908, was the railhead for the branch line to Winburg and boasted a school and a number of shops.

In the rural areas of the Free State the white population was almost exclusively Afrikaans-speaking, but, as has been shown with regard to Winburg and Senekal, there were substantial numbers of English speakers clustered in the towns. Many English people left when the period of British rule known as the

Sovereignty came to an end in 1854, but the withdrawal of Britain provided a further inducement for those who remained to throw in their lot with their Afrikaans-speaking compatriots. The presence of these early arrivals smoothed the passage of a further influx of English speakers when more settled conditions brought greater prosperity, and while it is true that an air of superiority was apparent in some quarters and that the English press was hypercritical of the Free State government, there was also a merging of identities. The fault line in Free State society was not so much between the language groups but, more fundamentally, between opposing opinions about where the country's destiny lay.

The Political Background

During the presidency of Jan Brand (1864–88), the Free State looked south. Because Brand was sympathetic to British culture and favored closer ties with the British colonies, he held himself aloof from nascent Afrikaner nationalism. This led to increasing estrangement between him and his burghers. In 1869 diamonds were discovered in Griqualand West. Britain and the Free State disputed control over the area, and as a result of Brand's conciliatory approach, Britain annexed the diamond fields in 1871. The payment of compensation to the Free State and the knighthood conferred on its president, as well as the Free State's official neutrality during the Transvaal War of 1880–81, undermined the esteem in which Brand had long been held by his burghers. The discovery of gold on the Witwatersrand in 1886 motivated Brand to seek closer economic cooperation with the Transvaal, but Paul Kruger, the Transvaal president, doggedly made this conditional on the closer political unity between the two republics that Brand and the Orange Free State Volksraad had eschewed.[26]

The death of Brand in 1888 brought opposition to his policies out into the open, with Christiaan de Wet strongly to the fore. The day after Brand's funeral a meeting was held in Winburg to promote the candidacy of F. W. Reitz. The number of votes garnered by Reitz in Winburg demonstrated the strong support he enjoyed in this district.[27]

As president, Reitz walked the tightrope of political ideology and economic reality: he sought to strengthen the Free State's relationship with the Transvaal without forfeiting the benefits of its bonds with the Cape. Kruger, on the other hand, exploited the strong desire for unity in the Free State by using every opportunity to press for his more limited desire for a defensive and offensive alliance. At the Potchefstroom conference between the Free State and the Transvaal in March 1889, Kruger secured a defensive alliance; at the Bloemfontein conference a few days later, a customs union between the Free State and the

Cape Colony was agreed upon. The disquiet caused by the political alliance with the Transvaal is demonstrated by the narrow vote (29 to 21) with which the alliance was ratified by the Volksraad.[28]

As a result of the vast wealth accruing from the burgeoning Witwatersrand, the Transvaal was transformed from a state that could barely balance its budget into a wealthy republic that was increasingly intent on self-sufficiency and independent action. The Delagoa Bay railway line provided the Transvaal with an outlet to the sea, free trade within the region was obstructed, and commercial and political relations with Germany were fostered. Joseph Chamberlain, who had become colonial secretary in 1895, was alarmed at the threat to British power and prestige.

When ill health obliged Reitz to resign in 1895, the succession struggle crystallized around J. G. Fraser, the chairman of the Volksraad and Brand's political heir, who favored a united South Africa, and M. T. Steyn, who was impelled by pan-Republican sentiment to ally his country more closely with the Transvaal. At this stage the Jameson Raid intervened. This was an illegal armed incursion into the Transvaal, engineered by Cecil John Rhodes, the prime minister of the Cape Colony and the most prominent mine magnate, that was intended to coincide with an uprising on the Witwatersrand and to justify British intervention in the Transvaal. The upsurge of anti-English feeling unleashed by the raid decided the political issue. Steyn won 83.5 percent of the vote to Fraser's meager 15.5 percent. Yet despite this popular vote, Fraser commanded the support of about one-third of the Volksraad.[29]

Steyn went into his first meeting with Kruger at Viljoensdrif in March 1896 convinced that, for good or ill, the Free State's lot was tied up with that of the Transvaal. Guided by this conviction, he tabled a draft resolution in the Volksraad on 11 June that amounted to the offensive and defensive alliance that Kruger had so assiduously pursued. This, in Fraser's view, marked a "complete surrender to President Kruger's political aims, and the absolute subordination of the legislature of the OFS [Orange Free State] to the business of giving effect to his desire to have the forces and resources of the State at his disposal in the hostilities between the British Government and the Transvaal" and "a wholesale betrayal of the OFS, which could only end in its destruction."[30]

Whether or not this is a fair statement of the case, the Free State was a hostage to fortune, for the appointment of Sir Alfred Milner as high commissioner in South Africa at precisely this time—in May 1897—and the rampant imperialism that this represented was perceived as a catalyst of inevitable ruin. For Steyn this perception was reinforced by his firsthand experience of Milner's maneuvering. Milner was contemptuous of what he called "the waiting game" and fanned the glowing embers of animosity.[31] He used the Bloemfontein conference with Kruger (31 May–5 June 1899), which the colonial secretary saw as a means of achieving a settlement, to bring matters to a head. In spite of Chamberlain's wishes, Milner deliberately excluded the moderating voices of W. P. Schreiner, the prime minister of Cape Colony; J. H. Hofmeyr, leader of the Cape Afrikaners; and Steyn himself.[32] The high commissioner refused to allow discussion of any subject other than the enfranchisement of the "Uitlanders," mainly British foreigners who had streamed to the Transvaal as a result of the discovery of gold. Milner's expectation was that simplification of the issues at stake followed by immediate publication of the proceedings of the conference along with the Uitlander grievances would reveal Kruger's intransigence and help to sway public opinion. When Kruger proved more flexible than expected, the conference was abruptly broken off.

Chamberlain was angry with Milner for limiting the discussion and for abandoning the conference precipitately. He still looked for a negotiated settlement,[33] but the widespread public airing given to the dispute cast Britain in the role of the defender of order, stability, and good government, a role that made British supremacy—a more credible *casus belli* than quibbles about franchise proposals—a matter of principle and obliged the government to apply sustained pressure on Kruger's government.[34] It was in pursuit of this policy of sustained pressure that ten thousand British troops were dispatched to South Africa.

Between April and September Steyn practiced conciliation, but on 2 October he accepted the inevitability of the coming war and mobilized his commandos, asserting that he preferred "to lose the independence of the Orange Free State honourably, rather than keep it in dishonour and disloyalty."[35] Steyn was faced with a difficult choice and made a decision that affected thousands of lives. As a result of his decision to go to war, the people of the Free State had to confront agonizing choices with incalculable consequences. The subject of this book is the various decisions they made: whether the men would fight (chapter 1), surrender (chapter 2), evade combat, or collaborate with the enemy (chapter 3); whether the women would cooperate with the occupying power or continue to support the burghers in the field, flee before the British, or submit to captivity (chapter 4); whether the women and men who were held captive would remain loyal or be won over by the occupying power (chapter 5); whether black people would range themselves with the Boers or the British (chapter 6); and, when the war finally came to an end, whether the conquered would be reconciled with one another and with the conqueror or regard peace as an opportunity for pursuing the war by other means or as a mere lull in hostilities (chapter 7).

A Brief Chronology of the South African War

1899	
11 October	The Boer ultimatum expires
12 October	Natal invaded:
13 October	Mafeking besieged
14 October	Kimberley besieged
20 October	Battle of Talana
21 October	Battle of Elandslaagte
24 October	Battle of Rietfontein
30 October	Battle of Nicholson's Nek/Ladysmith
	Defeat of Gen. Sir George White
2 November	Ladysmith besieged
23 November	Battle of Willow Grange
November	Western front:
23 November	Battle of Belmont
25 November	Battle of Enslin/Graspan
28 November	Battle of Modder River
December	"Black Week":
10 December	Battle of Stormberg (in the northern Cape)
11 December	Magersfontein (on the western front)
15 December	Colenso (on the Natal front)
18 December	Roberts supersedes Buller
1900	
January–February	Natal front:
6 January	Battle of Wagon Hill/Platberg
24 January	Battle of Spioenkop
5–7 February	Battle of Vaalkrans
14–27 February	Battle of Tugela Heights
27 February	Breakthrough at Pieter's Hill
28 February	Relief of Ladysmith
February–March	Western front:
15 February	Kimberley relieved
18–27 February	Battle of Paardeberg
27 February	Gen. Cronjé surrenders
7 March	Battle of Poplar Grove
10 March	Battle of Driefontein/Abrahamskraal
13 March	The occupation of Bloemfontein
March–November	Orange Free State:
17 March	Major *krygsraad* held at Kroonstad
31 March	Battle of Sannaspos

4 April	Battle of Reddersburg
9–24 April	Siege of Wepener
24 May	Annexation of the Free State
29 May	Battle of Biddulphsberg
31 May	Battle of Lindley
7 June	Attack on Roodewal Siding
15–31 July	Battle of Brandwater Basin
30 July	Prinsloo's surrender
6 November	Battle of Bothaville
3 May	Roberts resumes his advance
17 May	Relief of Mafeking
5 June	Occupation of Pretoria
June	Farm burning officially sanctioned
June–December	Transvaal:
5 June	Pretoria captured
11–12 June	Battle of Diamond Hill/Donkerhoek
27 August	Battle of Dalmanutha/Bergendal
1 September	Transvaal annexed
13 December	Battle of Nooitgedacht
September	Concentration camps established
29 November	Kitchener succeeds Roberts as commander in chief
16 December	Gen. Piet Kritzinger invades the Cape Colony
1901	
10–28 February	Gen. Christiaan de Wet invades the Cape Colony
28 February	Peace talks between Botha and Kitchener at Middelburg
March	Blockhouse system established
4 September	Gen. Jan Smuts invades the Cape Colony
7 September	Gen. Louis Botha invades Natal
17 September	Battle of Blood River Poort
30 October	Battle of Bakenlaagte, Transvaal
November–December	Drives in northeastern Free State (6–12 Nov., 8–12 Dec.)
25 December	Battle of Tweefontein/Krismiskop, Free State
1902	
February–April	Drives in northeastern Free State (6–8 Feb., 13–26 Feb., 5–17 Mar., 20 Mar.-5 Apr.)
February–April	Western Transvaal:
25 February	Battles of Ysterspruit and Tweebosch
7 March	Lord Methuen captured
23–24 March	Drives in Western Transvaal

31 March	Battle of Boschbult
11 April	Battle of Roodewal (Transvaal)
4 April–3 May	Smuts besieges Okiep in Namaqualand, Cape Colony
9 April	Meeting of Boer delegates at Klerksdorp
12–20 April	Drives in Eastern Transvaal
6 May	Zulu attack on Boer encampment at Holkrans, near Vryheid
31 May	Treaty of Vereeniging brings the war to an end

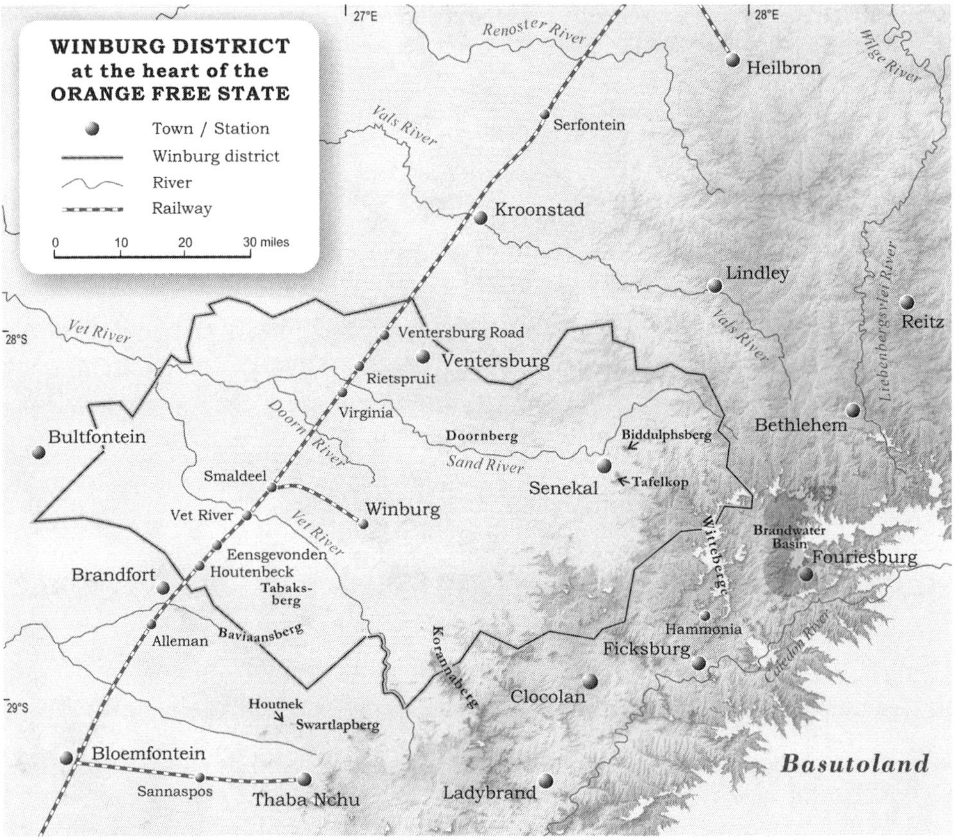
WINBURG DISTRICT
at the heart of the
ORANGE FREE STATE
Town / Station
Winburg district
River
Railway
0
10
20
30 miles
27°E
28°E
28°S
29°S
Renoster River
Wilge River
Vals River
Heilbron
Serfontein
Kroonstad
Lindley
Liebenbergsvlei River
Reitz
Vet River
Ventersburg Road
Ventersburg
Rietspruit
Virginia
Doorn River
Doornberg
Biddulphsberg
Bethlehem
Bultfontein
Sand River
Senekal
Tafelkop
Smaldeel
Winburg
Vet River
Brandwater Basin
Fouriesburg
Witteberge
Eensgevonden
Houtenbeck
Brandfort
Tabaksberg
Baviaansberg
Alleman
Korannaberg
Hammonia
Ficksburg
Caledon River
Clocolan
Houtnek
Swartlapberg
Bloemfontein
Sannaspos
Thaba Nchu
Ladybrand
Basutoland

1 Occupation and Insurgency

THE WAR IN THE FREE STATE may be divided into four phases. In the first two, characterized by conventional battles, the Boers at first asserted themselves; then, with the command passing to Lord Roberts, the British increasingly prevailed. The next broad period, following on the occupation of Bloemfontein, was characterized by irregular engagements and may, in turn, be subdivided into a period when the Boers still had the capacity to mount conventional operations and one when they were reduced to insurgency, with Marthinus Prinsloo's surrender in the Brandwater Basin marking the caesura. From the Boers' point of view, it was therefore a war of increasing hopelessness, and one must ask why the "*bittereinders*" (those who fought to the bitter end) persisted so long.

The First Phase of the War

The war started well for the Boers. Availing themselves of their good weaponry and superior numbers, at a time when only about twenty-two thousand British troops were in South Africa or on their way to the region, the Boers besieged three strategic towns: Kimberley and Mafeking in the Cape Colony and Ladysmith in Natal. The British commander in chief, Sir Redvers Buller, believed he could defeat the Boers with an army corps of forty-six thousand men. When they arrived on 31 October 1899, Buller divided his forces, sending a part under Lt. Gen. Sir William Gatacre to the northern Cape to discourage Cape Afrikaners from joining the Boer forces, and another under Lt. Gen. Lord Methuen to relieve Kimberley, while he would concentrate on lifting the siege of Ladysmith, where Maj. Gen. Sir George White was bottled up with eight thousand men. In the space of one week, all three generals suffered severe defeats: Gatacre at Stormberg (10 December 1899), Methuen at Magersfontein (11 December), and Buller at Colenso (15 December). The British government, press, and people were devastated by "Black Week."

The Second Phase

Just two days after the battle of Colenso, the British government made the decisive intervention of superseding Buller. F.M. Lord Roberts was appointed as commander in chief and Maj. Gen. Lord Kitchener as his chief of staff and ultimate successor. They sent a field force of 47,000 men to South Africa, and in addition to regular army reinforcements, the government took the innovative step of recruiting an auxiliary force of some 11,600 volunteers, especially irregular mounted infantry.

Sending Roberts to South Africa to retrieve the situation was a momentous decision. It was consistent with the doctrine of civilian control of the army, a principle that dated back to the Cardwell reforms of 1870–72. Officially established by an order in council of November 1895, civilian control was nevertheless difficult to implement in the face of the commander in chief Lord Wolseley's resentment of amateur interference in army matters, strained relations between the military and the cabinet in the run-up to the South African War, and the heroic image of Britain's top military leaders. While the supersession of Buller affirmed civilian control, the appointment of Roberts to succeed him implied a considerable delegation of authority to him, from which the cabinet could not easily retreat. Thereby the responsibility of bringing the war to a speedy conclusion was entrusted to Roberts, whose subsequent decisive actions inspired confidence. Clearly such a successful soldier should not be hampered in the execution of his mandate, and as a result the British cabinet was increasingly vulnerable to the demand that military necessity take precedence over political considerations. The conflict between civil and military interests intensified when Kitchener took over from Roberts at the end of November 1900. As administrator of the former republics, Sir Alfred Milner was desperately concerned that military decisions were being taken without regard to their impact on reconstruction and tried to undermine Kitchener's position, but although members of the cabinet were disturbed by the commander in chief's high-handed actions, Kitchener emerged unscathed from the contest.[1]

Furthermore, the army in South Africa showed adaptability in confronting the challenge. Buller had seen the urgent need for mounted infantry, while Roberts had the cavalry's sabers replaced with rapid-firing rifles; abandoned charges and frontal attacks, replacing them with outflanking maneuvers; deployed his artillery defensively; was innovative in his use of machine guns; and was prepared to strike away from the support of the railway line.[2] It was the last-named departure from previous practice that enabled Roberts to outwit Comdt. Christiaan de Wet, force Gen. Piet Cronjé's surrender with four thousand men at Paardeberg (27 February 1900), and march on Bloemfontein, which he entered unopposed on 13 March.

Here Roberts was obliged to spend the next month and a half resting his men; contending with an outbreak of a particularly virulent form of typhoid, which by April had already claimed close to a thousand lives; organizing the movement of reinforcements and supplies into the interior; and replenishing the horses essential to the cavalry, as Maj. Gen. J.P.D. French, astoundingly, had lost two-thirds of the animals in his command by the time he got to Bloemfontein.[3]

The Annexation of the Free State

On 14 March 1900, the day after Bloemfontein was occupied, military government of the Free State was instituted. Ten days later the Orange Free State was annexed and renamed the Orange River Colony, though the annexation was made known only two weeks later. On 31 May the new colony was placed under martial law, "as such law is understood and administered in British territory and by British officers." Months later an army order defined martial law more precisely as "the will of the conqueror . . . [which] is limited in its operation only by what is known as the customs of war and the discretion of those who administer it." These elucidations exemplify the enigma of martial law: it is the means by which an occupying power committed to legality at home abrogates the rule of law in order to give a semblance of legality to its military operations abroad.[4]

The premature annexation of the Free State was premised on the accepted "Small Wars" theory that once the enemy's capital was captured, the war was at an end. The Boers, however, felt little emotional attachment to Bloemfontein and had decided to move the capital to Kroonstad even before Cronjé's surrender at Paardeberg. A proclamation dated 19 March 1900 asserted that the war effort was unrelated to the question of the capital. On this basis the capital was successively moved to Heilbron, Lindley, Frankfort, and Bethlehem and eventually to wherever the president and his executive happened to be. Roberts's proclamation number 15 of 1 June claimed that because the country was now a British colony, those who persisted in the war were rebels and would be dealt with accordingly. Steyn's response on 11 June was that because the Free State was unconquered, the annexation was invalid and not recognized by his government.[5]

The Annexation of the Free State. (War Museum of the Boer Republics)

Roberts appointed Maj. Gen. Sir George Pretyman as military governor, initially of Bloemfontein and later of other occupied areas. A special police force drawn from the Coldstream Guards to keep order in Bloemfontein was soon replaced by the Provisional Mounted Police, a force of three hundred men. This, in turn, made way for the South African Constabulary in November 1900. Pretyman consulted with the erstwhile Republican officials J. G. Fraser and James Collins to assess the reliability of Republican civil servants, some of whom were reappointed. Thus George Falck, the administrator of posts and telegraphs, retained responsibility for postal matters, but the telegraph service was placed under military control. Officials recruited in the Cape Colony included L. A. Tancred as legal adviser to the government. Army personnel included Capt. A. G. Trollope, who served successively as director of education, administrator of districts under military control, and superintendent of refugee camps, and Capt. Percy Girouard as director of railways and telegraphs, with the railways renamed the Imperial Military Railways. The surveyor general's office was also taken over by the military, while the activities of the deeds office, auditor general, and high court were suspended for the duration of the war. Collins was appointed as resident magistrate of Bloemfontein, but many of the landdrosts reappointed as resident magistrates in other towns were soon replaced, because "some were actively hostile, some feeble and useless."[6] In order to get civil administration off the ground, minor functionaries such as magistrate's clerks, postmasters, postal contractors, and jailers continued in office.

In the months that followed, army officers were seconded as district commissioners to represent the governor in the conquered areas. As officer responsible for the civil side of the occupation, Pretyman was in constant conflict with Lt. Gen. Sir Thomas Kelly-Kenny, the general officer in command of Orange River Colony. Pretyman, who reported to both Roberts and Milner, kept the latter informed of the running battles between Kelly-Kenny and the district commissioners who were responsible to him.[7]

The Third Phase

The lull in Roberts's military activity provided the Boer leadership with an opportunity for critical reflection at a major *krygsraad,* or military council, which was held in Kroonstad on 17 March 1900. This meeting was attended by both President M. T. Steyn of the Free State and President Paul Kruger of the Transvaal, and far-reaching tactical decisions were taken. It was agreed that a more offensive strategy was called for with smaller, more mobile units, including corporalships of about twenty-five men, constantly harassing the British troops and their supply lines. In order to ensure the more effective operation of the commandos, wagon *laagers,* or encampments, would be dispensed with and there would be a tightening up of military discipline.[8]

On 31 March the Boer counteroffensive opened with an attack on Sannaspos, just seventeen miles from Roberts's Bloemfontein headquarters. While Comdt. Christiaan de Wet with four hundred men from Bloemfontein and Kroonstad concealed themselves in the dry riverbed of the Koornspruit, his brother and fellow commandant, Piet de Wet, with the commandos of Winburg and Bethlehem, was responsible for harrying Brig. Gen. R. G. Broadwood's army in the rear. When Piet de Wet's guns opened fire from the ridges to the east, the British fled westward in the direction of Bloemfontein, straight into the arms of the waiting burghers. Responding to what was readily seen to be a highly successful operation, a Reuters correspondent covering the war reported that "a feeling of joy pervaded the Bethlehem and Winburg burghers. . . . They felt their day of victory had dawned."[9]

Christiaan de Wet's success at Sannaspos was followed by two further attacks at Mostertshoek, near Reddersburg, forty miles south of Bloemfontein, and at Jammersberg near Wepener, sixty-six miles southeast of the city, both in the rear of the British army. He then occupied some ridges near Thaba Nchu with four thousand men, including foreign volunteers under Col. E. Maximov. Lt. Gen. Sir Ian Hamilton was ordered to clear the eastern flank of the Boers from

Houtnek in the line of his planned advance. He met with stout resistance on 30 April, but the following day the foreign volunteers had to retreat when they found that the Boers, on whose supporting fire they relied, had abandoned their positions during the night. It has been claimed that the British haul of prisoners included Cor van Gogh, a brother of the artist Vincent van Gogh, but Cor, who was fighting on the Boer side, had committed suicide nearly three weeks before.

The Imperfect Occupation of the Winburg District

On 3 May, Lord Roberts resumed his northward advance from Bloemfontein with thirty-eight thousand men and more than a hundred guns. The central column under Roberts himself was supported by the main mounted body under Major General French on his left and the Winburg Column, under Lt. Gen. Sir Ian Hamilton, on his right. Defending the central front before Brandfort against twenty-five thousand troops, generals Koos de la Rey and Tobias Smuts had only fifteen hundred to eighteen hundred men at their disposal. On the first day of the advance, the main column took Brandfort, whereupon the Boers fell back on the Vet River.[10]

Meanwhile Gen. Philip Botha and his subordinate generals, who were tasked with the defense of Winburg, occupied Baviaansberg and tried to occupy Tabaksberg in the vicinity of the farm Welkom. An artillery battle opened at 7 A.M., but after three hours the Boers, some one thousand strong with six guns, began to fall back. Thomas Mitchell, the owner of the farm (later described as a Scotsman who would not give sixpence to save Britain from ruin[11]), provided the Boers with water and milk and, having sped them on their way, welcomed the British with water and tea. He provided Broadwood with military intelligence and put his house at the disposal of Hamilton and his staff. The British flag was run up in front of the house, and that night some twenty thousand men bivouacked all around.

At dawn on 5 May, the march to Winburg continued. There was negligible resistance as Philip Botha sought to interpose his force of five hundred men, mostly Germans and Hollanders, between the town and the advancing multitude. The 7th Battalion Mounted Infantry raced them to occupy a hill, about three thousand feet high, commanding the southern and eastern approaches to the town. When the Hampshire squadron reached the summit, they were treated to the sight of the whole Boer force, five thousand to six thousand men strong, moving slowly northward.[12]

At noon Ian Hamilton sent his aide-de-camp, Capt. John Balfour, to demand the immediate surrender of the town. This could not be negotiated with Landdrost Jacobus van Zyl, because he had fled the town a few days previously. Discussions were in progress with the assistant landdrost, Cecil Bell, when Botha and his men entered the town from the northeast. Botha ordered the arrest of Balfour, whereupon, according to Winston Churchill's account, "the women screamed, the mayor and landdrost rushed forward in hopes of averting bloodshed. The Boers raised their rifles in menace, and the unarmed British envoy flourished his white flag indignantly."[13] Botha and his discouraged burghers had no option but to leave the town. Fourteen-year-old Maria de Villiers watched the arrival of the troops from two o'clock onward, marveling at the number of "cannons," which she surmised could not all have been intended for the conquest of Winburg.[14]

According to one report, the troops were well received by the townspeople. Pvt. J. W. Milne noted in his diary: "Reached Wynberg [*sic*] at about 2 pm, a good looking place with a lot of British women in it. As we marched through the streets a young woman shouted three cheers for the British. Some of them were handing packets of cigarettes to us." This welcome is confirmed by the dismayed testimony of Cornelis Plokhooy, a Dutch volunteer with the Boers. "I will never forget what we saw in Winburg," he wrote. "We rode along the main road, leading to the church, and saw small groups of fit young men, unarmed citizens of the Orange Free State, awaiting the arrival of the English. . . . Going a bit further, we saw—Oh, the shame of it!—Afrikaners and English with their wives, festively dressed, going out to meet the troops to welcome them as liberators." And according to another report, "the girls in Winburg went out with white fans to meet the English."[15]

However, a totally different picture emerges from a trooper's account of the Royal Canadians' entry into the town just two hours later. The trooper describes Winburg as "a sullen little place," where the houses were closed up and the stores shuttered, and scowling women stood in their doorways and "hissed in a noiseless way" at the men marching past. However, Sgt. M. C. Jackson of the 7th Battalion Mounted Infantry noted nothing untoward, commenting on the fact that "the inhabitants (female) were having afternoon tea on the verandas."[16]

Occupied Winburg was initially administered by military officers, but on 30 June seconded officers assumed civil responsibilities. Maj. W. J. O'Leary, assisted by Lt. Trafford Lewes, was appointed commissioner, to be succeeded by Capt. A. Lyon on 5 November. The commissioner was charged with maintaining order among the civilian population but had to liaise with the commandant, the commanding officer of the garrison—in this case, Col. G. E. Lloyd, succeeded by Col. J. S. Napier—to ensure effective occupation of the district.[17]

In an attempt to restore a measure of civilian administration under military oversight, landdrosts, now styled resident magistrates, were appointed. Two days after the occupation of Winburg, Maj. Gen. Sir Henry Colvile reappointed the Boer landdrost, Jacobus van Zyl, but the appointment was immediately countermanded by Lord Roberts, by whose order Lt. Gerald Cloete was to be appointed instead, to be succeeded in April 1902 by Capt. St. John Cole Bowen. The resident magistrate was assisted by fourteen justices of the peace. These justices were locals whose loyalty was unimpeachable or, Pretyman commented, "at least supposed to be." Their duty, we are told, was principally to keep the blacks in check.[18]

The Boers, meanwhile, continued to appoint officials, so anomalies were bound to arise from the parallel jurisdiction. The British authorities, for example, questioned the validity of the marriage of Frederik Pieterse and Johanna Fouché, contracted before Special Landdrost Gabriel van Dyk in the district of Winburg, "Orange Free State"—that is, an unrecognized official "of a State that has ceased to exist."[19]

In order to maintain law and order, Republican policemen like the Winburger Alexander Thom were initially reappointed by the British authorities. But distrust led to the replacement of local policemen by the Provisional Mounted Police. Owing to their limited numbers, police could barely venture beyond the confines of the towns. With the help of the police, the commissioner was required to collect all weapons, requisition horses, and destroy all carts and wagons. In her account of a peace mission in which she participated, Margaret Marquard, the wife of Rev. J. J. Marquard, the Dutch Reformed Church clergyman in Winburg, provides unconscious evidence of how limited the range of both civil and military authority was. She accompanied T.C.L. Bergstedt, David Roux, and Adriaan Swanepoel, who had received permission from Colonel Napier to parley with some Boers. They left Winburg by cart on 7 November 1900, and about fifteen miles from Winburg they passed the last British guards. After traversing countryside with "no human beings to be seen," they reached Izak Haasbroek's farm near Ventersburg, where armed Boers came out to meet them. On their return journey they encountered three mounted black scouts, and the mutual distrust felt was palpable.[20] Indeed, the efficacy of British occupation at this stage is neatly encapsulated in the formula that President Steyn later used in response to Lord Kitchener's banishment proclamation of 7 August 1901: "May I be permitted to say that your Excellency's jurisdiction is limited to the range of your Excellency's guns."[21]

Instead of the British occupiers going out to the farms, they resorted to a simple subterfuge. When farmers or their wives came into town to buy provisions, the British confiscated their vehicles so that they were unable to return to their farms. On 25 October 1900, country storekeepers were instructed that they were not allowed to sell food or groceries without a permit. When Hans Nel and his wife came into Winburg to buy provisions for the following month, they were not allowed to return to the farm, where their children, the eldest a fifteen-year-old girl, had been left on their own. The children were subsequently brought in, and the house, a mere twelve miles east of the town, was dynamited.[22] In this way "refugees" were created.

The commissioners had to keep an eye on the landdrosts, who were ex-burghers whose loyalty was questioned. Like Van Zyl, they were generally replaced by officials from the neighboring British territories, the Cape Colony and Natal. The landdrost's power to make appointments was a particular bone of contention. Emrys Evans, financial adviser to the military governor, cautioned that "educational machinery has been in the past one of the influences which have fostered the Afrikander Nation idea, and it requires careful investigation." So in July 1900, two schools in Winburg, including that of a Miss Smith, "quite an English girl," were obliged to close down.[23]

When Gen. Koos de la Rey deployed his commandos on the Vet River, he did not know that the Boers on his left flank had failed to prevent the capture of Winburg and had either dispersed or fallen back to the Sand River. His own burghers were flanked by the British and driven from their positions. The Boer retirement to Sand River throughout the night of 5–6 May left no rearguard to protect Smaldeel. The Royal Canadian Regiment made a dash for the village on 6 May but found that "the enemy had just left, blowing up the railway bridge as they went." The West Australian Mounted Infantry occupied Smaldeel the same day, and the 11th Infantry Division consolidated there the following day.[24]

On 9 May the whole British army moved on toward the Sand River. Richard Davis, an American observer, describes the sight of the massive British army advancing across the open veld, comparing it to a gigantic monster, a tidal wave, or an avalanche, obliterating everything in its path. When six thousand horsemen started carrying out a flanking movement, crossing the river below the bridge, the burghers galloped in the direction of Ventersburg, despite the fact that Comdt. Gen. Louis Botha of the Transvaal and President Steyn of the Free State were standing in the open road waving them back and urging them to make a stand. But as Davis points out, while the British forces were constantly renewed, these Boers were the same men who had held Buller back at the Tugela River in Natal for three months, who were then rushed to the western front to try to rescue Gen. Piet Cronjé from entrapment at Paardeberg, who were ordered to Fourteen Streams and then back again to Sannaspos, and who were now falling back on the Sand River, worn out by endless fighting against impossible odds.[25] "So," the war correspondent wrote, "they stood immovable, leaning on their rifles, silent, homeless, looking down without rage or show of feeling at the great waves of khaki sweeping steadily toward them, and possessing their land."[26]

Ventersburg was occupied on 10 May. It may well have been, in the words of Winston Churchill, "a miserable little place . . . dirty and squalid,"[27] but the reception accorded the British troops who entered it would have lent it luster in their eyes. After Josiah Daneel, a missionary too old for commando service, had surrendered it to Ian Hamilton, a local farmer by the name of Nicolaas Coetzee appeared on the scene with two fine oxen, which he presented to the Highland Brigade. The animals were slaughtered and distributed among the men. When Coetzee rode among the troops and scattered sovereigns in all directions, they must have felt really welcome. However, Coetzee's distressed wife, Martha, explained to Brig. Gen. Sir Hector MacDonald that her husband was not entirely accountable for his actions, and as many as possible of the coins were retrieved and returned and an official receipt was issued for the oxen.[28]

In order to protect Heilbron, which had been proclaimed the new Free State capital, Christiaan de Wet persuaded Louis Botha that the Transvaalers and the Free Staters should make a final joint stand on the Renoster River. The reaction from the Free State burghers was unenthusiastic. Thus the Senekal commando was supposed to assemble in the town on 16 May, but only twenty men reported.[29] When it became known that the British had broken through the Boer lines at Lindley and their road was open to Heilbron, Botha and De Wet agreed that the Renoster River front could not be maintained.

On 25 May, Lt. Gen. Sir Leslie Rundle advanced on Senekal in leisurely fashion. He sent Maj. Henry Dalbiac with sixty men of the Middlesex Yeomanry on ahead. Dalbiac entered the town, which the Boer forces had left; posted sentries; rounded up surrendered burghers; and had started foraging when shots were heard from the rise to the east of the town. He sped off in that direction with about thirty men, but he and three of his soldiers were killed in crossfire from the north and the south. Four more were wounded and thirteen were captured by the Boers. Shortly afterward Rundle arrived with the main force and Nicolaas Boer surrendered the town to him at the request of the landdrost, who had fled.[30] The Boer forces withdrew to the east of the town, where about four hundred men from the Ladybrand, Ficksburg, Smithfield, and Thaba Nchu commandos, as well as a group from Senekal under Comdt. Johannes Jacobs, assembled. They were under the overall command of Gen. Andries de Villiers and had five artillery pieces at their disposal.

The urban centers of the district, Winburg, Smaldeel, Ventersburg, and Senekal, were now all in British hands, but the Boers still controlled most of the countryside. This was vividly demonstrated by the ambush they were able to set for Rundle at Biddulphsberg, only eight miles from Senekal, a few days later. In the ensuing battle the Grenadier Guards were trapped between the Boers and a fierce veld fire. The horror of the situation is vividly evoked in a surviving letter from Trooper Harry Maile, who served in that regiment. He was severely wounded and would have died had the Boers not left the shallow ditches where they were ensconced to give him water, wrap him up, and get him to safety.[31] A three-hour truce allowed an opportunity for burghers and soldiers to fraternize, for as J. P. Bosman, one of the Boers who participated in the battle, put it, "At that moment of suffering, Tommy was no longer a hated enemy, but a fellow human being . . . a human being just like us."[32] Then the British bugle and the Boer whistle ordered the resumption of hostilities.

After the fall of Kroonstad, Roberts prepared to advance on the Transvaal. Some Transvaal leaders wanted to capitulate, but Steyn's intransigent response was that, if need be, the Free State would fight on alone. Kruger left Pretoria for the eastern Transvaal, from where he would go into exile in Switzerland. Roberts took Johannesburg on 31 May and entered Pretoria in triumph on 5 June. The fall of Bloemfontein had precipitated large-scale surrenders, and the fall of the northern capital had a similar effect. By the end of the month some six thousand Free Staters and eight thousand Transvaalers had laid down their arms.

On the day that Roberts took Johannesburg, Comdt. Piet de Wet launched a devastating attack on the 13th Imperial Yeomanry on the Lindley-Kroonstad road, compelling Col. B. E. Spragge, who had suffered 25 killed, to surrender with 464 men, but even before this victory Piet de Wet was already considering surrender.[33] A few days later his brother Christiaan demonstrated his determination to fight on with an equally devastating raid on garrison posts guarding the railway line near Roodewal, north of Kroonstad, resulting in extensive damage to British communications, the seizure or destruction of supplies worth more than one hundred thousand pounds, and the capture of 486 prisoners.[34] Boer successes, however, were vitiated by antagonisms among their leaders and their ingrained individualism, which resulted in a seeming incapacity for concerted action, culminating in the disaster of the Brandwater Basin.

Toward the end of May, Steyn had appointed Rev. Paul Roux of Senekal, who was serving as a commandant, a combat general, to the annoyance of the Winburg commandant, Sarel Haasbroek.[35] On 14 June, Roux led about one hundred men of the Senekal commando as well as one hundred men from Ladybrand under Comdt. I. A. Meyer in an attack on an entrenched post under Lt. Col. J. E. Capper at the Sand River bridge near Virginia. Meyer was to attack at 6 A.M. from the direction of Bloemfontein and Roux and the Senekallers would then join in from the direction of Ventersburg. Commandants Christoffel Froneman and Sarel Haasbroek were also supposed to take part in the attack, but they failed to appear. The attack, of which Capper had been forewarned, was repulsed with the loss of six men, four of whom were from Senekal. On a night march back to Biddulphsberg, the Senekallers encountered a large encampment at Doornberg. No guards had been posted and everyone was fast asleep. The sleepers turned out to be Haasbroek and his Winburgers.[36]

Roberts resolved to deny the commandos the northeastern Free State as an area of operation, thus putting an end to the menace to his lines of communication. By taking Bethlehem and driving the Boers into the Brandwater Basin, he would compel them to surrender.[37] After effecting a junction of their troops, major generals A. H. Paget and R.A.P. Clements marched on Bethlehem. The Boers occupied the approaches to the town, but under sustained attack they abandoned their positions prematurely and the road to Bethlehem was open.

The Brandwater Basin

The Boers now withdrew southward into the Brandwater Basin. This vast and well-watered valley with its excellent grazing, lush crops, and fruitful orchards seemed idyllic to the weary burghers, but Christiaan de Wet had no illusions about the threat that would close in on them. In terms of a krygsraad decision of 13 July, a phased withdrawal from the Brandwater Basin was supposed to take place. Christiaan de Wet with Philip Botha and Piet de Wet, accompanied by the president, two corps of scouts, and twenty-six hundred men, would leave first; followed by Paul Roux, Piet Fourie, and Christoffel Froneman with two thousand men; then Jan Crowther with five hundred men. Marthinus Prinsloo, along with the Rouxville commando and half of the Bethlehem commando, would stay to hold the passes with the help of Haasbroek's commando.[38] However, when Steyn and Christiaan de Wet left on 15 July, escaping unopposed through Slabbert's Nek, the Boers were left without strong leadership, and the lack of a clear command structure invited catastrophe. Nothing came of the phased withdrawal, and the British continued to close in. As the troops bottled them up, alarm and despondency spread among the commandos. The alarm felt by the burghers was exacerbated by a rumor that President Steyn had fled with the intention of crossing into the Transvaal, and it was feared they would now be regarded as rebels and their property would be confiscated.[39]

On Sunday 29 July, Rev. J. J. Marquard preached a powerful sermon on the text "On this mountain the Lord will provide," but the service was no sooner over than the news broke that, using former commandant Stephanus Vilonel as intermediary, Prinsloo, contentiously elected as chief commandant, had offered Lt. Gen. Sir Archibald Hunter the unconditional surrender of the Boer forces. As a result of Prinsloo's surrender, 3 generals; 9 commandants; 4,314 men; 3 field guns; 2,800 cattle; 4,000 sheep; up to 6,000 horses; and 2 million rounds of ammunition fell into the hands of the British.[40] The Senekal and Winburg commandos, totaling 354 men under commandants Gerrie van der Merwe and Lucas Rautenbach, laid down their arms on 31 July 1900.[41]

The Final Phase of the War

The surrender of the bulk of the Boer army in the field marked a further turning point in the war. After this the sovereignty of the Free State was questionable. Once the British occupied Fouriesburg on 26 July, only Harrismith and Vrede were still in Boer hands. At the beginning of the Brandwater fiasco, only seventy-eight hundred Free Staters, 35 percent of those eligible for military service, were still actively involved in the war. More than half of them surrendered. However, Prinsloo's surrender was repudiated by a number of officers, including Comdt. Sarel Haasbroek of Winburg and F.C. Hans Hattingh of Senekal, who escaped through Golden Gate with about fifteen hundred men. The presence of wagons and other encumbrances in the Brandwater Basin indicates that those who surrendered still constituted a conventional fighting force. Those who escaped left behind not only wagons but artillery as well and were now fully committed to guerrilla warfare. Although about twenty-five hundred burghers who had previously surrendered were re-commandeered,[42] the Free Staters still in the field lacked the capacity to reoccupy areas under British control. All they could do was to prolong the struggle on the basis of the "cardinal maxim" noted many years later by Henry Kissinger that "the guerrilla wins if he does not lose. The conventional army loses if it does not win."[43] Neither Steyn nor De Wet had any expectation of foreign intervention, so the final phase of the war was characterized by mutual attrition. The guerrillas suffered costs in the expectation of the costs they inflicted (expense, manpower, war weariness, dissatisfaction at home and abroad) being beyond Britain's prewar expectations and cost-tolerance level. In the long run the asymmetry in resources was too great, and the weakness of national sentiment among the Boers meant their political capability could not sustain them in the face of their opponents' overwhelming military capability. Consequently, the struggle was, for the most part, futile—even reckless, the historian André Wessels contends—because it meant that those who continued the war could not escape a share in the responsibility for the suffering of Boer and black civilians.[44]

The Boers who escaped from the Brandwater Basin headed for Heilbron to join De Wet, but he had been driven into the Transvaal. On 14 August they clashed with Hunter's column, and after almost a full day's fighting at Spitskop, eight miles south of Heilbron, they were forced to retire in the direction of Winburg, and Hunter was able to enter Heilbron the following day.[45]

When De Wet returned from the Transvaal on 25 August 1900, he immediately set about recruiting men, reorganizing the command structure, and reviving the war. He launched a recruitment drive to re-commandeer burghers who had taken the oath of neutrality. Henceforth officers would not be elected by their men, but appointed by him, and only those of proven ability would come into consideration. Three such officers were named as assistant chief commandants (generals) of the reconstituted commandos: Piet Fourie, J.B.M. Hertzog, and, later, Christoffel Badenhorst.[46]

As has been pointed out, however, the Boers lacked not only the military capability but also the political will to recapture areas occupied by the British. This was dramatically demonstrated on 27 August when a planned attack on Winburg collapsed under the weight of lack of coordination, poor discipline, and sheer muddleheadedness.

Learning through wiretapping that Maj. Gen. Bruce Hamilton and the men under his command were leaving Winburg by train, the Boers resolved to take the town with between eight hundred and one thousand men. Haasbroek would send one of his sons to guide a group under Comdt. Jan Olivier in an attack from the north, while he would lead an onslaught from the southeast. However, because the railway line to Kroonstad had been broken by other Boers, Hamilton was still in Winburg when the attack took place. Furthermore, because Olivier's commando slept late and their attack took place in daylight, they were easily driven off. In the course of their retreat, twenty-five men were captured, and Olivier himself and his three sons rode into a trap set by the Queenstown Volunteers.[47] According to Olivier's son Henning, Andries van Tonder told Olivier a hill was safe, although the enemy were concealed there, or he left some of his men on the hill but they abandoned it before his return. According to J. D. Kestell's account, Olivier, when called on to surrender, sat laughing on his white horse, thinking his burghers were playing a practical joke on him. However, according to S. J. du Toit, who interviewed Olivier in 1914, he sat weeping with anger and frustration because his burghers had failed him—or was he weeping, as C. J. Uys claims, because he had been betrayed by an unnamed former friend? Piet Kritzinger, who had already been disarmed, made a bolt for it and got away. No, says Kestell, that was Andries van Tonder.[48] Olivier's white horse, at least, is a constant.

Bruce Hamilton's account of what happened is altogether more prosaic. Following a dawn attack on Winburg, which was pressed for about an hour, the Boers fell back to the northeast and the southeast. During the pursuit along the Ventersburg road, eight men of the Queenstown Volunteers became detached about four miles from the town and found themselves near some retreating Boers. They occupied a cattle enclosure and were approached by Olivier and five other stragglers, who mistook them for Boers. Cpl. F. Hayes, who was a few hundred yards from the enclosure, made each of them a prisoner as he came up. He beckoned to fourteen other Boers to follow him and they also fell into the trap. Apart from Comdt. Jan Olivier, his three sons, one of them a field cornet, as well as a Field Cornet Swanepoel, were captured, "the best fighting men of his Commando," Olivier told Hamilton.[49]

On 13 September, Hector MacDonald surprised Haasbroek's Winburgers at Tafelkop on the Vet River, twelve miles south of Winburg. They managed to get away but lost sixteen of their wagons. Despite having to cross the Smaldeel-Winburg railway line in broad daylight, they were not attacked from either side. On the seventeenth MacDonald overtook them at Doornberg. Although they lost eighteen more wagons, the commando escaped unscathed. Wagons had been outlawed as "unnecessary impediments" six months earlier, but comfort proved more alluring than efficiency. Meanwhile the British had reoccupied Senekal, despite a vain attempt by Fourie's commando to resist them.[50]

Christiaan de Wet, who had suffered setbacks at Frederikstad (20–25 October) and Bothaville (6 November), marched south less than a week later in order to put into effect his long cherished plan to invade the Cape Colony. When Roberts heard that De Wet had crossed the Thaba Nchu line, he immediately ordered Maj. Gen. Sir Charles Knox to take command of three columns under lieutenant colonels T. D. Pilcher, I.J.C. Herbert, and J. S. Barker to pursue and engage him.[51] Constantly outwitting his pursuers, De Wet reached the Orange River, but finding it flooded and the Coldstream Guards waiting on the opposite bank, he decided to postpone the invasion. Although the attempted invasion was a failure, De Wet did succeed in drawing off British troops from the republics and in distracting attention from Kritzinger and Hertzog, who crossed into the Cape Colony in safety.

In January 1901 the fighting Free State burghers assembled at Doornberg in the Winburg district and reelected Steyn as president. The remnants of the Free State army and the nation were now synonymous, and it was with the leaders of the burghers still in the field, the de facto government of the republics, that the British would negotiate the terms of the Boer surrender a few months later. After the fall of Bethlehem, officials such as the government secretary, attorney general, treasurer general, and postmaster general had resigned, so the British military authorities were eager to capture Steyn, to whom the powers of the Volksraad had been delegated and in whom so many executive functions were vested.[52]

On the other hand, the position of military governor of the Orange River Colony having been abolished, Maj. Gen. Sir Hamilton Goold-Adams became deputy administrator of the Orange River Colony on 3 February 1901. The intention was that full civilian control should at last become a reality, but with towns cleared of their civilian populations, some towns destroyed, and the countryside laid waste, civil administration was severely hampered. In March,

Kitchener imposed the heavy burden of administering the concentration camps on these rudimentary civil structures. During Milner's absence on leave in England from the beginning of May to the end of August, Kitchener was acting high commissioner and therefore the only arbiter of both military and civilian matters.[53] The former was the top priority, and in February the War Office augmented his army with another thirty thousand mounted troops.

Hard pressed, De Wet resolved to take the war to the British by attempting once more to invade the Cape Colony. Accompanied by Steyn, he started south on 27 January 1901. By the end of the first week of February, twelve British columns were guarding the banks of the Orange River to forestall him. He found a weak point in their surveillance, and on 10 February he crossed the swollen river with more than two thousand men under commandants Froneman, Fourie, and Haasbroek.[54] Relentlessly pursued by Col. Herbert Plumer in pouring rain, De Wet made for the De Aar-Kimberley railway line, which was broken in two places. The teeming rain turned a low-lying area called the Duran Vlei into a quagmire, in which his convoy got stuck. When Plumer got there the next morning, forty wagons, a Maxim gun, and thirty prisoners fell into his hands. The exactions of the pursuit and the lack of adequate grazing took their toll, and De Wet's expectation that he would be able to get fresh horses in the Cape Colony was frustrated because a few weeks earlier the British had confiscated virtually all horses in the northern Cape. On 28 February the exhausted remnants of the invasion force crossed back into the Free State with considerable difficulty.[55]

While Steyn and De Wet were in the Cape, Kitchener, on his own and without consulting Milner, entered into peace negotiations with Louis Botha, the Transvaal commandant general, at Middelburg. Kitchener was prepared to be accommodating, but the Boers rejected his proposals. Kitchener blamed Milner, whose unrelenting insistence on unconditional surrender and refusal of amnesty to Cape rebels he branded as "vindictive." This failure obliged Kitchener to embark on more severe counterinsurgency measures. The completion of a network of eight thousand blockhouses covering thirty-seven hundred miles of the Free State and Transvaal was expedited at vast expense. The blockhouses, which were close enough to one another for converging fire, were connected by barbed wire; protected by ditches, walls, and floodlights; and equipped with land mines, bells, rockets, and flares to alert the fifty thousand soldiers and auxiliaries who guarded the blockhouse lines. These forts divided the country into paddocks to be systematically cleared by columns of mounted men.[56]

Increasingly suspicious of Botha's intentions, Steyn and De Wet responded to peace moves with the stirring affirmation: "The Republics are not conquered. The war is not finished. The burgher forces of the two States are still led by re-

A weary *bittereinder* and his emaciated horse.
(War Museum of the Boer Republics)

sponsible officers, as from the commencement of the war, under the supervision of the Governments of both Republics."[57] De Wet reorganized the Free State forces with a view to the continuation of guerrilla warfare, with each commando operating in its own area. He divided the country into six (later seven) military districts, each under an assistant chief commandant, with Froneman responsible for Winburg-Ladybrand.[58]

During April 1901, troops under colonels T. D. Pilcher and A. W. Thorneycroft "swept" the Winburg district. All that F.C. Hendrik van der Walt, in command of fifty men, could do was to make his presence known to divert the attention of the troops from the civilian population. On the approach of the enemy, a women's laager was directed to move out of reach with the livestock. At this stage of the war a symbiotic relationship between the fighting burghers and the fleeing women can be noted. While the efforts of the Boers were largely directed to protecting women from capture, the women, on occasion, fulfilled a commissariat role.[59]

In June 1901 field cornets Stephanus Cronjé and Johannes Beukes operated along the Vet River, keeping a close watch on a women's laager on the farms Kotzesvlei and Valsfontein. On two successive days in August, the British captured women's laagers guarded by burghers of the Vetrivier ward. In the

Winburg district, the protection of women often pitted the burghers still in the field in clashes with black scouts commanded by Oloff Bergh.[60]

The subdivision of the Boer forces determined the course of events. The British were compelled to divide their forces as well, and small, highly mobile patrols kept large numbers of troops occupied. Major confrontations were avoided; instead numerous skirmishes harassed the British forces. Sarel Haasbroek showed great initiative in independently disrupting British communications, making such effective use of the tactic of dispersion and evasion that Kitchener determined to make a special effort to capture him—along with his mentor, Christiaan de Wet.

On 7 August 1901, Kitchener, despairing of bringing the war to a speedy conclusion, issued his proclamation threatening Boer leaders who were still in the field after 15 September with permanent banishment from South Africa and the rank and file with confiscation of their property to pay for the maintenance of the concentration camps. Bill Nasson describes it as one of Kitchener's "blinding flashes of extremism," and the *Times History of the War* reports it as a "*brutum fulmen,*" as futile as it was misdirected. This is the way most of the fighting Boers saw it too. Former president Reitz mocked the pomposity of the document with its repetition of "whereas," dismissing it as a "paper bomb."[61]

Next Kitchener ordered a series of "drives" to capture the Boer leaders, starting on 18 August 1901. This involved four columns under Lt. Col. Edward Locke Elliot operating between Glen and Ladybrand, as well as columns under Col. J. S. Barker and Maj. Edward Pine-Coffin operating from Winburg, and Brig. Gen. M. F. Rimington and lieutenant colonels A. E. Wilson and J. Spens from Senekal. Haasbroek, however, eluded the elaborate trap that was set for him. Lieutenant colonels Elliot and J.E.D. Bethune failed to capture him at Korannaberg on the twenty-first, and Broadwood arrived too late to help ward off an attack on the Black Watch on the twenty-second. On 27 August, one Boer was killed and two captured; on the twenty-ninth fourteen hundred Boers were reported to be in the vicinity of Tafelberg; in the days that followed, conflicting orders sought to redirect the pursuing columns. On 1 September, Bethune attacked Witnek, where about a hundred Boers had been seen. The next day Elliot signaled to ask Bethune, "What was your bag yesterday and had you any casualties?" The "bag" turned out to be 1 Boer killed and 127 cattle and 230 horses captured. This supplemented Bethune's casualty list for the month of August, which detailed 2 Boers killed, 3 wounded, 18 armed and 48 unarmed prisoners, 960 refugees, 1,700 horses, 3,904 cattle, and 7,540 sheep, in addition to the crops destroyed. On September 9, Elliot's division once more set out from Winburg for a sweep in the direction of Harrismith. As in earlier sweeps, few armed Boers were captured, but much hardship was inflicted on the women and damage done to the agricultural economy.[62]

Again on 6 November, fourteen columns, comprising fifteen thousand troops, including Colonel Barker moving from Winburg, were ordered to converge on Paardehoek, sixteen miles north of Reitz, but still the commandos eluded them. The British signals, reproduced in Malcolm Riall's *Boer War,* reflect "a great deal of huffing and puffing by the column commander—Colonel [William] Lowe—at the lack of alacrity on the part of his subordinates," the irritation of the gunners in need of parts for their guns, the difficulty of coordinating the movements of so many men, and the frustration of their quarry eluding them and how the capture of livestock seemed to compensate for the failure to capture men. They also reflect frustration with Kitchener's failed attempts to counter Boer mobility with centralized control, telegraphic directives, and the superior numbers and firepower of mobile columns that "continued to be shuffled about the country in blind ignorance right to the end of the war."[63]

Before dawn on 4 January 1902 about 130 Winburgers encamped at the confluence of the Vet and Sand Rivers were surrounded by 600–700 soldiers. Most of the Boers got away, but 50 to 60 prisoners were taken, including three fifteen-year-olds, two fourteen-year-olds, a ten-year-old, and a nine-year-old. They were all deported to India. In November 1901 the Commando Law had been amended to allow fourteen-year-olds to be called up for military duty, and Steyn himself encouraged F.C. Hendrik van der Walt to give his nine-year-old son a rifle.[64] The completion of the blockhouse lines and the ensuing drives yielded a further meager crop of prisoners. Thus Michael Human and his sons, ages nine and thirteen; Jan Sennett and his fifteen-year-old son; Christiaan Pienaar; and seventy-year-old Daniel Wessels were captured on 10 February 1902. They too were shipped off to India.[65]

A factor that complicated the lives of the 17,000 burghers still in the field was the increasing number of their compatriots serving with the British. These scouts and guides were familiar with Boer haunts and practices. The bittereinders learned to be wary—for instance, never sleeping twice in the same place—but their morale was sapped, especially by the accelerating rate of defection from their ranks in the final months of the war, ultimately reaching a total of 5,464 men, one-third of the bittereinder strength. The various corps of scouts were united in the Orange River Colony (ORC) Volunteers, the Winburg branch of which was under the command of Stephanus Vilonel. Although the ORC Volunteers usually operated in conjunction with British units, there was an encounter on 18 April 1902 in which only Boers were involved.[66] Boer patrols were also involved in almost daily clashes with black scouts,[67] whom they regarded as rebellious subjects and to whom no quarter was given.

And so the war limped on from day to day until, at last, on 31 May 1902 at Vereeniging, Gen. Christoffel Froneman, assistant chief commandant for Winburg and Ladysmith, and Comdt. Frederik Cronjé of Winburg, who had been elected as representatives of the burghers of the Winburg district still in the field, cast their votes for peace.

The Option to Go on Fighting

As one surveys the inexorable course of the war and its inevitable outcome, one is struck by the fact that so many Boers chose to persist in the face of impossible odds. As the Free Staters fell back before the British juggernaut, they passed their farms and were confronted by the stark alternatives of leaving the commando and hopefully retaining what they had or pressing on and forfeiting everything. "Every Boer confronted this choice," Frederik Rompel wrote, "and half of the 20,000 Free Staters left wife and child behind, in spite of the fact that it would have been so much easier, so much more advantageous and reassuring for them to leave the commando to protect and care for wife and child."[68] An obvious assumption would be that their perseverance was a result of a strongly developed national feeling, but in the next chapter it is argued that this idea is anachronistic, that home and hearth exerted a greater appeal at this stage than the bonds of nationhood. Yet national sentiment played a part, because the war was a catalyst of Afrikaner nationalism. In this regard the social profile of the bittereinders and the role of patriarchy were significant factors.

Bill Nasson says, "In the closing phase of the war the broad profile confirms a conspicuous class differentiation in the social base of National Scouts and bittereinders."[69] This view enjoys wide support but probably more often as a value judgment than on the basis of research. It would seem to be too unnuanced on both counts. Oskar Hintrager drew attention to the phenomenon of richer burghers sitting at home because they had more to lose,[70] and Hermann Giliomee's contention that the bittereinders "were mostly commercial farmers and educated professional men" will not stand up to scrutiny.[71] It is true, as John X. Merriman pointed out, that "all, or nearly all, the prominent leaders were either progressive farmers . . . or educated men from the towns,"[72] the very people Hintrager identified as "Afrikaners" as opposed to "Boers."[73] These "Afrikaner" leaders who emerged during the final stages of the war were indeed motivated by a developed national sentiment. From them a powerful ideological impetus went out and the rank and file were transformed by it. This too Hintrager saw and commented on. By September 1900, he says, the Boers were "a nation of brothers under arms."[74]

Because of the patriarchal structure of their society, Boers were very amenable to the influence of their leaders. Good leadership promoted courageous action; as Rev. R. D. McDonald put it, "led by a brave officer even the coward becomes a hero."[75] Poor leadership during the early part of the war contributed to disillusionment, and when leaders abandoned the cause, the burghers were inclined to follow suit. Thus when Comdt. Frans Cloete decided to surrender, the bulk of his Edenburg commando did so as well.[76] During the guerrilla phase of the war, most of the old guard disappeared from leadership roles. In their place came dynamic commanders who evoked feelings of passionate loyalty in their followers. In this regard, Christiaan de Wet was preeminent, but De Wet's role is inseparable from that of President Steyn.

The longer the struggle lasted, the more the "cost-sunk factor" came into play; in other words, the massive extent of the sacrifice already made (De Wet's "rivers of blood") was an incentive to the Boers—indeed to both sides—not to give up.[77] The high mortality of women and children in the concentration camps was a particularly powerful inducement to fight on, and militant Boer women used it to keep their husbands in the field. This cost-sunk factor operated at both the national and the individual level, with leaders like Steyn and De Wet staking not only national honor but also their own prestige and future reputation on a favorable outcome.

The Dutch military attaché Carolus Asselbergs drew attention to endurance as a typical Boer characteristic, saying that their resilience could be attributed to a marked degree of toughness and tenacity.[78] Stubbornness may be identified as a psychological dimension of Boer hardiness, and in this characteristic Steyn led the way.[79] From the start of hostilities, he warned his officers that it was to be a struggle to the bitter end; he was instrumental in sabotaging every peace initiative; and, in the end, he resigned his office, thus avoiding the ignominy of putting his hand to the peace treaty. People use suicide as the ultimate psychological ploy to prove a point, and in a sense this is what Steyn did. He sacrificed himself in vindication of his honor and his duty to his people. But when he seemed willing to sacrifice his people as well, some were bound to call it mere obstinacy. The Transvaalers did just that at the Boer meeting in Klerksdorp that preceded the Treaty of Vereeniging.[80] Steyn retired from the fray with his image as the father of his people untarnished by surrender. His position was quite simply that unless the British were prepared to concede independence, the struggle must continue.[81]

F. F. Pienaar portrays De Wet in an unflattering light. He was ill-mannered and unkempt, tactless, brusque, and lacking in polish. He was notoriously short-tempered and freely laid into anyone suspected of being a laggard. Yet, far from repelling, these traits contributed to his image of powerful leadership in view of the hegemonic conception of masculinity in Boer society. With his charisma and reputation for military success, he drew to him men for whom being a man was synonymous with aggression, and to be weak was to be a woman.[82]

Religious and political feelings and discourse increasingly converged. As Jan Smuts said, "The Boer cause has become a Boer religion. Adversity has converted their political creed into a religious faith; and thus hope and faith and strength have been wrung from weakness and despair itself."[83] Boer civil religion lent ardor and authority to this nascent Boer nationalism. Paul Roux was a clergyman turned general, and secular commanders resorted to the Scriptures to justify their continuation of the struggle. Steeped in the Scriptures, the Boers identified with the people of Israel, and the concept of the faithful remnant spoke to their situation. They well knew that Gideon's army had to be reduced to a small band before it could defeat the Midianites. To outsiders the Boers' religious ardor was something extraordinary and, in combination with ignorance, mere fanaticism, but as a young observer, Karel van den Berg, perceived, "such faith, which is actually fanaticism, can undoubtedly achieve wonders."[84]

The course of events lent itself to different interpretations, and the vast size of the theater of war made it possible to put a favorable spin on engagements that occurred at a distance. According to Fransjohan Pretorius, the propaganda value of the war bulletins that were read out to the men on commando derived from the fact that "they contained truths, half truths and blatant lies."[85] In British circles it was widely held that if the Boers knew the true state of affairs, they would not go on fighting.[86] But the outcome of battles was misrepresented, the hope of foreign intervention was assiduously cultivated, Britain's problems abroad were exaggerated, and an uprising of Cape Afrikaners was anticipated.

From the start, Kruger's emissary Dr. W. J. Leyds had warned him that the hope of foreign intervention was illusory, that no major power would endanger its friendly relations with Britain. Yet Steyn claimed there was "reliable news" that Russians planned to occupy Herat and threaten India, and if the Boers held out for just six to eight more weeks, the British might be forced to accept terms.[87] In a similar vein, Steyn urged Schalk Burger, the acting president of the Transvaal, to keep up the struggle till a more sympathetic government came to power in Britain.[88] The "Khaki election," the general election of 1900, when the governing party was returned to power with an increased majority, demonstrated the folly of this delusion.

Reassurances about the role of foreign powers could achieve apocalyptic dimensions in the popular imagination. Folk wisdom and shaky geography coalesced with wishful thinking, and it was held that independence for the republics was Queen Wilhelmina's wedding wish that could not be denied, or that there was a bloodbath in Paris, where the harbor was full of sunken battleships and the English flag had been lowered.[89] Joubert Reitz satirized the foolish talk that was circulating among the burghers. The latest news, he wrote—although it was uncertain whether or not it was official—includes a French bombardment of Paris and the revelation that the French had bought Delagoa Bay and Kruger was there even now, awaiting the arrival of a mighty army of Russians and Americans.[90]

In addition to the hope of foreign intervention, the burghers were sustained by the anticipation of a general uprising in the Cape. An invasion in the early days, before the tide turned, might have secured general support from this quarter, but a general uprising was still depended on long after it was clear that it would not happen. According to an official Boer communiqué on De Wet's incursion into the Cape at the beginning of 1901: "De Wet's latest news is that the Cape Colony has risen to a man, and has already taken up arms."[91]

The whole nature of a man's commitment to the guerrilla band was different from commitment to a commando. The explanation for this change was both circumstantial and ideological. In a small group the members were far more dependent on one another, far more directly accountable to one another. The bonds of shared privation were stronger, the comradeship more intense. Reinforced by kinship bonds, the fighting unit was the burgher's family, the encampment his home, for, as Comdt. Lodi Krause famously put it, the homeless could no longer go home.[92]

A sense of mutual accountability would also be consistent with a reluctance to abandon the struggle, as it was feared that Cape rebels as well as those guilty of excesses would be abandoned to their fate. This applied to influential leaders like Christiaan de Wet and Christoffel Froneman, who risked prosecution for the killing of the captured peace envoy J. J. Morgendaal. Joseph Chamberlain instructed Milner that De Wet was not to be prosecuted, and Kitchener assured the Boer delegates that only three Boers would be exempt from the general amnesty provided for in Article 4 of the peace treaty. The record reveals a De Wet who was clearly uncomfortable on this score, objecting at the Klerksdorp meeting that the Boer delegates had only Kitchener's word that other names would not be added at a later stage.[93]

Apart from Article 4, the other major difference between the Middelburg proposals and the final peace treaty was Article 8, relating to the future status of black people. The Boer diarist Alie Badenhorst was convinced that black domination was the inevitable consequence of surrender.[94] The Boer delegates were profoundly disturbed by the threat posed by blacks, made vivid by the Zulu attack at Holkrans only days before their meeting. It was only when they were reassured that their interests would predominate under British rule that bittereinders were less reluctant to surrender.

Pretorius points out that being on commando became a way of life.[95] In any war, men are affirmed in their compliance with the values of masculinity—for example, independence, resourcefulness, ruggedness, and the capacity to ignore danger and endure adversity. A clearly defined command structure abrogates the responsibility for individual decision making and promotes socialization with one's peers. This is further fostered by the exclusion of women from the man's world of the fighting unit and the association of cowardice with women.[96] During the guerrilla phase of the war, enjoyment of commando life was untrammeled by ever present danger. Hendrik Ver Loren van Themaat captures the exhilaration very well: "In spite of all our complaints, we enjoyed this ranging over the free, open veld, this daily life of readily forgetting the past and unconcern for the future; tired at night but fresh in the morning, cheerful if there was good food, inured to weariness, phlegmatic about setbacks. Every day brings its tasks; when they are done, one can do as one pleases, even if it's lolling on one's back in the grass—such is life."[97] Ver Loren van Themaat wrote of one kind of exhilaration. To conclude, we may note another, more subtle kind of exhilaration: that which derives from the self-concept of being one of "the few," one of those who are privileged to have a heroic part to play in the history of their time. They share in the glory that Shakespeare's Henry V promises his men on the field at Agincourt.

2 The Failure of Protection

THE BRITISH BREAKTHROUGH at Pieter's Hill on the Natal front on 27 February 1900 and the surrender of Cronjé with 3,919 men on the same day on the western front, followed by the occupation of Bloemfontein on 13 March, convinced vast numbers of Free State Boers of the hopelessness of their cause. When Lord Roberts resumed his advance from Bloemfontein and the Boers fell back in disarray before the overwhelming superiority of his forces, Winburgers were bound to share in the general demoralization.

Two days after the occupation of Bloemfontein, Roberts issued a proclamation similar in tenor to one he had issued in mid-February when he entered the Free State. The February proclamation had promised that those who "desist from any further hostility towards Her Majesty's Government . . . and who are found staying in their homes and quietly pursuing their ordinary occupations, will not be made to suffer in their persons or property on account of their having taken up arms in obedience to the order of their Government," to which the revised version added the requirement of an oath of neutrality.[1]

This chapter tells how disillusionment with the war heightened the appeal of the proclamation. Yet the prospect of returning to a quiet life untouched by the war proved illusory. The British army simply did not have the manpower to provide the promised protection. Instead, surrendered burghers endured British harassment as a result of looting, requisitioning, the random operation of martial law, and the impossibility of differentiating between peaceable citizens and oath-breaking belligerents. The return of the commandos meant that surrendered burghers were also under pressure from their countrymen who demanded that they rejoin, and for those who refused, sanctions included imprisonment, abduction, confiscation of their goods, and even death.

Disillusionment with the War Effort

The appeal of the proclamation was almost irresistible, both in regard to its timing and in terms of what it promised. Two contemporary writers described the proclamation as "seductive," given the Boers' war weariness on the one hand and their deep attachment to their families and farms on the other. They were farmers, not soldiers, burghers who fought for hearth and home, not a professional standing army.[2] As one writer aptly puts it, "The Winburgers, like Afrikaners everywhere, were defending their home and their place; that was all."[3]

War weariness set in at an early stage. The descent into Natal had something of a carnival atmosphere about it, but the lack of any sort of overall strategy, the monotony of inactivity, and the realization that the war would not be brought to a speedy conclusion soon dampened the Boers' enthusiasm. Men started drifting off—with or without permission.

The law laid down that males between the ages of sixteen and sixty were liable for military service. In spite of this, more than 172 Winburgers in this age bracket had not gone on commando, at least 71 of them because they were ill or unfit and at least 50 because they were ineligible by virtue of their occupations—for example, shop assistants, railway workers, and government officials. The good faith of some of those who claimed illness was called into question by their fellow burghers, who did not accept that they were unfit for commando service. It is doubtful that all 50 men in reserved occupations were performing essential services, and some of them, such as William Fuchs of Smaldeel and Alfred Goldsmith of Ventersburg, were commandeered but refused to serve. In addition, at least 30 burghers from the Winburg district were so plagued by ill health that they were allowed to go home, where they surrendered on the approach of the British army. Of course, some whose illness persisted were prevented from returning to the front and had no option but to surrender when Winburg fell. For others, however, claims of unwellness appear to have been mere subterfuge. For example, George Loubscher went home to his farm in November 1899 and Johannes Venter to his in December; both subsequently acknowledged that when they did so they had no intention of returning to commando duty. There were persistent demands for home leave, and one Winburger went so far as to shoot a finger off in order to have his request granted. This was not a unique occurrence, as Count Adalbert Sternberg says that Boers even shot themselves in the foot or the arm in order to be sent home.[4]

Nothing could have been designed to have greater appeal to these men who delighted in domesticity than the resumption of family life and the quiet pursuit of their ordinary occupations promised in Roberts's proclamation. It is not surprising that their officers made every effort to prevent the burghers getting to know about it. F.C. Gert I. van Rooyen was present on an occasion when the proclamation was discussed. Christiaan de Wet produced a copy and said he held the officers responsible for preventing its dissemination. Copies were to be destroyed by officers and action taken against anyone found in possession of one. The officers' concern to keep knowledge of the proclamation from the burghers is confirmed by Paul Nel, who wrote: "I saw it when the Boers were retiring from Modder River. We had to keep it secret on account of the Boer officers."[5] But having seen the proclamation, Van Rooyen says, he surrendered at the first opportunity. It had a similar effect on Hendrik le Roux, who found copies in some looted wagons at Sannaspos.[6]

Nor could circulation of the proclamation be prevented. Burghers told one another about it, showed each other copies, pored over it in the stores they visited, corresponded about it. The proclamation was distributed by British agents, such as Antonie Baumann and Dr. Paul Gillespie, who was arrested by the Boers for doing so. Copies were scattered from the windows of passing trains, and this was how Philippus Meyer, whose farm was near the railway line, came to know about it.[7] Most commonly, British troops brought the proclamation to the farms they visited, where they found despondent Boers responsive to its message. Sometimes the husband was absent but the wife received it on his behalf. Indeed, it is striking that women, who by common consent were more ardent in pursuit of the Boer cause than the men, are so frequently mentioned as conduits of the peace message.

Between March and July 1900 alone, some six thousand Free Staters laid down their arms, a quarter of those for whom military service was compulsory and 40 percent of the initial mobilization.[8]

Between Two Fires

President Steyn tried to stem the tide of men leaving the commandos by the assertion in his counter-proclamation of 19 March 1900 that the Free State government was still in operation and that burghers were therefore still required to serve. Those who failed in their duty to the lawfully constituted authority were guilty of high treason. Following the annexation of the Free State on 28 May 1900, the British branded Boers who continued to fight "rebels," while Boer leaders, asserting the legitimacy of their government, called on Boers who had surrendered to rejoin the commandos. G.H.L. Le May formulates the dilemma neatly: "Many an individual was faced with the grim alternative of being treated by the British as an oath-breaker or by his own people as a renegade; and usually it was his own people who presented the immediate alternative more compellingly."[9]

The legitimacy of the Boer government obviously carried weight with Rachel van Rooyen, a woman from the Winburg district, who said: "The sheep, horses and mules were taken from our farm where we had left them when my husband took me away to evade British columns by instructions from the President and Boer authorities, as we considered ourselves under the protection of the Boer government." Jacobus Bornman, an eighty-two-year-old member of the Volksraad in President Brand's time, found himself precariously balanced on the horns of the dilemma. "The Boers were a few times on my farm," he wrote, "for example, De Wet . . . stayed on my farm one night and took some forage. I refused to sell it to him. Being an armed body of men, it was not possible for me to prevent it. In this way, I have also remained loyal to the laws of the Boers, but I have done nothing to help them."[10]

On the other hand, the primacy of the practical issue of power over the theoretical issue of legitimacy is neatly demonstrated in the story of Albertus Tempelhof of the farm Boschkop, just nine miles west of Winburg. On 2 November 1900 he was on his way to deliver milk to the hospitals in the town when he saw seven horsemen riding toward him and decided to turn back. They raced up and fired three shots, so he reined in his horses. One of the men, Roelof Botes, called him a rebel and ordered him at gunpoint to get down from the cart. Asked why he was not fighting, Tempelhof replied that there was no Free State government to fight for. His adversaries asked who was protecting him, and he replied that he was under the protection of the British government. When they pressed the point by asking who was protecting him that morning, his response was that the British could not protect him against every robber. Botes then drove off with Tempelhof's cart and all the milk on it.[11]

In the absence of the promised protection against both the invaders and their own countrymen, close to three thousand Free Staters rejoined the commandos in the course of 1900. Some of them evidently repented of their action in surrendering and did not wait to be commandeered. Thus Barend Meyer surrendered on 5 June 1900, had second thoughts just two weeks later, rejoined, and served loyally to the end. At about the same time, Jacobus Smit lamented his weakness in surrendering and felt justified in rejoining in light of British disregard of Roberts's promises.[12]

British Harassment

As early as January 1900, British officers had been warned to ensure "that soldiers are never allowed to enter private houses or molest inhabitants under any pretext whatever, and that every precaution is taken to suppress looting or petty robbery by any persons in any way connected with the Army." But this directive was more honored in the breach than in the observance. Barely six months later, when a British officer, Capt. F. P. Fletcher-Vane, reported an incident in which a farm was ransacked and wrecked, the response of his superior officer was, "Oh, but this woman's husband is on commando, so of course we have the right to loot the farm."[13]

This was how the Winburg district experienced the arrival of British troops in their midst. Hendrik de Bruyn was never on commando, but when the troops traversed his farm on 5 May 1900, they "simply looted" it. Thomas Mitchell of the farm Welkom, who accommodated Ian Hamilton and his staff advancing on Winburg, was pillaged by them despite his cooperation. A doctor asked Mitchell if some wounded men could sleep in a locked store. Early the next morning Mitchell found no wounded men in the store, which had been thoroughly looted. The next day Winburg was taken. That same afternoon the store of Jose Houlton was looted. Capt. G. Brindley of the 2nd Manchester Regiment, reported that he visited Houlton's shop, which was completely stocked. An hour later, when he had occasion to go there again, it was being plundered by men of Hamilton's column, who had cleared almost all the shelves. He advised Houlton to close up shop, but he was powerless to do anything about the looters, as they "immediately cleared off and there was no guard near."[14]

The next day, Smaldeel was occupied and three stores in the village were looted, those of William Holland, Bernardus Jaffit, and Armond Rasmussen. On 8 May, Sidney Lucas reported to the provost marshal that his shop had been targeted by soldiers. Less than a week later it was the Ventersburg business of Bergstedt & Gerlach that was looted. Capt. R. Cobbard testified: "When I arrived, the place was full of men of all corps, some hundreds in number, and was already practically looted. I saved the man's money and books—but could do no more." On 22 May, while Anton Schultz was detained on the farm Mexico, where he had gone to surrender, his store on the farm Leyden was looted. His wife said that she had locked the front part of the shop when she and two British officers who were engaged in requisitioning goods went into the back storeroom. When they returned they found that troops had broken the lock, entered the shop, and were helping themselves to the contents of the display cabinets.[15]

Not only shops, but private houses too were looted. On 5 May, Nathaniel Schnehage's house on the farm Doornfontein, six miles south of Winburg, was looted while he was detained in an outroom by members of Hamilton's column, and £286 in gold was removed from a locked *secretaire*. The following day, the home of Sidney Green, imprisoned by the Boers for refusing to take up arms against the British, was plundered by his countrymen. On 11 May, troops ransacked Jan Vorster's home near Ventersburg. Upon the occupation of Smaldeel, the home of Carl Schaumkel was broken into, and clothing, jewelry, and a treasured stamp collection were stolen. On 19 May, Charles Webb, a British subject and an old man, a gunner in the Crimean War, went to the farm Mexico to report his presence to the British commandant there and on his return found his farmhouse had been broken into.[16]

Officers seemed to have little control over their men. Indeed, a mind-set prevailed that troops had a right to plunder, as emerges from a letter that a soldier named Steuart Binny, caught up in the siege of Ladysmith, wrote to his mother in England: "I want to go to the Free State, and steal, and plunder—that's what I came out for."[17]

On surrendering and taking the oath of neutrality, burghers were issued with a protection pass, safeguarding their property. However, the insatiable needs of the army enjoyed priority, overruling the promised protection. When horses were requisitioned on 30 May 1900 and David Roux told the provost marshal that he had a protection pass from his predecessor, Maj. Count Albert Gleichen, Lieutenant Halm responded, "Oh—that's wastepaper! If Lord Roberts himself had signed it, you would have to give it to me if I demand it." And the disagreeable Halm, we are told, was "succeeded by as great a bully."[18]

From 4 November 1900 protection passes were abrogated altogether. Black auxiliaries were employed and expected a share of the loot, and the homes of women transported to the camps were routinely looted. The widow Johanna Cloete, whose husband had been killed early in the war, deposed the following: "On 24 March 1901 about 50 men of Gen. Bethune's Column came to the Estate [Foxhill Estate, owned by the mining magnate Abe Bailey], when I showed my protection pass to the officer in charge. This occurred in the front of the house and while we were conversing, a lot of the Troops entered the house and when I entered, I found that everything that had been locked was broken open, my furniture destroyed and a lot carried away, others again distributed some of the things amongst the blacks."[19]

The garrison that occupied Winburg had to be fed, so troops scoured the surrounding countryside requisitioning goods. They needed firewood, so on their very first day in the town, soldiers set about dismantling the grandstand of the Winburg Turf Club, which seated 248 people, in order to chop it up for firewood. In Senekal, St. Michael's Church was stripped of its pews. The officers needed accommodation, so houses were requisitioned. Winburg's flourishing library was destroyed; the books were "scattered completely," some even later being found on the town commonage.[20]

Margaret Marquard refers to the military exactions experienced in Winburg as "the state of plunder under martial law," the "ceaseless story of bullying going on," and "continued acts of wholesale and unblushing robbery," and she quotes Boer informants as saying that if they had known it was going to be like this they would not have left off fighting. Frieda Schrubstock, who ran a stall at Ventersburg Road station, complained of being bullied by the local commandant, a Captain Becker, who expected her to provision him free of charge. He apparently threatened her, saying, "You better look out, I am just as much as Puynkoffyn [his predecessor, Major Pine-Coffin]."[21]

Military occupation was accompanied by regulations that impinged on every aspect of daily life. Civilians were obliged to be in their homes after 8 P.M., and farmers were ordered to extinguish all lights by 9 P.M. Passes were required to move from place to place. If an alarm sounded, all residents of Winburg were obliged to stay indoors. A notice from the censor's office, dated 28 September 1900, is as informative for its high-handed tone as for its content: "Persons whose correspondence is carried on in any other language than English must expect considerable delay in the despatch and receipt of their letters. In cases where the services of a translator cannot be obtained, letters are liable to be detained indefinitely." Further evidence of the arbitrary exercise of power is that letters from the prisoner-of-war camps addressed "O.V.S." (for Orange Free State) were returned on the grounds that such a place was unknown.[22]

At first civilians were allowed the use of bicycles, but they had to be licensed at the commandant's office. With bicycles a rarity in Winburg, one can imagine the chagrin of Cecil Bell, now the magistrate's clerk in British service, when, just a month after he had surrendered the town, his new Singer bicycle became yet another casualty of the war. It was parked outside the courthouse when ammunition that the Boers had stored in the building was blown up by order of the provost marshal. A few days after Bell lost his bicycle, all bicycles in the town were confiscated and riding about on horseback or bicycle was forbidden until further notice. Wilhelm Koenig, the local hairdresser and soda water maker, had to surrender three bicycles, "as the authorities did not think it advisable to allow Civilians to possess Bicycles." When the war ended, his bicycles had disappeared without a trace. Bicycles belonging to farmers were also confiscated.[23]

The Vagaries of Martial Law

Winburg was an occupied town, and "the individual under martial law, in truth has little protection against military caprice, and his subsequent remedies are illusory."[24] Capt. F. P. Fletcher-Vane, who was commandant of Kroonstad, goes so far as to describe the powers of a commandant as comparable to those of a Nero or Caligula.[25]

The random application of martial law left people feeling aggrieved and unprotected. Funds were available for the payment of informers, and the Intelligence Department, which was driven by suspicion, assiduously followed up on reports received. In the search for concealed weapons, the flagstones of David Roux's wagon house were pulled up and the ground outside his office was dug up, as was Peter Kahts's garden. Men were arrested for "making signs" to Boers in the field. That was the charge brought against Aaron Pincus and Solomon Sorski, two members of Winburg's Jewish community who had been on commando until the fall of Bloemfontein. After surrendering, the two men were contracted to the British authorities to supply meat to the concentration camp but were arrested on 24 April 1901 for allegedly signaling the enemy. Acting on behalf of the Imperial Russian government, whose subjects they were, the French consul general in Pretoria insisted that Pincus was a noncombatant and had been compelled to go on commando. Despite this claim, the two men were sent to Cape Town to be deported. While they were awaiting deportation, the Imperial Russian Consulate intervened. Advised of the circumstances of their imprisonment, however, the consul made an about-turn, insisting, "It is immaterial to me whether they are kept in South Africa or not," and they were then dispatched to Bermuda.[26] This sudden loss of interest was probably a manifestation of anti-Semitism, for Nathan Berger contends that while other nationals had the protection of their governments, the Russian Jews of the Republics could not rely on the protection of the Tsarist government.[27]

St. John Cole Bowen, the resident magistrate of Winburg, acknowledged that men were sometimes deported on the strength of vague statements without any proof. There was no particular reason, he said, for the deportation of Johannes Meyer; whether or not a burgher was sent away "seems simply to have been a matter of what column the surrender was made to." Willem Fourie was kept in prison "probably on a vague statement without proof."[28]

The vagueness of charges brought by neighbors is well illustrated by the case of Willem Pretorius of the farm Rietfontein. On the strength of information supplied by Gert le Roux, Pretorius was made a prisoner of war because he was "suspected of being mixed up in engineering the Sannah's Post [Sannaspos] disaster." The depth of the malice that motivated informants can be deduced from the story of Dr. Esaias Snyman. After surrendering, Snyman became the medical officer in charge of the British military hospital in Ventersburg. He was highly regarded, but he was arrested and deported at the instance of "an informant (now deceased) who was activated by private spite owing to a quarrel between him and Claimant before the war."[29]

This informant was a burgher named Thomas Harvey, who ran the Free State Hotel in Ventersburg. When the war broke out, Harvey left the hotel to join Rimington's Guides. On 8 May 1900, only days after Winburg was taken, the 2nd Netherlands Ambulance, which was heading for Kroonstad, was apprehended by a British patrol. Among them, Boer nurse Betty Wessels noted, was an "Afrikander named Harvey." He accused the Boers of using ambulance wagons for conveying ammunition. Later that evening some fifty shots were fired at the ambulance, presumably by Harvey's patrol. Somewhere near Kimberley, Harvey came across Snyman's ambulance men and told them that he would do Snyman all the harm he could. As a result of Harvey's machinations, Snyman was sent as a prisoner of war to India on 30 October 1900. Furthermore, contrary to the orders of Bruce Hamilton and three days after the destruction of the rest of Ventersburg, Snyman's house was wantonly destroyed.[30]

Another doctor who was the victim of a dubious informer was Fritz Reich, who practiced in Senekal. Christiaan de Wet said of Reich, "Although he did not belong to our Field Ambulance, he did everything that he could for our wounded, as he had done for those of the enemy." After surrendering in May 1900, Reich was put in charge of the British hospital in Senekal. While thus employed he obtained a pass from Colonel Pilcher to buy provisions in Winburg and allegedly made use of the opportunity to engage in some espionage. As a result, the post of the Winburg Cattle Guard under Sgt. R. Allen was surprised on 28 June 1901, and Allen and ten privates were obliged to surrender. The British authorities discovered the source of the Boer intelligence from a captured artilleryman, Zacharias Hayward. Reich was arrested at the end of August 1901, imprisoned in Winburg, and three weeks later obliged to accept voluntary repatriation to Germany.[31]

On the face of it Reich deserved to have his subsequent compensation claim for damage suffered during the war, amounting to nearly £2,100, disallowed. However, there are a number of circumstances suggesting that in this case too military justice may equate with injustice. First, the evidence against Reich was obtained from an unheroic and no doubt unreliable source. Zacharias Hayward had been found hiding unarmed in a cave near Senekal. He was deported to India but offered to provide information in exchange for the chance of returning to South Africa. The first intelligence with which he whetted the military's appetite was that Hendrina Joubert, widow of the commandant general, was a conduit not only for intelligence but also for arms and ammunition.[32] Second, Reich was not put on trial, but imprisoned in Winburg for three weeks and then offered the alternative of voluntary repatriation. Third, on arrival in Germany he immediately approached the War Office with the urgent request that he should be afforded the opportunity of exonerating himself from "the absolutely untrue and monstrous accusation, that I was proved to be a spy." The response to this was that Roberts had made no such accusation against Reich and was "unable to cause any investigation to be instituted as to any remarks anyone else may have made." Reich was so agitated about the dishonor he had to endure that he next asked the German army, by whom he was now employed, to investigate the allegation. In a memorandum from the British government dated 5 March 1904, the whole issue of guilt was neatly sidestepped by the specious argument that because Reich was a citizen of the (nonexistent) Orange Free State at the time of the alleged incident, "in the opinion of the British Government therefore the service which the abovenamed rendered to his countrymen of that time could not do any harm to his honour."[33]

The case against Wilhelm Tripmacker was built on suspicions, assumptions, and absurdities. After Tripmacker had taken the oath of neutrality in May 1900, Col. J. S. Barker reported him as "a dangerous man," being practically the leader of the anti-British party and suspected of communicating with the enemy. He was sent to Bloemfontein as an "undesirable," but the German vice-consul protested that the treatment meted out to this "quiet, self-possessed and loyal man" was "unworthy a human being." The Intelligence Department was confident that its agents' investigations pointed not only to Tripmacker's guilt but to that of other German residents as well. A month later Tripmacker was allowed to return to Winburg, but he was soon rearrested and sent to Cape Town for deportation to India. The German consul general sent a protest to Milner, the high commissioner, and, having re-naturalized as a German citizen in March 1901, Tripmacker went to Germany the following month. "Maybe he was deported because he talked too much," mused Walter James, his business manager, and Maj. C. R. Lees came close to concurring with this view when he wrote, "I can get no further evidence that he did anything more than talk foolishly."[34]

The vice-consul for Germany vouched for the loyalty of the German community, but the British administration alleged "serious accusations" against some of them. Most of the Germans in the district were engaged in business, and whatever their initial sentiments may have been, dragging out the war was inimical to their commercial interests. What Major O'Leary said of T.C.L. Bergstedt (an American by birth) applies equally well to the German businessmen: "He is a man who well sees in what direction his interests lie, and is not at all likely to injure his prospects by political misconduct."[35] Those engaged in commerce desired stability and therefore favored the British cause with increasing vigor. At a time when the Continental press was vehemently anti-British, a protest meeting, chaired by Edward Rosslien, was held in Winburg on 17 February 1902 to refute calumnies against the British army. A declaration to this effect was signed by nineteen German businessmen,[36] including one who was an importer of arms and ammunition and had presumably done good business in the run-up to the war.

Garrisons Withdrawn

The Earl of Rosslyn drew attention to the deleterious effect of the British practice of occupying a town, exacting the oath of neutrality, and then leaving the inhabitants to their fate, for "it can never be said that this is a method of inspiring confidence or giving fairplay to a people who, sitting between two stools, are happier as they were than as they are."[37] His examples are Thaba Nchu, Dewetsdorp, and Ladybrand, to which we may add Senekal and Ventersburg in the Winburg district.

The garrison that occupied Senekal on 25 May 1900 was withdrawn on 26 August, because the troops were too thin on the ground for men to be spared from active service. The town was reoccupied on 15 September, and cleared of its population on 30 April 1901. By virtue of the surrender of the town, the inhabitants had become protected burghers, but the withdrawal of the British presence left them unprotected. As Oliver Edwards put it, they "were totally left to the mercy of the Boers." Interestingly, the same Edwards subsequently accused Nicolaas Boer of being "on most intimate terms with all the Boer officials after the British evacuation." Nicolaas Boer surrendered Senekal to General Rundle, took the oath of neutrality, and made himself useful to Maj. K. P. Apthorp, the commandant of the town. After the British left and the Boers returned, the Boer landdrost, George Cooper, asked Nicolaas Boer to read a dispatch from Christiaan de Wet, "and [he] could not very well refuse."[38]

Equally ambiguous was the situation of local farmer Christoffel Fourie. He had been on commando until he surrendered on 26 May 1900 and was allowed to return to his farm. He was taken prisoner by the Boers on 24 August but released by the returning British on 15 September. Two months later Cooper ordered Fourie to come into Senekal. When Fourie refused to comply, two armed burghers were sent to arrest him. He was paroled in the town, but when it was reoccupied by the British on 15 December, he was hauled before Gen. J. E. Boyce. Because the town was not garrisoned, Fourie once again returned to his farm until taken prisoner by British troops.[39]

The changing fortunes of war also produced an awkward situation in Ventersburg, where John Leech signed the oath of allegiance before Capt. C.G.H. Sitwell, the local commandant. When the British garrison was withdrawn, the list of fifty or sixty people who had sworn allegiance was left behind to be found by the returning Boers. Leech and some others were arrested and taken to Doornberg, where they were tried and then sent back to the village. Leech reported the matter to Gen. Charles Knox, and when Ventersburg was again occupied by the British, the Boers who had arrested him were themselves arrested.[40]

Punitive Measures

In terms of Roberts's proclamation of 1 September 1900, burghers were British subjects in consequence of the annexation of the Free State and were therefore obliged "to acquaint Her Majesty's forces of the presence of the enemy upon or in the neighbourhood of their farms, and, if they fail to do so, they will be regarded as aiding and abetting the enemy and will be liable to be treated as rebels." L. A. Tancred, the legal adviser to the ORC, contended that a subsequent proclamation could not validly undo the status of someone who had bound himself to neutrality, that reporting one belligerent to another was irreconcilable with the meaning of neutrality, and that enforcing such a requirement was not consistent with the behavior of a civilized state.[41]

Reporting to the British was a hazardous business. If such a message was intercepted, the sender was in danger from his countrymen. If he failed to report, he was at the mercy of the British. "So he was always between two fires," as one Boer put it.[42] There were Boers who failed to report the presence of Boers on their farms, so they were deported; there were also Boers who did report—in some cases "always reported"—and were deported anyway.[43] Had those who felt constrained to betray their compatriots known that they faced such arbitrary action at the hands of an all-powerful military administration, they may well have acted differently—but, then, they did not know.

Constant Boer attacks on Roberts's vulnerable lines of communication during the second half of 1900 drove him to distraction. Having tried the carrot of protection, he resorted to the stick of punishment, at times in contravention of the Hague regulations, to which Britain had acceded only months before entering the war. Members of the British cabinet were apprehensive of the increasing stringency of Roberts's proclamations but felt they had to support him in bringing the war to a speedy conclusion. In violation of Articles 44 and 50, Roberts made use of hostages and operated on the basis of collective responsibility. Night after night, Hendrik Erwee was forced to stand, unarmed, with the sentries on the Brandfort railway bridge. The prominent lawyer David Roux and the businessman and former member of the Volksraad T.C.L. Bergstedt were obliged to travel by train as hostages from Winburg to Smaldeel and back on 25 July 1900.[44] Because they were "protected burghers," this violated their right to "personal safety and freedom from molestation" to which they were entitled in terms of Roberts's proclamation of 31 May 1900.

It was also decreed that fines of at least 2s 6d (two shillings and six pence) per morgen (2.12 acres) should be imposed on the owners of farms where any damage was done to the lines of communication. In Winburg, fines totaling

£2,544 were levied on farms, some as far as eleven miles from where the railway line was damaged. The widow M. M. Nieman had to secure a bond on her property to pay a fine of £237, and Johannes Louw of Vermeulenskraal, two miles from Virginia Siding, was deported to Ceylon (Sri Lanka) because he could not pay the fine of £984 imposed on him. Johannes Wessels, who was never on commando and had surrendered at an early stage, was fined £200, and Lourens Erasmus was charged close to £1,000 for damage to the line on his property. Erasmus protested that he had never taken up arms, that his sons and all other male relatives had surrendered, that his infirmity made it impossible for him to have reached the bridge that was blown up, that he had no knowledge of Boer activity on his farm, and that the British officer who removed him and his family from his house, which was totally destroyed, was aware of his innocence. It is evident that the fines referred to above were not the only ones, as it was afterward acknowledged that the fines had been unfair and that "the cases of Mrs Delport, Mrs Venter and Mrs J. C. Wessels [should] be dealt with on the same lines as Mrs Nieman and L. F. Erasmus"—by an award of cash and stock. Mrs. Delport claimed repayment of £862 but was adjudged to be very well-off, so she got only £550, while Mrs. Wessels was refunded £130. Mrs. Dina Venter, whose husband had died in January 1900 and whose eldest child was only eleven, was fined £265 because the line was blown up twelve miles from her home. The fine was probably meant for Pieter Venter, owner of Ventersdal, which lay between her farm and the railway line. "I was a frightened woman," she said, "and do not read English so I paid up."[45]

On 16 June 1900 Roberts escalated his punitive measures by ordering the burning of a farm for every interference with the line. On the day the new penalty was promulgated, Christiaan de Wet's farmhouse was burned. In August, Roberts said that two farms should be burned every time the line was sabotaged; in September he urged the clearing of the country within a radius of ten miles of every incident; and in October he ordered Hunter to "lay the country waste."[46]

The failure of the protection policy left burghers exposed to arbitrary action by the British military, the malice of their neighbors, and pressure to rejoin on the part of the Republican authorities. With Roberts as commander in chief, military demands had increasingly superseded political expediency. When Kitchener took over command in November 1900, the urgent need to finish the war that Roberts had not been able to end induced him to ignore the social consequences of his military actions. Kitchener justified his policies with the assertion, "You will not conquer these people until you have starved them out," and fell back on arson and starvation, the "standard weapons of colonial warfare."[47]

Boer Harassment

If surrendered Boers were harassed by the British, they did not escape the attention of their compatriots either. In September 1900 De Wet had set about rebuilding the Boer forces by inducing those who had withdrawn from the struggle to rejoin. He justified Boers breaking the oath of neutrality on the grounds that, quite apart from the legitimacy issue, Britain had failed to keep the promise of protection made to those who had surrendered.[48] For religious people, oath breaking was no easy matter. Jan de Villiers of Senekal surrendered with Prinsloo and was permitted to return to his farm on swearing allegiance. As a man of honor he strenuously resisted calls to rejoin, but in the end he felt compelled to do so, having seen the British break every promise. A relative wrote that her family had always despised "hands-uppers" and "oath breakers," but now members of that family, men of principle, fell in the latter category. This left her confused, unsure about right and wrong. She had the greatest respect for Jan de Villiers and realized that "this terrible war brings problems that we have never had to deal with before."[49]

A typical conscription notice from Senekal, dated 16 September 1900 and addressed to Frans Jordaan, reads: "Herewith Burgher F. Jordaan is called upon to join a commando immediately, failing which he will without further notice be taken prisoner of war and all his goods confiscated."[50] Some burghers did not need much persuading. Willem Prinsloo was told that he must rejoin or he would be shot, "so I went back to commando."[51] In addition to Frans Jordaan and Willem Prinsloo, many other burghers, all from the Senekal ward, had rejoined before the year was out.

It is not that the Senekallers were more valiant than their Winburg neighbors, or more perfidious; it is just that the Winburgers were better policed—or, to use the vogue word, "protected." Indeed, Philippus R. Meyer knew whom to blame for his actions. Having surrendered in May 1900, he remained on his farm until December when "a Boer commando came to my farm and apprehended me as a traitor and took me along. I had no option and had to choose between one of two evils i.e. being shot as a traitor or taking up arms again. I remained with the Boer Commando till July 1901 when I was apprehended at Druivenkop in the district and deported to Bermuda." He concluded, "I would not have taken up arms again if I had been protected according to the terms of Lord Roberts' Proclamation." With unconscious irony, Cornelius Esterhuyzen said, "I obeyed the orders of the Boers because I did not know how to behave myself," and Jacobus van der Watt, who had huge amounts of stock taken by the Boers, justified himself by saying, "I had to humour them, being unprotected."[52]

Attempts by the Boers to induce men to rejoin were sometimes frustrated by the proximity of British forces. Boers who in August 1900 came to the farm Zoutfontein, six miles southwest of Winburg, to take Nicholas Wessels prisoner were prevented from doing so by the approach of British troops. Joachim Koekemoer had a similar narrow escape. Johannes Bornman was ordered by Comdt. Jan Erwee to join his laager before morning or face arrest, but his dilemma was resolved when the Boer commando had to move off during the night.[53]

In the Winburg district, recruiters met with resistance and some coercion was used. Burghers were taken prisoner for refusing to rejoin, but some were able to get away from the commandos. De Wet had said that burghers should not be compelled to go on commando, "because I was of [the] opinion that a coerced burgher would be of no real value to us, and would besides be untrustworthy." Capt. Danie Theron, however, ruled that "those who do not obey must be forced by means of loaded rifles to do their duty."[54]

It was not just a question of rebuilding the Boer forces, however. Because surrendered burghers were obliged to provide the British with information, they constituted a real danger to the commandos if left on the farms. Two of Danie Theron's scouts visited the farm of Paul Heymans, a surrendered Winburger, pretending to be British in order to trap him into telling them where the president was. However, another burgher, who was in Heymans's house at the time, shot them in the belief that they were in fact British. This tragic mistake convinced many Boers that surrendered burghers had become virtual enemies and should be forced to rejoin the commandos.[55]

De Wet, however, was strongly opposed to having burghers of doubtful commitment on commando. This became evident when the Winburg commando joined him at the end of January 1901 with a view to a second attempt to invade the Cape Colony. At a time when he needed every man he could muster, he questioned the presence of burghers who, he said, could have joined earlier and demanded that they be sent home.[56]

One can imagine how moving about the countryside with conscripts who had to be watched all the time sapped the energies of the fighting burghers. This can be illustrated with reference to numerous instances from the Winburg district. Willem Barnard was constantly guarded and was not allowed to have a rifle. "The whole time I was watched," he testified, "and before Prinsloo's surrender I did not have an opportunity to escape." Jan Lidderd was forced to rejoin for about three months, surrendering on 11 September 1901, "the first time I got an opportunity to escape to the British." Adam Senekal, a deserter from his commando, was imprisoned by the Boers in Bloemfontein jail. After surrendering to the British, he was again arrested by the Boers. He was taken on commando but never bore arms and deserted again after six months. Gert C. van Rooyen was twice arrested for refusing to rejoin. On the first occasion he was held by Gen. Paul Roux from 18 June 1900 and "treated most shamefully." Released on 1 July, he was rearrested with eleven others on 23 August and held captive until 7 September when they agreed to rejoin. Cornelis Botha obtained permission for them to go home, ostensibly to prepare for their return to the commando. Instead Van Rooyen was paroled by the British to go to Durban.[57]

Johannes van Zyl resorted to extreme measures to escape his Boer captors. He claimed that when he surrendered on 4 May 1900, he was assured by no less a personage than Ian Hamilton that he had nothing to fear from returning Boers. Then, in August, the Boers came to his farm. They visited him more than once, confiscating horses and forage and threatening to shoot him and to burn his house down because he refused to rejoin. On 14 November his brother-in-law, who was on commando, warned Van Zyl that if he wanted to save his life and property, it was imperative that he rejoin. A commando was encamped just outside his house, so Van Zyl could not get away. He pretended to agree, resolving to escape at the earliest opportunity. He was closely watched on commando, so he could not do so. On 29 November he asked permission from F.C. Hans Hattingh to go out on patrol. Van Zyl deliberately moved toward the British lines, and as a result he and the rest of the patrol were captured. In a sworn statement Johannes Schimper confirmed that the patrol was captured in these circumstances.[58]

Some burghers were held captive in Senekal, but when the British troops under Gen. J. E. Boyce arrived, the Boers fled, leaving many of their prisoners behind. Some of the prisoners had been given permission to return to their homes for one day to gather up some possessions in preparation for their being moved to Hammonia in the Ficksburg district. One of these was Ocker Meiring, whose farm was about half an hour's ride from Senekal. When Meiring returned the following day, he found that the Boers had evacuated the town. He went home again before the British arrived the following day.[59]

Close to a hundred Boer prisoners were taken to Hammonia, to be freed by Maj. Gen. Sir Charles Knox on 28 December 1900. One of them, Christoffel Botha, was taken from his farm by two armed men on 1 December by order of Landdrost George Cooper of Senekal. After interrogation by Commandant Froneman, he was allowed to remain in Senekal on parole. Ten days later he and about ninety other surrendered burghers were taken to Hammonia. On 28 December they were released by General Knox, "who in an address told us that he was glad to see that we had remained so loyal and that nothing more would be done to us and everything that we possessed would be protected by them."[60]

How incapable this promise was of being fulfilled is demonstrated by the case of Antonie Schutte. Less than a week after his release, he and Charles Jelliman obtained permission from the military authorities in Senekal to go into the veld to round up their cattle. They were captured by the Boers, who treated Schutte as a spy. He was handcuffed to a wagon every night for two months, was made to drive a mule wagon, and was often threatened with being shot. "I had to promise to take up arms again to lessen my terrible hardships, which was really against my will, but I can swear I never fired a shot."[61] There is no evidence of disloyal conduct toward the Boers on Schutte's part—either then or subsequently.

Willem Kok reported that he was kept chained for four days "because I would not take up arms again." On the other hand, Georg Brink, who was also badly treated, acknowledged that his ill treatment had occurred because his captors were "particularly incensed with me on account of what I have done for the Imperial Troops since they occupied the country."[62]

Some surrendered burghers had more than one unpleasant encounter with their fighting compatriots. Michiel Eksteen testified: "About the end of August [1900] I was taken prisoner by men of Truter's Commando, one of them a nephew of mine. I was taken before Commandant Haasbroek at the laager which was about 20 minutes ride from my place. Haasbroek told me that they were justified in trying me, shooting me and confiscating my property. I was about 11 days with the commando and escaped during the night."[63] In September Eksteen was among those who were arrested by the Boers and taken to Senekal and from there to Hammonia. Again there is no evidence that Eksteen had entered British service at that stage. The rough treatment he received may have alienated him to the extent that he subsequently did so, although even then it was in the relatively harmless role of cattle inoculator.

Once captured by the Boers, F.C. Petrus van Rooyen was anxious to avoid recapture. While he was on commando, he had received a letter from his wife about Roberts's proclamation. He discussed the matter with Philippus and Zacharias Koekemoer and they all decided to surrender. Van Rooyen then went home on sick leave and handed himself over to the British. When he was freed from Boer imprisonment at Hammonia, he went home, took a mare that had a foal, and rode the mare into Senekal to get permission for himself and his wife to stay in the town. Upon receiving permission, he concealed his wife's pass under the mare's mane and released the animal, which returned at speed to its foal on the farm, where his wife found her pass in its prearranged hiding place.[64]

Christiaan de Wet was insistent that receipts should be issued for any goods that were requisitioned, but it was inevitable that those whose loyalty to the cause cost them dearly would feel that their countrymen who had abandoned the struggle deserved no such consideration. According to the testimony of Johanna Penn, some Boers came to the farm Sweethome, where her husband was a bywoner, in September 1900. They took a number of bags of corn, for which they refused to pay, and compelled her husband to go on commando with them until April 1901, when he succeeded in escaping. Christiaan Eksteen, who was in the British secret service in the Doornberg, had 400 sheep taken from his farm by Commandant Haasbroek. Between May and December 1900, Gideon Pienaar suffered constant losses of stock and grain because he refused to rejoin; for the same reason, Johannes Otto and Jacobus du Toit had their property confiscated and were put across the British fighting line on 6 June 1901; and when Boers visited the farm of Petrus Botha on 12 January 1901 and removed 650 sheep and 47 head of cattle, his herdsman was told that they had done so because Botha had sought the protection of the British government and was in its employ.[65]

The line between requisitioning and looting became even thinner if the victim was a British subject. Thomas Mitchell operated a business, Mitchell & Co., General Merchants and Direct Importers, the storerooms for which (previously looted by British troops) were on his farm Welkom. Two of his employees, Abraham and Klaas, provide a graphic and circumstantial account of the depredations visited on these stores. First there was a party of Boers who broke the door open and looted goods. They came almost daily, using carts to carry off their plunder. Then women came from the farms and simply helped themselves and left without paying. On 26 December 1900 the original party of Boers returned, and one of them, Piet Meiring, smashed the windows of the house, which he then looted. Between January and March 1901, F.C. Johannes Beukes visited the house several times, and he and his men vandalized Mitchell's office. They removed books, silverware, and money from a sideboard drawer. Pincus Scott found and took with him a tin trunk containing photograph albums, silverware, three watches, and a solid silver inkstand, which had been buried in the garden.[66]

Edwin Orsmond had stores on two farms, and he and his storekeeper, Gerrit Cooper, filled pages and pages of an account book recording goods taken from them between May 1900 and May 1901 by eight different officers on behalf of generals Froneman and De Wet.[67]

Extreme Measures

Burghers who were known to be in British service could expect short shrift. Andries Keyter was publicly thrashed, receiving an unbelievable fifty lashes with a stirrup leather from Combat Gen. Philip Botha on 24 October 1900.

Johannes Louw, who, as postmaster of Ventersburg, was never on commando, was confirmed in his office by the British on 8 June 1900. However, when the Boers reoccupied Ventersburg on 6 November, he was dragged from his office, publicly flogged, and forced out of the town. Pieter van den Berg, who supplied intelligence to the British, was also publicly flogged and put over the fighting line. Frederik Bekker was made a justice of the peace in July 1900. Less than three months later, a party of Boers came to his house, and, not finding him at home, their leader, P. A. Vogel, turned on Bekker's wife. When she refused to tell him where her husband was, Vogel struck her with the flat of his hand, drawing blood from her mouth. He threatened to shoot her and to remove her to the Boer camp on the grounds that she was a British spy.[68]

British intervention may have secured the release of Adam Human from captivity at Hammonia, but his wife had to flee a few days later when Boers fired on her house, insisting that they would shoot her husband wherever they found him. Human was very conscious of being "between two fires."[69]

The themes of disillusionment with the war effort, the attractiveness of Roberts's proclamation, renewed recruitment, formal arraignment, the failure of protection, Boer harassment, and the fortuitous arrival of British troops all converge in the story of Cornelis Botha. Having taken the oath of neutrality, he remained quietly on his farm until 23 August 1900 when he and his two sons were taken prisoner by Boers on the orders of Commandant Olivier. Accused of high treason because he had advised J. Fick not to take up arms again, Botha was sent on foot to Ladybrand. He appeared before Judge J.B.M. Hertzog but was acquitted and allowed to return to his farm. In September, Botha went to see Gen. Hector McDonald to ask for protection. McDonald said he had other matters to attend to and could not protect him on his farm. In December the Boers again ordered Botha to go to Senekal, where he would be imprisoned. He refused, and on 8 June he was instructed that he and his family were to hold themselves in readiness, as they were to be removed to Kroonstad and all their property confiscated. However, before this warrant could be executed, Col. Beauvoir de Lisle's column arrived at the farm and Botha left with them to Kroonstad, now in British hands. After January 1901, Botha was regularly employed by the British as a guide.[70]

Surrendered Boers who served with the British columns risked execution. On 11 October 1901 the Free State Executive Council reviewed sentences imposed on six collaborators by Gen. Christoffel Badenhorst and his krygsraad on 18 September. These men had been caught while carrying out a reconnaissance near Smaldeel on 8 September. It was decided that although James Eva had deserted from a commando, he had been in the country for only eight months and was therefore not to be regarded as a burgher, but would be sent to the enemy. James Adendorf, who was only eighteen and had been influenced by his father, would be imprisoned and would receive twenty-five lashes. In the case of Nicolaas Kotze, Johannes Kotze, Theodorus Wasserman, and Hendrik de Bruyn, however, the death sentence was confirmed and carried out. De Bruyn was a Winburger who served in the Farmers' Guard at Smaldeel. The two Kotzes and a brother, David, had been members of the Winburg commando but surrendered in May 1900. They were removed to the Bloemfontein concentration camp, where David fell ill. After his death, on 10 March 1901, his brothers joined the Farmers' Guard—only to be captured by the Boers just fifteen days later. To add greater poignancy to this sad story, the Kotzes' father, Nicolaas Kotze, was with the patrol that captured them.[71]

The case of Stephanus Vilonel calls for special attention. Vilonel was the able and courageous commandant of the Senekal commando before he fell out with De Wet prior to the battle of Sannaspos and was reduced to the ranks. When Gen. Andries de Villiers was severely wounded at the battle of Biddulphsberg on 29 May 1900, Vilonel offered to take him to Senekal for medical attention. Here he entered into secret negotiations with the British about his future. When De Villiers died, Vilonel was offered the vacant position of combat general. He declined the honor on the grounds that he had decided to surrender, which he did in the second week of June 1900. Shortly afterward he wrote to F.C. Hans van Rooyen of Ladybrand, seeking to persuade him to surrender with his men. Vilonel's letter was intercepted, and in a sting operation he was captured and brought to trial. He was not arraigned before a krygsraad at Zuringkrans in the Winburg district, because it was feared that certain officers who were present there had already negotiated with the enemy in the vicinity of Ficksburg.[72]

The trial took place at Reitz before Judge J.B.M. Hertzog and two assessors, Thomas Brain and Johan Luyt. Vilonel was sentenced to five years' imprisonment with hard labor, the judge remarking that he was fortunate to escape the death sentence. On 11 July 1900, Vilonel's unsuccessful appeal was heard at Fouriesburg by a full bench of Hertzog as acting chief justice and Frederik Cronjé and Hendrik Hugo as acting judges, Chief Justice Melius de Villiers and Judge Hendri Stuart having surrendered when Bloemfontein fell. Vilonel conducted his own defense, insisting he had acted throughout according to the dictates of his conscience.[73] After the fall of Bethlehem, the Boers no longer had any prisons, so Vilonel was made to accompany the commandos into the Brandwater Basin, where, as we have seen, he was employed by Prinsloo to negotiate the Boer surrender to General Hunter.

In a skirmish on 18 April 1902, only weeks before the end of the war, five or six members of the ORC Volunteers were captured at Spitskop, near present-day Marquard, their commanding officer, Vilonel, escaping only because of the speed of his mount. Much confusion surrounds the identity of some of those captured, but three who were tried by a court-martial chaired by Froneman, sentenced to death, and executed on a farm in the vicinity of Senekal can be positively identified as Johannes and John Allison of Dewetsdorp and Sybrand Meyer of Winburg.[74]

Sometimes, it would seem, the formality of a trial was dispensed with. A civilian guide named Carmichael, "an old Scotchman who had been a travelling pedlar all round this district before the war, so knew it by heart and all the people in it,"[75] was with the rear guard of Pilcher's column withdrawing from Korannaberg on 9 April 1900 after an engagement the previous day. Carmichael went back to look for a path along which he believed some of the Boers had retreated, when, according to the evidence of Dr. Francis Wilson and other local residents, he suddenly came face-to-face with a party of Boers, who fired at him, killing his horse under him. He ran into a gully for shelter but was allegedly pursued and gunned down by the Winburgers Johannes Peyper and Antonie Terblanche.[76]

The circumstances surrounding the death of Willem P. Pienaar of Mooifontein, six miles north of Winburg, are not unambiguous. According to Pienaar's wife, he was never on commando and surrendered on 27 June 1900 while on a visit to the Transvaal. Given a pass to return home, he took his rifle with him, "actually being on commando." On 1 November, Pienaar heard that Boers were on his other farm, Kaalgaatje, where they were helping themselves to fodder. He and his wife went there to try to stop them, but before they reached the farm, ten British policemen appeared on the scene. The Boers opened fire and Pienaar was mortally wounded. "We knew nothing of the police this day," his wife testified, "but they often came to the farm." The police left her with her wounded husband and rode away to Winburg, promising to fetch him in the evening, while the Boers moved off to their base about six miles away.[77]

The Search for Options

For burghers who were disinclined to fight, there was no place to hide. If they had the means, they could flee the country. Michael de Swardt took refuge in Basutoland (Lesotho) because "the Boers were advancing to that part of the district where I resided"; Stephanus Jacobs was very wealthy and went all the way to Europe "in order to get away from the Boers who were trying to capture him."[78] But as far as the ordinary man on the farm was concerned, once his house was burned down and his means of livelihood had been taken away or destroyed, he had the stark choice of rejoining the commandos or taking the next step in securing British protection.

By September 1900, Margaret Marquard tells us, there was a substantial number of "tame Boers" in town seeking refuge from the "wild Boers." Andries Venter was so pestered by these wild Boers that he had to "come in" for protection, and because Casper Venter's farm was close to the Boer stronghold of Tabaksberg, Maj. George Marshall advised him to "come in," as he was going to destroy all the grain in that part of the country. And if "coming in" did not avail, one could always be "sent away." Herein, the kindly Colonel Cappe advised Abraham de Villiers, lay his "only means of safety."[79]

The failure of the protection policy marked a turning point in the war. Roberts had promised more than he could deliver. The devastation of scorched earth and the concentration camps was the result of the failure to protect surrendered burghers. Unable to end the war in any other way, Roberts of Kandahar and Kitchener of Khartoum resorted increasingly to the methods of pacification practiced in Afghanistan and the Sudan. The perceived failure of Britain to honor its word steeled Boer resolve and the war went on and on.

More than half of the six thousand Free Staters who laid down their arms between March and July 1900 rejoined during the course of the year. With new recruits the strength of the burghers in the field approximated the number mobilized at the beginning of the war. It did not take long for those who surrendered to become disillusioned by the failure of the protection policy or, as they experienced it, the perfidy of Britain. For this reason, De Wet aptly said that Roberts was his best recruiting agent. In the end the promise of protection was replaced with the threat of exile. If the domesticity of the Boers made the promise alluring, it also made the threat terrifying.[80] For those who feared deportation there seemed to be only two options: collaboration or renewed resistance.

3 From Neutrality to Collaboration

THE PREVIOUS CHAPTER has shown how untenable notions of neutrality proved to be. Surrendered burghers came under pressure from their compatriots in the field and from the British, as President Steyn had foreseen, and more than half of them found this pressure irresistible. In consequence some 25 percent of the Winburgers who surrendered under Roberts's proclamation rejoined the commandos, and about 30 percent slid into collaboration.

The image of descent into an undesirable situation—"slid"—is a deliberate one, because, as Gen. Ben Bouwer said, Boers did not surrender in order to collaborate, and Jan Smuts pitied the deluded people who believed the promises of the proclamations and embarked on the "smiling but treacherous road" that would lead them to collaboration. The Dutch historian G. J. Schutte refers to "the slippery slope of collaboration" that was so familiar to Netherlanders from the German occupation. And from his wide experience as a war correspondent, Robert Fisk wrote of "the steady, sad slippage into collaboration which all occupied people must suffer."[1] Not only was the burgher who withdrew from the struggle compromised by his commitment to the conqueror; his conscience also became habituated to alienation from the national cause.

This chapter is titled "From Neutrality to Collaboration" to reflect the many gradations in this process of alienation and to emphasize the essential unity of the phenomenon. Obviously one must give due weight to the gradations, distinguishing between actions that, both in intention and in outcome, did less damage than other actions. Obviously, too, there was no inevitability about one disloyal action leading to another. But the danger of disregarding the unitary nature of the phenomenon is that too much emphasis is likely to be given to certain acts of collaboration—specifically, membership of armed formations toward the end of the war—to the neglect of others, such as the giving of information, which may have cost lives over a much longer period. Furthermore, disjoining the "*hendsopper*" (Boer who surrendered) from the "joiner" (Boer who collaborated) has tended to excuse the former while excoriating the latter, obscuring the fact that lack of commitment to the Boer cause doomed the Republican war effort from the start.

Before turning to gradations of culpability, this chapter addresses some general issues relating to economic considerations, national feeling, and level of commitment that underlay the phenomenon of collaboration in all its forms.

Economic Considerations

Disloyalty to the Boer cause has been attributed most frequently to the bywoner class in society. There is a profound irony in this attribution, for we see two contradictory trends at work in the traditional historiography of the war. On the one hand, deep socioeconomic fissures in Boer society have been glossed over as inconsistent with an idealization that served the purpose of subsequent myth formation by reading a simple, tranquil, monolithic, egalitarian Afrikanerdom back into the past, while on the other hand, Boer collaboration has been readily explained away in terms of class-based behavior.

The assumption that it was mainly the bywoners who defected is widely held but has never been statistically validated and lends itself all too easily to the subjective elaboration that they were not only poor but disreputable as well. How ironic that Lord Milner should make precisely this subjective leap, though in the opposite direction, in his characterization of opponents of British rule in the Free State: "At present, our bitterest opponents rule the roost, and mock at the more pacific men, who get nothing for their pains, but the sneers and bullying of a pack of extreme fanatics and rowdy bywoners."[2]

The Afrikaans historian Gustav Preller did the same thing. On the strength of the "dozens" of collaborators known to him, he disparaged them as "people on the lowest rung of development, ignorant, uneducated and totally unprincipled." Yet elsewhere he reported on some sixty Free Staters, "fine young Boers, noted in the fatherland in their own locality for their uprightness and love of their neighbors," who were happy to offer themselves to the British for active service against their own people.[3] Both the emotive language and the contradictory statements from a single source alert us to the operation of bias. In more measured tones, Donald Denoon informs us that most of the National Scouts in the Transvaal were bywoners before the war and concludes that the rupture in Afrikaner ranks can therefore be attributed to "economic differentiation."[4]

Economic differentiation is a far more useful concept than "bywoner," which is too fluid to be meaningful. Not all bywoners were desperately poor. Cornelis van der Merwe was a bywoner, but his mother owned 10,600 acres, and the brothers Johannes and Josias Delport, who were bywoners, were beneficiaries in the wealthiest estate in the country. By the same token, being a landowner cannot simply be equated with wealth. Much would depend on the productivity of the land and on the extent of a farmer's indebtedness, his stock holding, and his industry. Andries Venter had an average-size farm, but as it was bonded for £1,100, he was not well off, and Antonie Nel had a large farm but practically no livestock.[5]

We tend to think of "poor whiteism" as a phenomenon of the early twentieth century, but white rural immiseration was a reality in the Eastern Cape as early as 1860. In the Free State there was no problem while land was plentiful, but the subdivision of farms to provide descendants with individual holdings resulted in uneconomic units, unsustainable in the face of recurrent droughts and agricultural plagues. Enormous tracts of land were bought up by speculators and government officials. The destructive wars against the Basotho, in which some white farmers lost everything they possessed, were followed by a worldwide depression. The mineral revolution brought new opportunities, but farmers who lacked the ability to adapt to rapidly changing circumstances were left behind by it. Undercapitalized, small farmers were driven off the land; uneducated, they lacked the means to advance themselves in an urban environment. Over generations the victims of economic and social deprivation coalesced in a depressed class from which they could no longer extricate themselves.[6]

In 1895 the problem was discussed at the Free State synod of the Dutch Reformed Church, and the Volksraad proposed to make government farms available to the landless. In the debate it emerged that there were already more than five thousand children in the state who were barred from going to school by poverty and more than two thousand burghers who were too poor to buy their own rifles. There was abject poverty in Ficksburg, where we read of a mission by the Salvation Army. From the postwar claims for compensation it is evident that this organization also operated in Bloemfontein, Kroonstad, Wepener, and Senekal. Furthermore, the fact that prisoners of war on St. Helena mockingly referred to Christian Endeavor, a popular evangelical movement, as "the Dutch Salvation Army" demonstrates their familiarity with the organization.[7] There was also the phenomenon of the Poor School, where class consciousness led to the segregation of children whose parents could not pay school fees into a separate classroom, as at Winburg, or even a separate venue, as at Ficksburg. The Poor School in Winburg had thirty-six pupils, 20 percent of the total enrollment.[8]

Albert Grundlingh points out that the victorious march of Afrikaner nationalism and capitalism and the consequent "embourgeoisement" of society produced a situation in which Afrikaner history came to be conceptualized as a success story. Empathy with the disadvantaged was lost, and poor relations from the past became an embarrassment. As the bywoner disappeared from Afrikaner consciousness, he also disappeared from Afrikaner history.[9] As a result, we have tended to underestimate the extent of landlessness in the Free State. A full-scale analysis would be necessary in order to determine the extent of landlessness, but here are two indications suggesting that it was probably greater than is generally believed. In the Winburg concentration camp register, 108 males are described as farm owners, although 32 of them had holdings of between 400 and 800 acres, 28 were lessees of farms, and 30 were the sons of farmers or bywoners on their fathers' farms. On the other hand, 96 are described as bywoners, 25 as laborers, and 34 as artisans of various kinds. Using very broad categories, we may therefore describe 47 percent as landed and 53 percent as landless. If we look at the destinations of 100 former POWs who left the Winburg camp in the course of 1902, we have the interesting situation that 27 went to a farm owned by someone with the same surname and initials, 28 to one owned by someone with the same surname but different initials, and 2 to a farm jointly owned; on the other hand, 47 went to a farm owned by someone with a different surname and 4 to relief works. Coincidentally the percentages are 47 percent for the first category and 53 percent for the second.[10]

If there was a preponderance of bywoners among the collaborators, there was also a preponderance of bywoners among the bittereinders. So while we may dismiss the facile identification of bywoners with collaboration, it does not dispose of the economic argument altogether. Not only did poverty leave a man vulnerable to paid service, but it also raised questions about the privilege that wealth bestowed and inhibited identification with a nascent nationalism.

The premium Boer society placed on wealth is evident from the property qualification that limited high civil and military office to the more prosperous. Although egalitarianism was the official ideology, elected officials came largely from the ranks of the large landowners. In addition to the fact that the members of the Volksraad constituted a wealthy élite, to a large extent those who elected them did so too, because the propertied and generally better educated were more likely to be enrolled as voters. This becomes evident from an examination of the Winburg voters roll.[11] Plotting the distribution of a sample of 489 members of this group yields a wealth profile that is at variance with the pattern for the population at large.

This sample includes men over the age of sixty, who were not liable for military service, so the concentration of wealth in the hands of the elderly becomes apparent. Of the 1,539 enfranchised burghers, only a minority appear to have been on commando. The clear implication of this is that, both in terms of wealth and age, those who voted for the war did not correspond with those who actually fought it. In adversity, therefore, the poorly motivated Boer combatant easily turned against the superior beings who determined the course of events. An embittered POW whom Preller encountered exemplified this attitude: "It would have been better," the man said, "if those who opted for war also had to fight the war! . . . There came a time when your 'statesmen' should have known to make peace. When they failed to do so, I called it a day."[12]

It was easier for a wealthy burgher to evade military duty than for a poor man. A curious provision of the Commando Law allowed someone who was called up to send a substitute or otherwise to buy his way out. Frank Irons provided a substitute with a horse, saddle, and bridle, as well as a rifle, and paid him eight pounds per month for seven months; and Daniel Gouws, who did not have a substitute, was permitted to give a wagon, a span of oxen, and a cart instead.[13]

Some landowners, we are told, forced their bywoners to go on commando, and some used their whips to keep them at the front. There was a sense of grievance among some bywoners even before the war that they had to perform commando service without compensation to protect the property of others even though they themselves had none. That this was no new perception is demonstrated by complaints that it was the poor burghers who fought the Basotho War of 1867–68 and petitions for aid alleging that it was an indisputable fact that the commandos consisted mostly of poor burghers who had to protect the property of the wealthy. In the 1890s concerns were already being expressed in the Free State about whether bywoners could be relied upon to take up arms in the national cause.[14]

The fact that rich men like Hermanus van der Linde of Ventersburg took no part in the war did not escape notice. "Mr H. van der Linde was called up and went to Winburg and now he is having a good time sitting at home fit and well,"[15] wrote an aggrieved burgher. Economically based dissatisfaction was part of the motivation of Adriaan Strydom, who surrendered in May 1900 "because I owned no land. Why should I have sacrificed my life and family for others?"[16] Bill Nasson points out: "At the start, the war provided social cement, but once things began to go badly, not only did it flake off, but economic and social divisions worsened."[17] This is what happens in a war: class divisions are transcended, but only as long as everything goes well.

Pan-Republican National Sentiment

Economic considerations also have a bearing on the strength of pan-republican national sentiment. Patriotic mobilization could not even ensure full initial participation, let alone sustain it. Toward the end of January 1900, Gen. Philip Botha complained to President Steyn that there were still many burghers who were not on commando, and Christiaan de Wet lamented the hemorrhaging of his forces in the Winburg district, where so many burghers laid down their arms. In contrast to the educated urban middle class, Nasson points out, the ordinary Boer "inhabited an agrarian world thick with localisms, resilient family loyalties, and devoted ties to farmsteads."[18] On commando he yearned to be with his family in the house he had built, surveying the crops he had grown, possessive of his cattle, perhaps his only wealth.

Any suggestion of Free Staters fighting for the Transvaal intensified popular resentment. S. F. Malan sought to demonstrate the role of determined pan-republican nationalism in the Free State. While conceding that there was hesitation about committing the Free State to a military alliance with Kruger's Transvaal, he insists that the ardor of a common patriotism outweighed considerations to the contrary. Yet Malan too readily adduces cultural trends as political evidence. He avails himself one-sidedly of Free State and Afrikaner nationalist sources, particularly the newspaper *De Express,* and it is questionable whether the requisitions, resolutions, and newspaper articles on which his argument relies truly reflected popular opinion. These initiatives all emanated from a highly politicized and articulate minority. The ordinary man on the farm attended meetings as quasi-social occasions and was easily swayed by the rhetoric. Furthermore, Malan does not allow due weight to the powerful influence of the Free State presidency, whose incumbents regularly used the advantage of their constitutional role, personal prestige, and superior education to impose their point of view on the members of the Volksraad.[19] The crisis of the times, combined with the powerful leadership of Steyn, led to an abandonment of the Free State's previous alignment with the Cape, in the course of which the interests of the state were subordinated to the needs of its northern neighbor.

Dissentient political views did not simply disappear, and later opposition to the war was expressed in aspersions on Kruger and his "Hollander clique" or was articulated in terms of the political sentiments of J. G. Fraser, Steyn's presidential rival. Alfred Goldsmith, a Ventersburg teacher, declined to fight because, he said, "it is not the Free State's war, it is the Transvaal's," and Christina Louw said of her husband, Johannes, "He was always a staunch follower of Mr J. G. Fraser in his political views and was ever opposed to the policy which involved the Free State in the present struggle."[20] Various contemporary commentators remarked on the difference between the Free Staters and the Transvaalers, generally citing the greater susceptibility of the former to British influence.[21]

Relations between the republics were characterized by strain and recrimination. Sophie Leviseur observed, "The Transvaalers and Free Staters have never loved each other, and even in that war, fighting side by side, there was no love lost between them." After the fall of Winburg, one contemporary witness noted, the discouraged Free Staters held the Transvaalers to blame for the loss of their country, and after the vain attempt to halt Roberts at the Sand River, another reported, the feeling gained ground that it was "all over with the Free State" and Free State burghers said openly that they would not fight for the Transvaal.[22] Their great trust in the Transvaalers, to whom they had looked up, was shattered. With regard to the Volksraad, without putting too fine a point on it, once it came to fighting, most of its members seemingly changed their minds about the will of the people.[23]

Lack of Commitment

While there were staunch followers of Steyn and staunch followers of Fraser, it is striking that many Free Staters were swept about by every wind. Grundlingh comments on the alacrity with which some burghers changed sides, even to the extent that burghers captured in the field immediately offered their services to the British, and this is borne out by the present research. "I surrendered under Lord Roberts' Proclamation in May 1900 and then went to the British," says Nicolaas Kotze. Lourens Prinsloo surrendered on 26 May 1900 and after that "was always employed by the British as a guide and scout." The Winburger Cornelis Bruwer was a member of the Transvaal Artillery until 6 May 1901 and a guide in the service of the British less than a month later. Grundlingh attributes this phenomenon to the fact that the decision to defect was preceded by a period of gestation during which the idea took shape.[24] P. J. du Toit's diary provides a record of just such a mental process—from his reflection in November 1900—"Why prolong the agony and allow the country to go to ruination and poverty? The sooner there is put a stop to the war, the better. But how? We are under strict control and orders of our generals, and if one deserts, your property is confiscated by your own people"—until his surrender six months later.[25]

An additional explanation for apparently effortless shifts in loyalty is the lack of commitment of some and the shallowness of the commitment of many. There were also those whose participation was equivocal and whose explanations of their role ranged from the ingenuous to the tortuous. The prize must surely go to Pieter Meyer: "I was taken prisoner in October 1900 during fighting at Ventersburg. I was not fighting myself. There was fighting going on. I saw the British troops fighting but I did not see whom they were fighting with. I don't at all know who the English were fighting but I think somehow it must have been the Boers." And for a varied wartime career, few could compete with Michiel

Gildenhuys, who was on commando, surrendered, was captured by the Boers, escaped, was recaptured, went back on commando, was captured by the British, and moved from Green Point, to Seapoint, to the Winburg concentration camp and service as a guide.[26]

This equivocation may be linked to an aspect of Boer mentalité. Interaction among the Boers was beset with caution. Oskar Hintrager, an astute observer, commented on indeterminacy in the Boers' social intercourse: the un-affirmative handshake, followed by desultory conversation about noncontroversial matters, and as late as the 1940s, Karel Schoeman, who grew up in a Dutch-speaking home, was aware of a striking ambivalence that resulted in an avoidance of confrontation and forthright opinions, something that struck him and his mother as typically Afrikaans.[27] The equivocation of the common Afrikaans expression "*Ja-nee*" (literally "yes-no"), signifying qualified agreement or cautious disagreement, exemplifies this attitude. At the time of the South African War, pragmatism would seem to have been a striking Boer characteristic that set them apart from their principled Dutch kinsmen, and this is an interesting theme (and subtext) in letters home from Dutch teachers in South Africa.[28]

Pragmatism is the most convincing explanation for the behavior of many Winburgers during the war. The claims for compensation seldom provide a rationale for burghers' actions, but when they do, the justifications are never of an ideological nature. Some surrendered because they did not want to fight or were tired of fighting;[29] others because they considered the struggle to be hopeless.[30] Some said their horses were worn out; others that they had corn to harvest. This one surrendered for fear of material loss and that one in hope of material gain.[31] The records indicate that at least a dozen Winburgers trekked around the country in a bid to save their livestock.[32] Willem Prinsloo rejoined the commandos because he was threatened by the Boers, and Chrisparus Bester and Anthonie Grobbelaar rejoined for fear of being deported by the British. Willem Naudé and Marthinus van Dyk took service with the British in hopes of monetary advantage.[33]

All of this suggests that Malan is wrong about a pan-republican nationalism extending beyond an urban leadership group to the rural rank and file. As we have seen, one foreign observer of the contemporary scene, Oskar Hintrager, distinguished between educated, urbanized "Afrikaners," the mainspring of nationalism, and the less sophisticated rural majority, the "Boers." Another observer, L. C. Ruyssenaers, commenting on the phenomenon of sixty burghers defecting in one night, describes the Boers' sense of nationhood as superficial. R. W. Schikkerling also noted the weakness of the Boers' national sense, and at Slabbert's Nek, the Rev. General Roux sought to motivate the Boers, whose national consciousness was poorly developed and among whom self-interest still predominated, with reference to Isaiah 66:8: "Shall a land be born in one day? Shall a nation be brought forth in one moment?"[34]

If a strong sense of national consciousness was lacking, there was strong local feeling among the Boers. The commando banded members of a community together in defense of their district or ward, and the corporalship intensified the sense of kinship and comradeship. The burghers of Winburg's Zandrivier ward wore blue hatbands and called themselves "Blue cranes." This local pride, the *Times History of the War* perceived, was at once a great strength and a great weakness, for while men might fight fiercely in defense of hearth and home, they were disinclined to fight for a more abstract concept.[35]

We now turn our attention to manifestations of Boer disloyalty: evading combat, opting out of the war, the "objective collaboration" of working with the new authorities, participation in the peace movement, providing intelligence, employment by the military establishment, and serving under arms.

Evading Combat

The occurrence of cowardice is concealed in a historiography conceptualized in terms of imperial and republican masculinity. A national army is a "total institution" (Erving Goffman) in which socialization into conformity is reinforced by coercion. During the South African War, British soldiers found guilty of cowardice or of abandoning a post were sentenced to death, although few such sentences were carried out. In spite of this severe sanction, in October 1900 the prevalence of surrenders among the troops led to the promulgation of Army Order 208, in terms of which a court of inquiry would examine the conduct of the senior officer or soldier present with a view to a possible court-martial, and Army Order 110 of May 1901 made a court-martial mandatory.[36] This resulted in a bizarre situation when not long afterward some British soldiers were captured by a Winburg commando. The Boers were about to release the soldiers in the vicinity of Smaldeel when their officer anxiously asked Comdt. Jacobus Theron for a document certifying that they were outnumbered and had been surrounded by the Boers.[37]

The Boers were members of a citizen's army and individualists; therefore they were in greater danger of showing "unmanly" fear. There was a general reluctance among them to go into battle. When Gen. Philip Botha ordered one thousand men to check the British right flank at Tabaksberg in the battle for Winburg, only sixty-six obeyed. At the height of the battle, the general went after a burgher who had absconded; whereupon the rest of his men abandoned their positions. During the first phase of the war, the men were conscripts, compelled by law to go on commando, but, as Howard Hillegas points out, not compelled by law to fight;[38] it was only in the guerrilla phase that they were, for the most part, volunteers.

Apart from the striking number of Winburgers who were never on commando, there were those who were not called up because of ill health but proved themselves fit enough by their subsequent actions. As an invalid, Abraham Pelser was not commandeered, but he was able to flee with his livestock whenever the British approached. Because he maintained this practice to the end of the war, one must assume he had a fair degree of mobility. Another invalid, Gerhardus Buitendach, was not commandeered but did a spell of commando duty as a substitute for Edward von Staaden before taking up service with the British in the Farmers Guard. Sarel van der Walt was never on commando because of his defective eyesight, but this did not prevent him from serving as a guide to British troops and as a member of the ORC Volunteers.[39]

One way of evading combat and safeguarding one's livestock at the same time was to hide in the broken terrain in the eastern part of the Winburg district or to take refuge in another country. Stephanus Blignaut took up residence in a well-stocked hut hidden in a ravine,[40] and by July 1901 Basutoland hosted 2,043 white Free Staters, of whom 483 were men, along with more than 20,000 cattle and 110,000 sheep.[41]

A failure of nerve in the thick of battle might be ingeniously argued away. During a skirmish at the Modder River, Winburg commandant J.P.J. (Kootjie) Jordaan could do nothing to prevent Andries Botes from absconding on the pretext that he was going to fetch reinforcements. In the POW camp at Green Point, Botes's jitters made him the butt of his countrymen's indulgent jokes. This is typical of the tolerant response that burghers generally showed to the occurrence of "*bangziekte*" (scared sickness). By contrast, when Christiaan Wheeler, who had avoided going on commando by feigning illness, went over to the British, his lack of courage was contemptuously alluded to in the comment, "He is now in the Farmers' Guard at Glen—fighting from a blockhouse seems to be to his liking."[42]

Opting Out of the War

Historians of the occupation of France (1940–45) refer to the willingness to capitulate as "attentism,"[43] and Albert Fabre-Luce asserted that open attentism was tantamount to accepting the total occupation of France and that collaboration was full-blown attentism.[44] With the Free State government still functioning, the commandos still in the field, and the occupation of the country still limited, the wholesale refusal to perform the military service required by law was the primary collaboration.

Thousands of Free Staters laid down their arms because they were dispirited and convinced that there was no prospect that the final outcome could be anything but disastrous for the country and for themselves individually. In coming to this conclusion they anticipated the decision reached at Vereeniging fully two years later, encapsulated in Jan Smuts's statement that if Boer independence was forfeit, "it clearly becomes our duty to stop the struggle in order that we may not perhaps sacrifice our people and our future for a mere idea which cannot be realized."[45]

This was the choice that Winburgers confronted after the fall of their capital and the annexation of their country: survival or an unattainable ideal. The Free State government in the field refused to recognize the annexation or to countenance what they regarded as treasonable dereliction of duty on the part of their subjects.[46] But the Boers were individualists, and a unilateral decision to abandon the struggle must also be seen in the context of the whole Boer ethos of making war. Initially men served under officers of their choice; they constantly took home leave, with or without permission; they declined to expose themselves to unnecessary risk; they disobeyed orders; they simply drifted off. They were farmers, and on the farm they made decisions for themselves, taking orders from no man. Their military indiscipline was notorious and was commented on by various observers, such as the foreign military attachés Carl Reichmann, Pavel Stakhovitch and Vasili Gurko, Julius Allum, Omius van Oostrum, and Georges De Villebois-Mareuil.[47] Yet the Boers' characteristic patterns of behavior derived not so much from indiscipline per se as from a combat culture of individualism that asserted the elective nature of their involvement. Hintrager characterized the Boer attitude in battle as: "I'm not staying here. It's a dangerous place for me. I'm not going to get myself shot by an Englishman."[48] They habitually contracted out of untenable situations, and many of them came to regard the entire war as untenable.

"Objective Collaboration"

Stanley Hoffmann distinguishes between objective or involuntary collaboration, necessitated by the impossibility of maintaining parallel bureaucracies in occupied areas and subjective or voluntary collaborationism, whether for ideological or servile ends. Given the fluidity of human conduct and concepts, these categories—working *with* or *for* the enemy—cannot be rigorously distinguished. "Objective collaboration" was a reluctant acknowledgment of reality, justified by some on the grounds of saving what could still be saved, but Charles de Gaulle consistently rejected the concept, because in his view it sought to safeguard France's physical integrity at the cost of its moral integrity.[49]

In every occupied Free State town there were burghers who accepted administrative appointments in the belief that British occupation constituted the new reality and that by acknowledging that reality and coming to terms with the verdict of defeat, they could still be of service to their people. As happened in France, however, it was a case of "He who sups with the devil needs a long spoon," for the occupying power made ever greater demands while agreeing to few concessions. In the Free State, too, the moral measure of the policy had to be found in its outcome rather than in its intentions.

The Winburg doctors who served as medical officers in various concentration camps demonstrate the ambiguities inherent in medical practice in a country at war. Their situation is epitomized in the provost marshal's comment on Caleb Schnehage: "Pro-Boer in sentiment, he has worked for a long time as a doctor in the Refugee Camp and done his work very loyally to British interests."[50] Schnehage and Victor Werdmüller served with the Free State ambulance service before taking up appointment in the Winburg camp. Conrad Kops, who had a country practice twenty-seven miles south of Winburg, was appointed medical officer at the Aliwal North concentration camp in 1901 and later that year transferred to the Winburg camp. Gilles van de Wall, a doctor at Senekal, was appointed principal medical officer in the Kroonstad concentration camp and served most conscientiously in that capacity for the last ten months of the war. Alfred Baumann was district surgeon in Winburg until 1896 when he went to Europe for specialist study in ophthalmology. When war broke out, he returned to the Free State and, in apparent contrast to his brothers Gustav, Herbert, and Otto, all of whom were prominent in the Boer war effort, took up appointment with the British as medical officer in the Bloemfontein concentration camp from April 1901 until April 1902.[51] However, this contrast probably puts an inaccurate construction on his seemingly univocal action, for according to G. Saron and L. Hotz, President Steyn himself asked Baumann to abandon his studies to do duty in the camps.[52]

J. G. Fraser is paradigmatic of the well-intentioned leader who, seeking to influence the British to ameliorate the condition of his compatriots, inevitably became increasingly compromised. In order to win greater trust from the British, he was drawn into greater compliance with the wishes of the British. Approached by Milner with a request for his cooperation, Fraser responded: "My Lord, I am a burgher of this State, and a member of the Volksraad. Provided that nothing is required of me derogatory to my allegiance in that regard, I am willing to do all in my power to help you in rendering your occupation as easy to our people as possible, and I will be glad if you will permit me to bring to your notice any hardship which may be caused by inadvertence or ignorance of local conditions on the part of your subordinates."[53] Margaret Marquard mentions two occasions when Fraser was asked to intercede with the British authorities: to get a passport for Anna Murray to travel from Bloemfontein to Winburg, with a view to resuming her teaching career, and to overrule the closing of down of Anna's school in Winburg by the military authorities. On both occasions the moderate concessions sought were turned down. In June 1900 Fraser protested to Pretyman against the terrorization of the burghers who, in consequence of the annexation, could claim the rights of British subjects. He urged the British to make war on the bittereinders and protect the surrendered burghers, and in January 1901 he deplored the conversion of the country into "an inhabited desert." His protests went unheeded.[54]

Local functionaries like policemen and postmasters who had held office under one regime were reappointed under the next, lending life a semblance of normality. As has been shown, the lure of a return to normality, promised in Roberts's proclamation, exercised great appeal. The presence of ever hungry British troops in Winburg created a ready market. On their entry into the town, Sidney Lucas said, he worked a day and a night to meet their demand for bread, and in the space of less than six months at least fourteen licenses for bakeries and ten for restaurants were issued in Winburg—apart from lemonade and ginger beer outlets, billiard table operators, and other facilities to meet the soldiers' needs. Ordinary farmers also stood to benefit. Indeed, this was implicit in surrendering under the proclamation, which called on burghers to return to their daily avocation. If one was a farmer, one would supply one's agricultural produce to the market—which was, in effect, either the British military authorities or the British civil administration.

Nowhere was the fact of British conquest so painfully evident as in prisoner-of-war and concentration camps. Here, too, burghers took up occupations in the service of the British but to the benefit of their compatriots. It is difficult to quantify the reprehensibility of such service. If those who were of greatest benefit to the British were the most culpable, then one would have to place Comdt. Helgaardt Theunissen of Winburg, the hero of the battle of Stinkfontein (after whom Smaldeel was renamed in 1906), at the top of the list, as the British were loud in acclaiming his invaluable role as camp commandant at Green Point and later Simonstown. It is an accepted military convention that an officer performs this role without incurring blame. However, the ambiguity of Theunissen's position is exemplified by the fact that in November 1900 he frustrated an escape attempt by prisoners of war by reporting it to the military authorities. He had a comfortable relationship with the occupying power and facilitated the peace movement. Seemingly it could be said of him, as it was said of Caleb Schnehage, that he was pro-Boer but loyally served British interests![55]

The British were happy to regard the Rev. J. J. Marquard as "Chaplain to the [POW] Camps," because he subserved their interests—in contrast to the Rev. Christoffel Snyman of Ventersburg, who was deported because as a Dutch

Reformed minister he had a great deal of power but was "not using it sufficiently in the interests of the British."[56]

If one did not have the talent or the education or the vocation to be a camp commandant, a camp doctor, or a camp clergyman, one might become a camp policeman or an issuer of rations instead, and then the financial rewards are most likely to be remarked on. Thus it was known that Ockert van Schalkwyk, who was appointed "an Overseer or something," received generous rations. If one was a carpenter by trade, how wrong was it to take up paid employment in the carpenter's shop of the Winburg concentration camp, as Hendrik Kruger did?[57] Apart from earning some money to care for his family, he could serve the camp community by making much needed beds and coffins.

The Peace Movement

Burghers who were convinced that the Boer cause was hopeless tried to persuade their friends and relations to surrender or banded together to promote peace, and it is noteworthy to what lengths they were prepared to go, what dangers they defied, in the pursuit of this goal. Johannes van Zyl was given a pass to go to Clocolan, where he got "a great many" Boers to give up the struggle, and while spying on the Boers at Wonderkop, Paul Lange of Senekal persuaded eight of Froneman's scouts to surrender. Just how injudicious it could be to take a reluctant fighter on board is demonstrated by the case of Petrus Els. He had surrendered in May 1900, but F.C. Abraham Botes ordered him to rejoin. When Els next surrendered, it was with seven companions, including Botes himself, in tow. Botes subsequently joined Hendrik de Kok in meeting his son F.C. Rudolf Botes and eleven men of Haasbroek's commando to persuade them to surrender.[58]

In November 1900, T.C.L. Bergstedt and David Roux persuaded Margaret Marquard to accompany them and the surrendered field cornet Adriaan Swanepoel on a peace mission to Haasbroek's commando, facilitated by Colonel Napier. A few days later Bergstedt and Frans Schimper tried to effect a meeting with De Wet and President Steyn. Although no meeting took place, a letter to the president was handed over at Schimper's farm. The next day, eight armed burghers arrived to arrest the peace envoys on the orders of Comdt. Jan Erwee, but thanks to the intervention of Philippus Froneman, they were not taken prisoner.[59]

Such sporadic attempts to end the war prepared the ground for more formal structures. In December 1900 Chamberlain impressed on Milner the British government's wish that means should be found to induce Boers to surrender. Milner conveyed Chamberlain's thinking about the use of emissaries to Kitchener, who, in an interview with a surrendered burgher, Meyer de Kock, held out the hope of a Boer share in government once peace was restored. At a meeting chaired by De Kock, the establishment of a Burgher Peace Committee was proposed. Before the end of December 1900, a central Burgher Peace Committee was established in Pretoria, and six local committees were in place in the Transvaal by the end of January 1901. The same pattern was followed in the Free State. In December 1900 a main committee was set up in Kroonstad under Piet de Wet with subcommittees in other towns. The Winburg committee consisted of George Perry, Frans Schimper, Stephanus Vilonel, Stephanus Jacobs, James Adendorf, H. S. Viljoen, D. C. Botha, J. C. Pretorius, and P. N. van der Merwe. Viljoen was an erstwhile member of the Volksraad from the neighboring Bethlehem district while Botha, Pretorius, and Van der Merwe were landowners from Ficksburg who, as prisoners of war in Green Point and Simonstown, had been recruited to do missionary work in the Bloemfontein, Kroonstad, and Winburg camps and in June 1901 were given permission to go to their home district, provided they were "prepared to exercise their influence in Boer laagers in the vicinity."[60]

Intelligence

With regard to the Boers giving information to the British, one should perhaps differentiate between those who were coerced and those who did so freely. Men were deported for not reporting the presence of fighters on their farms. Hintrager says the Boers feared deportation more than death; as a result, many did report such visits to the British authorities. Others rejoined the commandos or fled before the troops for fear of being "sent away." Nicolaas Jordaan, an invalid who had never been on commando, and Antonie Grobler, who had been invalided home, went with the commandos for fear of deportation. Chrisparis Blignaut rejoined, and Johannes Erasmus, who had never been on commando, fled from his farm for the same reason. Willem Niemann joined in Haasbroek's escape from the Brandwater Basin in order to avoid deportation with those who surrendered under Prinsloo.[61]

While a sense of obligation, or a measure of coercion, applied to this category of informing, other information was provided with varying degrees of enthusiasm. Some people gave information in order to harm others. As a result of informing, people learned to distrust one another. As Maria de Jager recalled, "One couldn't trust even the people on the farms, because the enemy used so many threats and promises and there was much treachery."[62]

Informing might also result from the level of cordiality that was established between the military authorities and the surrendered Boers, which itself was tied up with the preexistent relations with English speakers. In the Free State "the English" could never be a demonized enemy to the same extent as in the Transvaal. The president was surrounded by English speakers; of the twenty officials who accompanied him to Kroonstad after the fall of Bloemfontein, no fewer than thirteen had non-Afrikaans, mostly English surnames. The Boer forces included thoroughly acculturated English speakers like F.C. Lester Thring of Kroonstad. Educated people like the Marquards communicated mostly in English. Steyn always wrote to his wife in English, as did Abraham Fischer. English was widely used among the cosmopolitan population of towns like Winburg,[63] and among the younger set the habitual use of the language was a mark of sophistication.[64]

Proficiency in English meant ease of communication between the victors and the vanquished. We often read of prisoners, whether Boer or British, striking up conversations with their captors. One example out of many is that Boers captured at Stormberg and British soldiers were observed to be "hobnobbing, swapping tobacco pouches and cigarettes and behaving in the most comradely manner imaginable."[65] We know from Cornelis Plokhooy how warmly some burghers welcomed the entry of the British into Winburg. Those who found common ground soon fraternized. Some town Afrikaners, Margaret Marquard noted, were "quite friends" with the British officers, singing Sankey hymns together.[66]

The tension between sociability and patriotic duty is palpable when the Boer nurse Betty Wessels tells us about one of her British patients, Dr. J. G. Willis, who was suspected by the Boers of being a spy: "He says they treat him like a criminal, he is guarded and has no one to talk to, what could I do[?] I should very much like to help him, but how[?] I won't do any harm to my country." It is in the context of such sociability, heightened by the sexual dynamics of gallantry and flirtatiousness, that we must locate a voluntary exchange of information. In his diary entry for 23 September 1900, Major Pine-Coffin, the British commandant at Ventersburg Road, tells of his socializing with some Boer ladies. How interesting, then, to read a statement from the same officer to the effect that Eleanor Daniels "gave us information of great value."[67]

There were English speakers who remained loyal to the Boer cause to the end. For someone like F.C. Reggie Cleaver, who grew up in the Winburg district but served with the Transvaal forces, for example, it was a simple matter of honor.[68] A friend from his school days was the "British Afrikaner" F.C. Walter Coleman of Bloemfontein. F.C. Lester Thring of Kroonstad had a brother who was an officer on the British side. Maj. F. L. Thring had never been to Africa before, and it was only after Lester was captured that they met and had interesting chats about the war.[69] So too the Winburger Richard Acton, who was English speaking and a Roman Catholic to boot, was faithful to the Free State "from a sense of duty,"[70] while his elder brother, Francis Acton, fought and died on the British side.[71]

This loyalty was all the more noteworthy since English speakers had to contend with some hostility. To a certain extent this was justified. Preller says: "We all had English friends and acquaintances who quietly disappeared when the war clouds started gathering," and he quotes Vere Stent, editor of the *Pretoria News*, as saying, "We English never change our allegiance nor our nationality."[72] This was well demonstrated by John Logue, who had been in the country for fifty-one years and was an enfranchised burgher but had no difficulty in stepping back into his Englishness the moment the troops appeared on the scene: "When I saw the Proclamation I went up to the first Troops that came along and told them who I was. And they said I need fear nothing and that a pass was unnecessary as I was an Englishman and I was never interfered with." When the good burghers of Winburg town were first called up for commando duty, many of them were found to have "absconded" or "disappeared." The list includes many who were probably English speakers, judging from surnames such as Barnett, Creighton, Fitzgerald, Forbes, Gray, Markey, Miller, Milroy, Shaw, Smith, and Welch.[73]

Before the outbreak of the war, British subjects who applied for a "document of neutrality" were allowed to stay in the Free State. Otherwise they were supposed to leave the country by 18 October 1899, but this was not enforced and few were obliged to leave. When John Stimpson, who had lived in Winburg for seven years prior to the war and served the British administration as chief constable of Brandfort, showed his document of neutrality to a Boer patrol, he was knocked down by the field cornet, who said, "I am damned sick and tired of you British subjects."[74] English speakers on commando, both the willing and the unwilling, could have a hard time of it, and those who had recent ties with Britain were in an invidious position. Sidney Green of Senekal, an Englishman by birth but an enfranchised burgher, was commandeered to the Basutoland border with Charles Aitken of Winburg and others. When they refused to serve, they were held as prisoners in Bethlehem until released by Major General Clements. The brothers Samuel and Harry Draper were on commando until 1 April 1900 but "took no part whatever in any of the fighting previous to our surrender owing to the fact that we considered we weren't justified in doing so although we were burghers of the state." W. Ward was British by birth and was employed as overseer of the ORC government stock farm at Ventersburg Road. However, his eighteen-year-old son, John Ward, was a Free Stater by birth and had gone on commando, was captured at Paardeberg, and then sent to Ceylon. Now the father wanted him back and undertook that "as a born and loyal Englishman I will be answerable in every possible way for his future," which ended in John joining his father and his two younger brothers in British service.[75]

Away from the commando, English speakers fell easy prey to the flattery of acceptance by the British. William Holland was a burgher but was treated, he tells us, as a British subject. He was trusted implicitly by the military authorities and responded by rendering them every possible assistance.[76] So without denigrating the loyalty of some English burghers, the presence of others provided something of a fifth column.

If the notice of the British could so charm "colonials," it is not surprising that it affected Boers as well. English speakers in South Africa have a long history of condescension,[77] and a Boer who felt inferior was likely to be very pliable in the hands of a British officer who treated him with cordiality. Prisoners were routinely questioned, and because they had not been groomed about what they might say, they were at times very forthcoming. When P. J. du Toit defected, he had a couple of whiskeys and a cigar with Lt. Col. W. B. Hickey and a whiskey with Major J. H. Travers and decided that Captain Hosler was "a fine chap and a jolly good fellow." He was astonished by the cordial way in which he was received by an erstwhile enemy and concluded it "was simply astounding and this from an enemy I was trying to kill a few days previously. If our men in the field only knew what was in store for them, how gladly wouldn't they come in."[78]

Service with the British Army

The British actively recruited Burgher Police, later called Farmers' Guards, who assisted the South African Constabulary, as well as scouts and guides from the prisoner-of-war camps. For those captured at Paardeberg, captivity and exile must have seemed endless. It is hardly surprising, therefore, that ten out of twelve Winburgers on St. Helena who volunteered to serve with the imperial forces in February 1902 had been held on the island fortress for nearly two years. In his diary H. de Graaf drew attention to the disorienting effect that lengthy imprisonment was bound to have, especially since many had received no news of their families. Prisoners from the district who volunteered to serve as scouts or guides were transferred to the Winburg concentration camp, where they could live with their families. Kitchener believed that the primary motive of men who joined the various burgher corps was "to recover sufficient breeding cattle before it is too late to enable them to restock their farms and make a living in the immediate future."[79]

The lure of cattle was a powerful one. Dating back to Trekboer times, the primitive accumulation of cattle was not only synonymous with wealth and worth but also something of almost mystical importance, a marker of manhood, because only men worked with cattle. Guides were clearly well paid; Johan Griesel earned ten shillings a day in this capacity—double what a British soldier was paid—and could therefore reassert his masculinity by making generous provision for his family.[80]

Such collaboration was not necessarily accompanied by conviction; it could reflect an unthinking yearning for life on the open veld rather than pro-British sentiments. In the absence of conviction, strong anti-British feeling might suddenly erupt to undo whatever benefits had already been gained or were anticipated by virtue of apparent adherence to the British cause. This is what happened to two conductors, Stephanus Smith, who was arrested for "filthy language against British soldiers," and Petrus Taljaard, charged with using "treasonable and seditious language."[81]

Service under Arms

At some point along the continuum of cooperation an invisible line was crossed. Cattle guards were armed and could find themselves in combat with their fellow Boers. Thus we are told of the Winburger Andries Viljoen that he "had to fight the Boers several times when they tried to take the government cattle."[82] Guides and scouts accompanied regular fighting columns, Bergh's Scouts served under a British officer, and the ORC Volunteers were constituted as a uniformed formation within the British army. Here, unless the men concerned were so hard-pressed as to have abandoned principle, more powerful motives than material gain must have come into play. This was Milner's view of the National Scouts. Although many of them had mercenary motives, "there were some men who were honestly convinced that the war had become criminal from the moment it had become hopeless and that their duty to their countrymen was to do all they could to bring it to an end."[83]

This pragmatic decision was bolstered by an application of the civil religion of prescinding from what happened to what God willed. According to the predestinarian view, what God foreknows must necessarily happen. This, it was generally held, implied that his will may be deduced from events in the history of his faithful people. The classic revelatory event in this extension of the idea of sacred history to secular history was the battle of Blood River, and the impression of divine favor conferred by this event was held to be clearly confirmed by the resounding Boer victory over the British in the battle of Majuba in 1881 and the early successes of the present war. Those who favored the continuation of the war appealed to God's will and accused their opponents of lack of faith.

The greater the weight of empirical evidence against the covenant theology of this civil religion, the greater the need to hold firm as its proponents' faith was being tested. But military reverses and the looming inevitability of total collapse compelled some religious people to agonize about their own hermeneutic and to reappraise the implications of their theology. If God makes it clear to us that he wills our defeat at the hands of the British and we go on fighting against them, are we not then fighting against him? Emma de Kok shared this concern with Margaret Marquard, who was clearly impressed, though unconvinced. She recalled that Jeremiah had told the people of Judah that it was in submission to Nebuchadnezzar that they would be saved. Although she wondered if this was not something the Dutch Reformed clergy should ponder, she prayed that God would not allow them to proclaim anything other than his will to the commandos.[84] Thus the predestinarian mind-set kept coming up against the inscrutability of the divine will, a constant preoccupation among the Boers.[85]

Stephanus Vilonel took the ultimate step of defecting to the British side and leading a body of armed men, the ORC Volunteers, against his countrymen. Piet de Wet did so too. Vilonel's section of the Orange River Colony Volunteers consisted of 220 men operating from Winburg; De Wet's was based in Heilbron and had 248 members.[86] Early in 1901 Piet de Wet wrote to his brother, Christiaan, to justify his actions, defending himself against the charge of cowardice, insisting that the war had become a foolhardy delusion, and claiming that there was no longer a Free State government against which he could commit treason.[87]

In March 1901 Vilonel stated that he surrendered because "our independence was hopelessly lost . . . and that it was absolute folly to continue the struggle, as it would only lead to total destruction of private property and ultimate destitution."[88] In a letter dated 11 January 1902, Vilonel represented the course he had resolved on as a patriotic repudiation of Steyn's stubborn adherence to a war policy that was leading inexorably to the downfall of his people: "If you wish to proceed with the needless continuance of a devastating war, which can only result in the total decline and destruction of your own people, making ex-burghers of both Republics into hewers of wood and drawers of water, you will be the cause that I and other ex-officers and burghers take up arms against you in civil war, to thus accelerate the end."[89]

Vilonel's reference to "civil war" is highly suggestive. Those who favor the term "Anglo-Boer War" correctly identify the principal antagonists, but this description of the war obscures not only the fact that there were other participants but also that the war was fought for alternative outcomes—different perceptions of a future South Africa. It was not only Britain that took up arms against the Boer republics; there were also black subjects of the republics, as well as fifty to sixty thousand predominantly English-speaking South African loyalists who did so. These "loyalists" came mainly from Natal and the Eastern Cape, where an imperialist ideology prevailed that from the late 1870s distinguished these regions from the Western Cape with its tradition of colonial nationalism centered on humanitarianism, the drive toward self-government and constitutionalism, and the premium placed on English-Afrikaner cooperation. By the end of the century, these different political traditions formed the basis of a party system, and the "peace ministry" formed by W. P. Schreiner in 1898 could not survive the tensions between colonialism and imperialism, as a result of which the prime minister was forced to resign. Milner's subsequent controversial suspension of the Cape parliament, which was supported by ultra-loyalist members of the Progressive Party, was perceived by John X. Merriman in imperialist versus colonialist terms as a "raid upon the liberties of this country."[90]

Furthermore, in the Cape there were hundreds of Afrikaans-speaking families whose sentiments were symbolized by the portraits of Queen Victoria that took pride of place in their parlors. They were content with the freedom and prosperity they enjoyed, and although they might sympathize with their northern neighbors, they were not going to jeopardize life and liberty in such a hazardous venture as rebellion. Indeed some of these men felt so strongly that they joined local militias to defend their towns against Boer invaders. Although Afrikaners constituted the overwhelming majority of the white population of the colonies, the rebels from the Cape and Natal were too few to have a significant impact, and after the first few months of the war their numbers dwindled sharply.[91]

The objective of a unified, modernizing, and prosperous South Africa was passionately articulated by L. March Phillipps, who entered the war on the loyalist side.[92] This appeal resounds even more powerfully in the words of H. S. Oosterhagen, a disillusioned Dutch supporter of the Boer cause who bitterly contemplated the corruption and obscurantism that he had vainly fought for and that would be swept away by a British victory: nepotism, oligarchy, jobs for pals, the sacrificing of honesty when there is money to be made, perjury in claiming loot as private property, everyone doing as he pleases, disobedience, and the hypocrisy of applying the Scriptures, as well as the law, to others but not to oneself. Another Hollander, Karel van den Berg, had been powerfully moved by the Boer cause and had taken up arms in defense of it but had to confess that a good British administration would be of benefit to the country and would produce more satisfactory conditions.[93]

For Free Staters who were disillusioned with what they came to see as the intransigence of Steyn and De Wet, no constitutional mechanisms were in place to articulate their opposition. When Steyn's term of office expired, the Volksraad could not be convened, because only ten out of fifty-nine members had not surrendered or fallen into the hands of the British. As a result, Steyn was reelected by the commandos; those outside the combat were already "civilly dead." Aware of this fall-off in support for the war, Comdt. Esaias Grobler, who had been in charge of the southern forces but surrendered after the fall of Bloemfontein, proposed that a quorum of members of the Volksraad should meet and serve notice on Steyn that the continuation of the war was contrary to their wishes.[94]

This was also the burden of the appeal that a Burgher Peace Committee addressed to the moderator of the Dutch Reformed Church in the Cape Colony on 8 March 1901. P. J. du Toit defended his actions in the same way, asserting that his decision to aid the British cause was motivated by patriotism: "Because I am convinced in my own mind that nothing in the world can save us, then why should I wait to do my share towards bringing this horrible and miserable state of affairs to a speedy termination, for the sake of the country at large, for the sake of humanity, and lastly for the sake of the women and children in refugee camps, and the prisoners of war on Ceylon, St Helena and [in] India? This I consider the duty of every true patriot."[95]

If the decision to defect was, in some cases, a principled one, it might also be a courageous one. It seems strange to speak of the decision to actively serve against one's people as calling for courage, yet Margret Boveri, who wrote on the phenomenon of treason in the twentieth century, postulates what one might call an existential courage of despair. This insight, quoted by Grundlingh, is most apposite. In the midst of the devastation and misery of war, Boveri contends, the displaced, disoriented person "must search out his own way and make a new life for himself, drawing only from his own resources. . . . Once he has lost his home, the last prop is removed and he must face the world alone and unprotected. . . . The courage to seek a new way . . . is the blossom which grows among the poisonous roots and weeds of treachery, lies and inner dissension which dot our landscape."[96]

Ethical decisions are reinforced by the mechanism of social approval. The esteem of being singled out was, no doubt, in some cases an incentive to disloyalty. Marthinus van Dyk was in a Winburg hospital recovering from a wound when he was approached by Col. J. S. Barker, who recruited him as a guide to his column. According to Maj. E.H.M. Leggett, who was responsible for much of the enlistment work for the ORC Volunteers, Vilonel raised and commanded this body at the invitation of no less a personage than Lord Kitchener. Once the decision was made, the warmth of being accepted would serve to reinforce it.

This is one aspect of how our moral conduct is affected by what is regarded as acceptable by those around us. The horizon of expectation of family and friends is also determinative of what we do. Grundlingh comments on the phenomenon of defector families. This is to be expected not only because we most influence those who are closest to us but also because our own actions are most likely to be encouraged or inhibited by their expectations of us. Among the many examples from the Winburg district are the following: David Senekal and his four sons all served on the British side; Frans Schimper, a justice of the peace since the British occupation, had three sons who served with different columns for eighteen months; the three sons of Johannes Petrus Koen were all in British employ; and four sons of Andries Venter, who was never himself on commando, were in government service.[97]

Some families were radically divided. Apart from horizontal divisions, one is also struck by the generational divide, such as that in the Cremer family. Hendrik Cremer, the commandant of Winburg who died in the Boer cause, had a mother, Philippina Cremer, who was virulently anti-British, but he also had a son, Jan Cremer, who was killed on 23 February 1902 while fighting for the British in the Farmers' Guard.[98]

Other families appeared to be divided because the actions of some members did not match the professions of others; or because those professions were empty, people's political actions being based on expediency rather than on the rhetoric of what they thought they believed; or simply because one day's actions were overtaken by the next day's events. A Boer War love story is illustrative of these complexities of human behavior.

Cecilia Senekal was engaged to Pieter Schutte, who served in the Free State Artillery and surrendered with Prinsloo. Schutte was exiled to Ceylon, where he died just four months later at the age of twenty-two. Cecilia was devastated and cut herself off from all human contact for four days, weeping on a lonely hill and giving expression to her feelings in a poem, "Blauwe Bergen," which, sung to the tune of "Clementine," achieved great popularity. Eventually, four years after the war, Cecilia married Pieter's elder brother, Cornelis Schutte, who also had been a prisoner in Ceylon. In the poem Cecilia's grief is articulated in overtly political terms: the Boers were sold out by Prinsloo; the British were cruel murderers; her fiancé was a sacrifice for freedom. There is certainly nothing in Cecilia's patriotic stance that would prepare one for the discovery that her brother, Bartel; two uncles, Frederik and Adam Senekal; and at least five cousins—Hendrik, David, Pieter, Zacharias, another Hendrik, and Joachim Senekal—all entered British service.[99]

The crisis of the time forced men and women to make decisions. They did so in the circumstances prevailing at a particular moment and on the basis of the information available to them. The circumstances might change dramatically as the tide of war swept to and fro. As has been shown, burghers who compromised themselves on the occupation of Ventersburg and Senekal had no way of knowing that the British garrisons would be withdrawn. On a wider scale, in the light of the return of the Boer commandos to the occupied areas of the Free State, many Boers who had surrendered under Roberts's proclamation concluded that they had been misled or had misread the situation and rejoined the Boers. Others were convinced that they had chosen rightly in terms of the alternative futures realistically available to them and to the country. The resultant close contact with the British and the continuing choices they confronted led to other decisions, the outcome of which could not be foreseen. Those who committed themselves fully to the British cause did so in the expectation that a British victory would secure them a meaningful and honored role in society. Thus the loyal address presented to Joseph Chamberlain in February 1903 was signed by Piet de Wet and others, including the Winburgers Frans Schimper, Stephanus Jacobs, and John Leech, speaking on behalf of "the loyal Dutch people whom we represent."[100]

However, the British abandoned these "loyalists," and it is superb irony that, in the end, it was Afrikaner nationalism that covered up their tracks.

4 War against Women

THIS CHAPTER CONSIDERS the varied responses of Winburg's women to military occupation. For the most part they continued to play a support role in relation to the fighting burghers, but some were friendly toward the British, assisted them, and even collaborated with them. The British were offended by the accusation that they were making war on women and sought to justify their actions as consistent with their self-image of chivalry. Five credible reasons for the devastation of the countryside are noted here, and the women's experience is described in terms of their sense of betrayal, the ruthlessness of the military, and the violation of female space. Finally, the famed militancy of the Boer woman is examined.

When the men went off to fight, most women stayed at home and took on entirely new and unfamiliar responsibilities. The independence of spirit that characterized Boer women was heightened as established gender patterns were subverted by new circumstances. Not only did women have to exercise authority over male farmworkers; they increasingly had to take on farming operations themselves. The adjustment to these unfamiliar roles was not an easy one, but in time some women proved more successful farmers than their husbands. The Free State newspaper the *Friend* reported that women were "working the farms and exhibiting energy, endurance and knowledge that many men have not and never will have,"[1] and Margaret Marquard noted wryly that Mrs. Niemand was farming with gusto since her husband, Piet, was not there to nullify all her good work.[2] Women were well aware of how the breakdown in the distribution of labor affected traditional power relations. One woman wrote to her husband: "I am assuming the role of boss in your absence, all right? One day when you return, I shall still want to be boss. From habit."[3] One can imagine the outrage felt by women who prided themselves on having proved themselves a man's equal in adversity when their husbands returned to the farms in the early months of 1900 to indolently reclaim what Bob Connell calls the "patriarchal dividend," defined as "the advantage men in general gain from the overall subordination of women."[4] The women had arduously taken on new responsibilities so that the men could fulfill the gendered role of "protectors." Small wonder, then, that the men were chased back to the commandos to resume that role.

While wars are rivaled only by childbearing in defining and mobilizing gender roles, they are also noteworthy catalysts of changing identities as women engage with their situation.[5] As the South African War intensified, women were obliged to venture onto even more powerfully gender-determined masculine terrain. We read of women carrying a coffin, filling in a grave—even speaking at a graveside.[6] In this situation of societal flux, women may on occasion have handled firearms. In Ceylon, Gen. Paul Roux's wife, Hester, is alleged to have boasted that she accompanied her husband on commando and "used her rifle to much advantage."[7] We can accept, however, that this was so contrary to established norms as to excite general disapproval.

Most women, it would seem, were uncompromising in their determination that the men must fight or forfeit their love forever. From Margaret Marquard's letters we learn that the women of Winburg stood in fear of their husbands abandoning the struggle.[8] Those who did so were scorned, and many were driven back to the commandos by the women's taunts and derision. In the first phase of the war, home leave was an ordinary occurrence, and even after the occupation of the urban centers, large areas of the countryside remained under Boer control, so the farms continued to be a source of encouragement, refreshment, supplies, and intelligence.

Responses to Military Occupation

Confronted with the presence of the enemy in their towns and on their farms, Boer women had to make moral decisions. Their initial response might be to have nothing to do with the troops, but this was not a decision that could be sustained. Often their first experience of British soldiers was of pitiable wretches begging for food. On the day that Winburg was occupied, the soldiers came asking for bread, and Margaret Marquard records such a change of attitude: "The first ones we refused . . . then pity prevailed and as evening came we gave."[9] The hunger of the soldiers was a source of amazement. "The Tommies eat everything they lay their hands on," Maria de Jager exclaimed. Being an enterprising woman, she made the soldiers pay threepence for a cup of milk,[10] but selling food to the enemy, as opposed to giving it, scandalized some. Frederik Rompel, correspondent of *De Volksstem,* says, "What the women have they give to the poor Tommies," but a haughty officer demanding food, even in return for ample payment, could expect to be refused.[11]

A similar challenge to indifference arose with regard to the sick and wounded. When Betty Wessels joined the 2nd Netherlands Ambulance, she initially recoiled from the prospect of nursing enemy soldiers but later adapted to doing so. Pity overrode partisanship, and Boer nurses in hospitals and Boer women on the farms earned high praise for the care and compassion with which they tended to the needs of enemy soldiers.[12] An Australian war correspondent wrote: "Women, with gentle fingers, shifted bandages, or washed wounds, or gave us little dainties that come so pleasant in such a time. . . . England does not treat her own men better than the Boers treat the wounded British." Florence Liebenberg and her daughters felt no compunction about working without payment in the British hospital in Winburg.[13]

Yet for the women involved in such duties these relationships were perceived to be fraught: the kindly person encountered socially was still a representative of the remorseless enemy being fought against. Margaret Marquard records indulgently that a fellow townswoman was won over by the kindliness of some officers, but she was clearly taken aback when she called on the townswoman and found her entertaining a British soldier in her front parlor.[14]

After Bloemfontein fell, some women felt that further resistance was in vain and were the conduit by means of which Lord Roberts's proclamation reached the men on commando, with dramatic impact in the case of Martina Coetzee. Martina informed her husband about the proclamation and says, "Three days after I had given him notice about the said Proclamation he came straight home and surrendered on the following day."[15]

There were some instances of active collaboration. Anna Immelman and Mrs. Brown, the mother-in-law of Otto Heesche, provided the British with valuable information; Hansie Rademan was specifically left on her farm so that she could send in information; Adriana Bobbert rendered unspecified services; the wife of Frederik Bekker was accused of being a spy; Hester J. Prinsloo visited the Boer laager as a British spy; and the estranged wife of Abraham Meintjes acted as a guide to the British at Witnek, accompanying the troops on horseback. She showed them where families had taken shelter in the ridges and where they had hidden or buried their possessions. In the course of the raid, her grandfather, Hendrik Reyneke, was killed when he looked out of his house to see what was going on.[16]

Once the removal of women to the camps became the norm, any woman left undisturbed was presumed by the Boers to be colluding with the enemy. So women who were suspected of collaborating were ordered to trek with the commandos. When Jurina Maree refused to do so, Commandant Froneman encamped near her homestead with the purpose, she believed, of attracting the attention of the British, who removed her from the farm and burned down her house. Maria Eksteen, who was accused of being a British spy, was jubilantly put over the enemy lines.[17]

If this is a very short list of collaborators, its brevity is due less to the famed steely resolve of the Boer woman than to the distortions created by archival records, which, reflecting the power relations operative in a society, provide only "a sliver of social memory."[18]

Notions of Chivalry

The charge that Britain was waging war on women achieved wide currency. Ordinary women taunted their captors that it was not civilized conduct for an army that could not beat the men to fight the women instead. De Wet accused the British of doing so, and in the House of Commons, opponents of the war were outraged by the government's attempts to justify the use of concentration camps on the grounds of espionage by Boer women. The Irish MP John Dillon wanted to know from St. John Brodrick, the secretary of state for war, "if any civilized nation in Europe ever declared war against women."[19]

The accusation was a painful one to a nation that was reveling in the revival of chivalry.[20] Patriotic propaganda represented the conflict as a "gentlemen's war" at a time when "officer" and "gentleman" were held to be synonymous and when "having been born an Englishman seemed to carry with it a moral imperative to defend the weak and helpless."[21] A gentlemen's war presupposed worthy enemies, not a host of harridans disrupting gender norms by engaging in military activity that obliged British officers to abandon their proper role as protectors of women and behave in an ungentlemanly manner toward them. Such an intersection of class and gender discourses is illustrated by two entries in Pine-Coffin's diary. One is to the effect that he had tea with some Boer ladies; the other observes: "We had some trouble with some of the Dutch women, and had to throw them on to the wagons."[22]

The distinctions between "ladies" and "women," officers and others, also informs the conduct of Maj. W. J. O'Leary toward Cornelia Cronjé, wife of Gen. A. P. Cronjé, who had been turned out of her home, along with her daughter, Ella, and Miss Vlotman, a governess, by order of Lt. Gen. Sir Archibald Hunter. "As they are of a superior station in life," O'Leary wrote, "and as Mrs Cronjé is an old and infirm lady, it was deemed by Colonel Hon. J. Scott Napier, Commandant, and myself, advisable that they should be put up in Ford's Hotel till arrangements could be made for their removal south."[23]

However, the impression of chivalrous conduct begins to wear thin when we read Ella Cronjé's version of what happened. She tells of the harassment they suffered from 6 July, when Lt. H. Morris and his men of Brabant's Horse ransacked the house, helping themselves to anything they chose; of the lack of civility on the part of some of the officers of the Highland Brigade, who came in September; and of the taunts that accompanied the burning of their home by Col. W. L. White and his men on 18 September. After spending the night in the open, they were put on an open wagon and taken into Winburg, which they reached after dark. An officer's bored response to their privations was, "You are only common working people and used to such a rough life." On 23 September, Colonel Napier offered them the choice of being sent to the Cape Colony or going in open railway trucks to the concentration camp in Bloemfontein along with the other families made homeless on the same day. From the treatment accorded them up to this point, it is clear that Napier's gentlemanly instincts were not shared by all of his brother officers. Furthermore, because the officer who dismissed the Cronjé party as "only common working people" was a major who accompanied Napier, it was probably Major O'Leary himself, in which case the apparent graciousness of putting them up in Ford's Hotel may have been a subterfuge to justify what was considered unwarranted expenditure.

One way of dealing with the dilemma of the gentlemen's war against women was to deny the seriousness of the situation in the camps, the source of all the agitation; another was to hold the inmates themselves responsible for the unfortunate mortality rates; a third was to portray the camps as essentially a humanitarian enterprise. All of these expedients were essayed.

Initially, unfavorable reports emanating from the camps could be written off as mere mischief making. They were too insistent, however, for this to be an adequate defense, and once information on the death rate started coming to light and the House of Commons debated Emily Hobhouse's explosive report on what she had seen in the camps, the question of "methods of barbarism" was pertinently raised.

The first Colonial Office Blue Book (parliamentary report) on the camps was notorious for putting the blame for the high mortality rates in the camps squarely on the inmates themselves. Their indifference to hygiene, their use of barbarous remedies, and their neglect of their children were cited as contributory causes, and this theme was enthusiastically taken up by the press and the public at large. But blaming the mothers is to mock the victims of misfortune and, as the *Manchester Guardian* pointed out at the time, has no bearing on the moral question raised by the mortality rate.[24]

Defense of the Concentration Camps

On 2 August 1901, Joseph Chamberlain stated in the House of Commons that the concentration camp system was the only humane alternative to leaving the women and children on the "desert veld."[25] However, this claim is contradicted, first, by the fact that women whose homes were burned down were initially—and in the final months of the war—left to fend for themselves; second, by the unwillingness of many to take up residence in the camps; and, third, by the measures taken to prevent those who were in the camps from leaving them. Chamberlain's statement is also gainsaid by other more credible motives.

The first camps came into existence in September 1900, but the sporadic destruction of homes had occurred as early as December 1899 in the Jacobsdal district. It happened from the moment that British—and more especially colonial—troops, volunteers from the Cape Colony and Natal, appeared on the Free State scene. The Colonial Division was described in the *Times History of the War in South Africa* as "a body of men who could hardly be surpassed in the art of foraging," and a British official observed that "a swarm of locusts are not as bad as Brabant's men. They have robbed and wrecked everywhere."[26] But sporadic robbing and wrecking is not the whole story. The deliberate attack on private property in pursuit of a scorched-earth policy, generally associated with Kitchener and before him with Roberts, in fact started with Methuen, who in January 1900 wrote to Roberts that he was denuding the country "in order to starve out the Boers."[27] Presidents Kruger and Steyn protested the actions in a joint letter dated 3 February 1900; Roberts replied two days later: "The most stringent instructions have been issued to British troops to respect private property as far as is compatible with the conduct of military operations. All wanton destruction or injury to peaceful inhabitants is contrary to British practice and tradition, and will if necessary be rigorously repressed by me."[28]

In fact, no provision was made for the occupants of the houses destroyed during the first eight months of 1900. In May a Boer patrol found a woman with a day-old baby without even a blanket in the veld near a burned-out farmhouse in the Winburg district.[29] On 21 June, five days after a proclamation by Lord Roberts that officially launched the scorched-earth policy, the *Cape Argus* reported: "Between Bloemfontein and Boshof some thirty or forty homesteads have been burnt down and utterly destroyed. Many others have been burnt down also. Their homes destroyed, women and children have been turned out on the veld in the bitter South African winter."[30] If the camps were a humanitarian measure, they were, at best, in the nature of an altruistic afterthought when the stream of refugees into the towns made it impossible to continue to ignore their plight.

Again, in the last six months of the war, when the Free State had been thoroughly devastated and there was widespread fear of hostile blacks, women and children were no longer brought into the camps. Trooper Tuffin of the 2nd Dragoon Guards, who visited a farm between Winburg and Senekal on 19 January 1902, reported that there were about thirteen women living on it and goes on to say: "They had no furniture and nothing to eat what [*sic*] we could see but they looked well on it anyway."[31] In spite of this sanguine assessment, the women and children who survived those last months of the war in the open veld, some 25 percent of the women of the Winburg district,[32] were pitifully destitute and debilitated, and some died in peacetime as a result of what they had endured in time of war.

The term "refugee camps," Emily Hobhouse pointed out, implies that people were glad of their protection. "It is absolutely false. They are compelled to come and are wholly prisoners,"[33] she wrote as early as 31 January 1901. Women whose houses had been destroyed begged to be left on the "desert veld"—one even falling on her knees. So notorious were the camps and so great the fear of being sent to one of them that many women formed themselves into women's laagers, some accompanied by men, and trekked about in an attempt to escape capture. At the end of the war, according to General Froneman, there were still about eighty families trekking about his division (Winburg and Ladybrand).[34]

In later years women who remained outside the camps—"stayed out" was the common term—told of their achievement with considerable pride. A Winburg woman, Hester S. Prinsloo, recalled how privations were surmounted through resourcefulness. She fled with her seven children, sister, parents-in-law, and a number of domestic workers in January 1901. Although their wagons with all of their possessions, as well as their sheep and cattle, were seized by Hamilton's column, they themselves managed to evade capture. Commandant Haasbroek ordered Cornelia Naudé to flee from her farm in September 1901, but she was captured with sixty other women only two days later. By contrast, another Winburg group fled before the British for nearly two years.[35]

The mountainous terrain of the eastern Free State provided shelter for some. Among the Winburg women who took refuge in a cave were Maria Wessels and her four daughters, all in their twenties. Hendrina Prinsloo was one of a group who hid in a cave on the farm Holfontein, where her son, Hermanus Prinsloo, a half brother of the future South African president P. W. Botha, was born on 23 August 1901.[36] It is not difficult to imagine how the mother's trauma would have shaped her children's upbringing, contributing to the mind-set that the younger brother later had the power to impose on others.

A British soldier records that on the last day of 1900 his unit "visited the farm of Du Buisson, where we found no less than six women or girls concealed in the mountains. A great scene ensued, and the Colonel decided to take them in to Senekal. Their clothes were taken out of the caves in the mountain side. Eventually the Colonel decided (I cannot but think wrongly) to leave them, so we took what we wanted and left them." When Lt. Col. R. B. Firman found two women living in a cave with their children, he wrote a letter, dated 27 July

1901, saying: "To Mr M. Lourens: Sir, I am leaving your wife and Mrs Uijs in the wretched place they have to live in. If you had any compassion on your women, you would surrender to superior force, and not prolong a hopeless struggle."[37]

Women hiding in caves flies in the face of the war secretary's assurance on 25 February 1901 that the camps were "voluntary camps formed for protection. Those who come may go."[38] While it may be an overstatement to say that women were imprisoned in the camps, at the Winburg camp they were threatened if they went too close to the fence, the gates were guarded by soldiers with fixed bayonets, and they had to have passes to leave.[39] Obtaining a pass was further complicated by the emotional obstacle that women whose husbands were in the field had to apply to a fellow countryman who had thrown in his lot with the British. Maria de Jager and a few other women wanted to go into Winburg to buy medicine, which is precisely what the camp authorities wished to prevent, as they objected not only to the contents of the patent medicines but also to the self-sufficiency their use bestowed.[40] When the superintendent's clerk said the women ought to be in prison, Maria responded, "We are in a prison, but we have to make our own food. We'd like to be in one where we don't need to cook."[41]

Reasons for the Devastation

Helen Bradford suggests five credible reasons for the devastation visited on the Boer republics, devastation of which women were the immediate target: it was retribution for the affront that Black Week and all subsequent reverses offered to British arms and British superiority; it provided an outlet for a particular brand of masculinity; it punished a variety of offenses; it alleviated the supply question; and it dealt with the reality that women were complicit in the war by providing the Boers with intelligence and supplying their commissariat needs.[42]

The army was frustrated by the successes achieved by irregular forces, and for colonial troops from the Eastern Cape and Natal—more British than the British themselves—this was a particular affront. Colonial troops from Natal were also eager to avenge Boer destruction of property in that colony. According to the diary of Charlie Moses, British patrols that were involved in an attempt to relieve Mafeking destroyed a number of farmhouses on the Free State border as early as 28 December 1899. Although this cannot be confirmed, Maj. Gen. J. B. Babington burned homes in the western Free State during the first week of January, and when the main army of forty thousand men entered the Free State on 11 February 1900, Rimington's Guides in the vanguard celebrated their presence on enemy soil by wrecking a farmhouse.[43] This was the beginning of a trail of abuse of which a foreign observer said: "Following the advance troops, most of the time, I was on several occasions the eye witness of the most disgusting scenes of plunder and did not on any occasion see any officer intervening and saying even one word to put an end to this disgrace."[44]

As an exercise of power, house wrecking was also linked with looting and vandalism. Clearly farm burning was enough of a reality to be used as a threat in the Winburg district as early as 4 May 1900, when the men of Hamilton's Horse visited the farm of Nathaniel Schnehage. Schnehage was powerless to prevent his possessions being carried out by soldiers. "I asked them why my house was being looted, which I had a right to know according to the Proclamation of Lord Roberts, and they replied: You had better be quiet, otherwise we will burn your house down." A similar threat was directed to Margaret Marquard on 27 August 1900 on the specious grounds that she had flown pigeons to the Boers with letters under their wings.[45]

Many firsthand accounts witness to an orgiastic element in the burning of houses and the slaughtering of animals that accompanied it. Some of the men involved were no doubt surprised by their own conduct, which needs to be contextualized in a whole culture of Victorian masculinity. Their violation of female space seems to be at variance with the chivalric ideal of protecting the weak, but the construct of manliness was learned in homosocial groups and was acted out in homosocial groups in appropriate behavior as evaluated by other members of the group.[46] This is well illustrated in the following passage from a letter written by a British soldier:

> We were only there for a few minutes but we did do a little damage in a short time. I put the butt of my rifle through a large looking glass over the mantelpiece and put my foot through a sideboard with glass doors. One of the others smashed up a piano and an organ. The women didn't half scream. I thought they would go for us, but it was an awful sight. I should not have thought that I could have done such a thing, but when you get in with the regular soldiers and have a good gallop we get a bit excited and don't care what comes next.[47]

A commonly held view is that the men enjoyed the looting and destruction while their officers were merely performing a "painful duty." However, when Rev. Eustace Hill, who ministered to the troops in the Senekal area, preached a sermon against looting, he aroused the ire of an officer who referred disparagingly to "parsons and old women."[48] A Canadian report speaks about "the officers standing by laughing at the fun their men were having,"[49] and in a letter home, Lt. Douglas Rich from Queensland wrote, "The best part of this game is sacking the houses, although we poor devils of officers don't get

Wanton destruction: Rimington's Guides taking their ease in a Boer house amid the remains of a smashed piano. (War Museum of the Boer Republics)

much of the fun as in most cases it is forbidden and we have to keep the men back."[50] Women's writings, too, suggest that the contrast that was assumed to exist between considerate officers and crude, disorderly soldiers was not always borne out by experience.[51]

Intimately interwoven with the male chauvinism of the officer caste were exaggerated notions of Anglo-Saxon superiority. The women whose space was violated by the destruction of their homes and the looting of their possessions, the women and children who suffered privation in the veld and in the camps, as well as the men who stubbornly went on fighting instead of fulfilling their domestic duties were dehumanized in British eyes to the stereotypical "bearded men, shrew women and dirty children."[52]

Roberts acquiesced in farm burning before he officially sanctioned it in June 1900 for attacks on the railway, on which he was dependent. Other reasons were adduced, such as espionage and the treacherous use of the white flag, but the more the conditions under which farms could be burned were systematized, the more they were ignored. Thus Capt. March Phillipps wrote of operations in the Free State in November 1900:

> Farm burning goes merrily on. . . . We usually burn six to a dozen farms a day; those being about all that in this sparsely-inhabited country we encounter. I do not gather that any special reason or cause is alleged or proved against the farms burnt. If the Boers have used the farm; if the owner is on commando; if the line within a certain distance is blown up; or even if there are Boers in the neighborhood who persist in fighting—these are some of the reasons. . . . Anyway we find that one reason or another generally covers pretty nearly every farm we come to, and so to save trouble we burn the lot without enquiry.[53]

As early as 8 August 1900, Maj. Edward Pine-Coffin noted in his diary: "I intend making a complete clearance of this country, both men and women,"[54] and Roberts's proclamations of 14 August 1900, which designated burghers under arms "rebels," and of 14 September, which threatened greater severity, gave subordinate officers license to unleash devastation in the districts of Winburg and Bethlehem during September, October, and November.[55]

On 26 October 1900, William Williams, a British justice of the peace at Ventersburg, advised Pine-Coffin (at Ventersburg Road) by means of a message concealed in a cigarette case that Boers were concentrating in the village. Roberts agreed that "no doubt an example should be made of Ventersburg," and on 28 October he gave orders, which were passed on to Bruce Hamilton, that every house belonging to a Boer from which the owner was absent should be destroyed. After destroying the village, Bruce Hamilton posted the following notice: "The town of Ventersburg has been cleared of supplies and partly burnt, and the farms in the vicinity destroyed, on account of the frequent attacks on the railway line in the neighborhood. The Boer women and children who are left behind should apply to the Boer commandants for food, who will supply them unless they wish to see them starve. No supplies will be sent from the railway to the town."[56] On 1 November, Pine-Coffin recorded in his diary with apparent satisfaction: "Ventersburg Town was burnt today. All refugees sent off. I collected several more families and sent them away, sending men in one direction and the women in another, so that after the war they will have some difficulty in getting together."[57]

Margaret Marquard tells us that eleven family groups were removed from their farms in the Doornberg area and brought into Winburg on 20 September.[58] The homes of nine of them were burned down, but the homes of the other two, Catharina Fourie and Martha le Roux, were spared because their husbands

Violation and despair: a farmhouse goes up in flames.
(War Museum of the Boer Republics)

The burned-out ruin of the Ventersburg church.
(War Museum of the Boer Republics)

had been prisoners of war since February. However, the fact that the family head had surrendered did not necessarily make any difference. The home of Bernardus Wessels was burned down as early as July 1900, although he had been captured in February 1900 and was a prisoner of war in Green Point. Houses belonging to the following Winburgers were destroyed in September: Jacobus de Bruyn, who had been captured on 5 May and was also a prisoner in Green Point; the widow Jacobs, whose house was unoccupied, her sons being in Ceylon; a Mrs. Ferreira, age seventy-five, whose surviving sons had surrendered with Prinsloo and were in overseas camps; Louis Venter, a prisoner since 10 May, so only women and children were left on the farm; Abraham Coetzee, who was taken prisoner in May and died at Green Point on 8 July 1900; Willem Venter, who surrendered on 10 May; Mrs. Elizabeth Venter, a widow; Sarel van der Walt, who was never on commando on account of his poor eyesight and surrendered on 10 May; and Jacobus du Plessis, who was captured at Paardeberg on 27 February.[59] It is a bitter irony that in time three of the six males mentioned here—De Bruyn, Venter, and Van der Walt—found themselves in British service.

After Kitchener took over command at the end of November 1900, all pretense of farm burning being only an exceptional punitive or deterrent measure was dropped, and houses, crops, and animals were routinely destroyed. When Capt. R.A.H. Moody was asked why the home of F.C. Ignatius de Bruyn, who had surrendered on May 5, 1900, was burned, he responded noncommittally that the house "occupied by Mrs Du Bruyn and family was burnt down by my orders. I considered it my duty."[60]

Boer property was also taken to meet the army's needs. Livestock was driven off; means of transport confiscated; and doors, floors, and roof timbers of houses removed for firewood. At the farm of John Leech near Ventersburg, a truckload of imported furniture still in fifteen original packing cases was used by a column under Col. E. C. Williams and Major Pine-Coffin for firewood. When their guide, William Thomson, pointed out that Leech was a loyal British subject, Pine-Coffin brushed his objection aside, saying it was a military necessity to have some means of cooking the men's food.[61] An example of confiscation by the military is provided by an order issued by Capt. A. Lyon, the commandant of Smaldeel, on 29 September 1900, regarding Jacobus Theron's property: "Koos Theron . . . being still in arms, I hereby order that all his stock is to be driven in to Smaldeel also any carts, waggons [*sic*] etc. he may be in possession of."[62]

In ordering Major General Colvile to garrison Winburg once Ian Hamilton moved on, Roberts noted that "as it is impossible to send you supplies, you must supply yourself from the country. Make the people bake bread, and collect livestock for your wants." This was all very well except for the fact that Hamilton had spent three days denuding Winburg of all the provisions he could carry for eleven thousand men and twelve thousand animals. When Hamilton subsequently sent a note from the farm Dankbaarfontein, nine miles north of Winburg on the Ventersburg road, saying that he could do with another day's supply—thirty thousand pounds of meal, four hundred pounds of salt, and all the tea available—Colvile felt justified in refusing to help, as he himself had to forage for the four thousand men of the 3rd Brigade, "all hungry."[63]

When Roberts's troops spent three days on the farm of Gerrit Meyer, they cut down seventy fruit trees. Leeuwarden, the farm of the noncombatant Cecil van Heyningen and his wife, Martha, was situated on the railway line one and a half miles from the Doorn River military camp, where more than four hundred men were stationed, and near a concentration camp for blacks. This thickly wooded farm was denuded of all wood. Apart from the fifteen hundred loads of wood removed by the military authorities, every tree was cut down, and every bit of wood, whether furniture or floorboards, was taken from the farmhouse.[64]

Once the construction of blockhouse lines got under way in March 1901, a further category of military need was added to the reasons for destroying Boer property. The buildings of Bernhard Dehler, who had surrendered in May 1900, posed no military threat, because they were inside the military camp at Ventersburg Road. In spite of this, they were destroyed because "they wanted stone etc. for blockhouses." The house on Welverdiend, where Martha du Plessis lived, was broken down so that the materials could be used to construct a blockhouse.[65]

Proximity to a black camp was another hazard. Hendrik de Bruyn was never on commando, and his son was shot by the Boers for collaborating with the British, yet his farmhouse was totally destroyed. The fact that not even the foundation survived is explained by reference to such a camp at a half-hour's distance. The corrugated iron from the house occupied by Pieternella Meyer was used "for the native superintendent of the native refugee camp." [66]

Finally, the devastation of the republics was carried out as a simple matter of military necessity. Captain Phillipps provides a striking description of the frustration of a conventional army fighting a people's war: "They are all round and about us like water round a ship, parting before our bows and reuniting round our stern. Our passage makes no impression and leaves no visible trace."[67] A century later Mao Zedong formulated the relationship between insurgents and the populace at large in what he termed "protracted war": "The people are like water and the army is like fish," meaning that in this kind of warfare, control of the civilian population is crucial to success.[68]

With the women able to provide food and shelter for family members or passing patrols, every farmhouse was a potential supply base. Every farmhouse was also a source of intelligence. But more than that, every farmhouse was a spiritual supply base of the will to fight. So the women had to be taken hostage to break that will. Roberts discerned that "unless the people generally are made to suffer for the misdeeds of those in arms against us, the war will never end."[69] Confinement, he was coming to realize, was the answer to evasive guerrilla warfare.

Women who "stayed out" were not merely avoiding being sent to the concentration camps, nor did they drive herds and flocks before them merely to preserve their property. We often read of these women acting under orders from Boer officers because their laagers served as a Boer commissariat. Johannes van der Merwe, who, after his surrender with Prinsloo, stayed out with his wife and daughters to supply goods to the Boers, and the widow Maria du Preez, who provided money and supplies, were by no means unique in their auxiliary military roles.[70]

As a result of the scorched-earth policy, the fate of the women was not only incidental to the fate of their property; it was a means of achieving the same goal. When Gen. Hector MacDonald was ordered to lay waste the Korannaberg and Doornberg regions of the Winburg district and asked his superior how he should interpret the term "lay waste," Lt. Gen. Sir Thomas Kelly-Kenny defined it as follows:

> Gather all food, wagons, Cape carts, oxen, goats, cows, calves, horses, mares, foals, forage, poultry. Destroy what you cannot eat or remove . . . burn all houses and explain [the] reason is that they have harboured enemy and not reported to British authorities as required. Give no receipts. . . . The question of how to treat women and children and what amount of food and transport to leave them will arise. As regards the first part they have forfeited all right to consideration and must now suffer for their persistently ignoring warnings against harbouring and assisting our enemy. As regards the second give them the bare amount to reach Winburg and there confiscate all transport. The object is to destroy or remove everything which may help the enemy or his horses or oxen to move or to live. Definition ends.[71]

How Women Experienced the Scorched-Earth Policy

It is chilling to read accounts of the laying waste of the Free State because of the sense of betrayal, because of the denial of common humanity, because of the orgiastic element in the destruction, and, most strikingly, because in dealing with a predominantly female civilian population, some rather nasty manifestations of the hegemonic masculinity of the victors came to the fore.

Traditional hospitality could be sadly misplaced. Phillipps admits to the awkwardness of arriving at a Boer home and being offered refreshments and then having to tell the Boer women that the purpose of the visit was to burn the place down.[72] This kind of disillusionment was visited in equal measure on the people of the Winburg district, as is evident from the experience of Mrs. Johannes Potgieter. She had come to regard a certain British officer as "a very kind man and a real gentleman." She welcomed him into her home, where he often had meals with her. He assured her that her house was safe, but when there was a fight nearby, she was turned out. It was raining hard, and she wept and pleaded for the children's sake, but her house was burned, and she was put on a wagon and taken to the Bloemfontein camp, where she subsequently died. Of Marthinus and Maria Stander we are told that the husband was unfit and had therefore never been on commando. After May 1900 he never moved far from his home lest he should be suspected of communicating with the Boers in the field. British soldiers often passed the farm and were often fed by him. In October there was a fight, and the Boers passed along the main road, never stopping, closely pursued by the British. The next day, the British burned down their house, allowing the couple no time to get clothes or food.[73]

The troops were perceived to be ruthless in carrying out these operations. This may be illustrated with reference to the way some people in the Winburg district were removed from their farms. When the eighty-year-old mother of Adriaan Eksteen was removed from the farm Peru, the officer in charge said, "She will go even if she were dead." Eksteen's wife, Susanna, was removed from the farm in spite of her advanced pregnancy and a letter from Dr. Francis Wilson certifying her unfit to travel. They got as far as a neighboring farm, where the baby was born. At this stage J. Halkett, assistant provost marshal of Pilcher's Horse, wrote: "Mrs. J. Eksteen Jun. having to our regret been moved from her house, by mistake, when she was not in a condition to travel, Dr Wilson has been left to take charge of her, and also her mother-in-law and grandmother to care for her. All these persons must remain on the farm Karba."[74]

It was disquieting for Boer women to observe the evident pleasure that many officers and men seemed to take in their work. There were some who regarded the women with pity and comforted them with small acts of kindness, but for the most part they were perceived as destroyers who enacted fearful scenes of devastation—and seemed to enjoy it.[75]

Most shocking to the Boers was the suffering inflicted on animals. The burning or dynamiting of farms was accompanied by the wholesale slaughter of livestock in order to lay waste the countryside. An entire brigade might spend

A few of the 1,700 horses slaughtered by British troops in the vicinity of Winburg. (War Museum of the Boer Republics)

a day cutting the throats of sheep. Animals were run down, bayoneted, burned alive, dynamited, and shot by firing squads.[76] In the vicinity of Winburg one British column was responsible for killing seventeen hundred horses and sixty thousand sheep. On 3 September 1901 they killed approximately one hundred horses on Rietfontein, the farm of Stephanus Jacobs. Sworn statements about the slow torture inflicted by inept executioners were made before Comdt. Jan Theron by six residents of the district.[77]

What the residents of the farm Vermeulenskraal experienced on the night of 8–9 November 1900 well illustrates the "rather nasty manifestations of the hegemonic masculinity of the victors" referred to earlier. Johannes Louw, the owner of the farm, and his brother-in-law, Andries Hauptfleisch, occupied two houses one hundred yards apart. They had both taken the oath of neutrality, their homes were a mere five miles from the British camp at Virginia Siding, a ford at a distance of five hundred yards from their homes was permanently guarded by ten or twelve soldiers, and they received daily visits from the British camp, so there was no possibility of any communication with Boer forces in the field.

On the night in question, a patrol of forty men under two officers, one of whom was known to Louw and Hauptfleisch by the name of Jarvis, arrived at the farm. Hauptfleisch; his wife, Christina; and their eleven-month-old son were asleep when ten men, including the two officers, burst into their house. Jarvis ordered the frightened family into a corner of the dining room, where a soldier with a fixed bayonet guarded them. Meanwhile the soldiers, each of whom carried a grain bag, hacked open locked cases and chests of drawers, filling their bags to overflowing. Hauptfleisch begged Jarvis to allow his wife an opportunity to get dressed, but Jarvis ordered them out of the house with her still in her nightdress. Outside they could hear the squawking of poultry, and in the morning only one hen and three chickens were left alive of their 250 fowls and ducks. It was about 2 A.M. when they were conducted to the Louws' house, where they were put into a room with Johannes and Christina Louw and their children. They learned that the Louws' house had also been plundered and that Jarvis had taken possession of a cashbox containing thirty-four pounds and another box with watches and other articles to the value of at least seventy pounds. A guard was put over the two families, and the officers then went to sleep in the front room.

At dawn the officers woke and summoned the families to the front room. Jarvis had the boxes in front of him and said he would return the contents if the two Louw girls made breakfast for them. This they did, but afterward only some items from the boxes were returned, Jarvis retaining about sixty pounds in cash and valuables. They had been told that the men were to be deported and the women and children removed to Virginia Siding, so Hauptfleisch again asked Jarvis about a dress for his wife. A soldier was called to accompany her to her house. It was now clear daylight, and she was mortified to have to walk past all the soldiers outside in her nightdress. There were no clothes left in the house. However, a dress—but no stockings, shoes, or head covering—was retrieved from a bundle carried by a black man.

The melancholy group set off under guard of a Corporal Bell and ten men. In contrast to the men who were laden with booty and poultry, some of them carrying six to eight fowls, Bell was empty-handed and confided to Hauptfleisch that it was "by no means pleasant" for him to be associated with "this abominable work." When they were about one thousand yards away, the two homesteads, two wagon houses, and the schoolroom went up in flames.[78]

A woman not being allowed to get dressed strikes a prurient note, especially if it seems to have been a common practice. Pine-Coffin records: "Burnt a spies [*sic*] house and took the spy, his wife had not time to get her clothes on."[79] The officer specifically identified here—Lt. E. P. Jarvis of the 55th Company, 14th Battalion, Imperial Yeomanry—also figures in another incident. Daniel Erasmus testified that the looting of his farm "was led by Lieutenant Jarvis, Colonel North's subordinate . . . [who] lay down on my sister's bed and behaved himself in a most indecent and unbecoming manner, notwithstanding the presence of the ladies."[80]

On arrival in Ceylon, Louw and Hauptfleisch directed a protest to the governor of the colony for transmission to the secretary of state for war. Lt. Col. L. Jones of the 3rd Cheshire Regiment, who was asked to investigate a charge of theft against Jarvis, reported: "There appears to be no direct evidence against Lieutenant Jarvis and there are several residents here [at Brandfort] who are prepared to speak very highly of him." Consequently, Maj. Gen. Sir Charles Knox, in command of the district, concluded that, "owing to the length of time that has elapsed since the alleged theft, etc. took place, I have found it impossible to get much information bearing on the subject."[81]

The suggestion of "indecent and unbecoming" behavior on the part of this officer raises the whole question of sexual misconduct. Rape is a universal concomitant of war, combining male dominance over women with the victor's dominance over the enemy, so it would be surprising if Boer women on isolated farms were not seen as ready prey for sexual abuse. Margaret Marquard mentions "a miserable story" of violence done to Catherine van Deventer by a Colonial, but does not elaborate.[82] Such occurrences are bound to have been underreported. The victims' culture imposed reticence in sexual matters, and the perception of imposed sex as something shameful to the victim would have further inhibited exposure of such incidents to the light of day. In any case the only authorities to whom a woman might turn for redress were enemy males. The primary group cohesion of the regiment would inhibit possible witnesses from stepping forward, and the patriarchy of the period operated to the discredit of rape victims, who were further sullied by prying interrogation. Consequently, Boer women, like their British counterparts, were skeptical of receiving justice. Even if not hostile, an officer would be able to act only if the perpetrator could be identified.[83] Private Frederick Tucker tells of two Boer women walking down the ranks, looking hard at every man but unable to identify their assailant.[84] During the entire course of the war only fourteen cases of rape, attempted rape, or aiding and abetting rape were brought to trial by the military authorities in both the Free State and the Transvaal, and nine acquittals ensued.[85]

Some depositions alleging sexual assault were made before Boer officials. Two from the Winburg district were sworn to before General Froneman in his capacity as a special landdrost. The testimony of Anna van Loggerenberg (corroborated by Susarah Pelser) recounted how two troopers arrived at her home on 9 February 1902. Without a word one of them pushed her onto a bed and attempted to rape her. When she screamed the second soldier roughly held her mouth shut, "but I defended myself to such an extent that they could not succeed in their purpose." In the records the description of what happened is often veiled. The frequency of assailants not "achieving their purpose" or not "fully achieving their purpose" suggests a shying away from a traumatic reality, but in the case of Johanna Nel, the bizarre outcome provides a self-authenticating touch. The soldier who was forcing himself on her was apparently so disconcerted by the inconsolable crying of her children that he went into the room where her baby was, kissed the child, and went away.[86]

Not only did Boer women experience the war as waged against them, but they also, in contrast to the men, projected an image of themselves as defiant and undefeated. Over and over we read of the apparent equanimity of the women who witnessed the destruction of their homes before they were transported to the camps. Boer homes were the center of family, community, and religious life, and the horror of their destruction can hardly be imagined. To some extent the women may have been numbed by this most traumatic of experiences, yet at times their demeanor derived from the marshaling of inner resources and was not mere passivity.[87] In his description of farm burning Captain Phillipps makes special mention of the calmness of the women in the face of adversity. Sometimes they might beg that their home be spared, sometimes they might demonstrate anger against the troops, but for the most part "they make no sign, and simply look on and say nothing."[88]

After the farm burning there followed the journey to the concentration camps. The first families whose houses were burned in the Winburg district spent the first night in the open. On 20 September 1900 they were then transported on open wagons to Winburg. The Fourie family group were given some tinned beef and flour along the way but had no opportunity of doing anything with the flour, as the proximity of commandos necessitated a wild dash for safety. When the wagons stopped, the twenty children were driven by thirst to drink from pools of water along the road. After reaching Winburg nearly all of these children were very ill with dysentery, and one of them died. After a delay in Winburg and a further delay in Smaldeel, they were sent on open railway trucks to Bloemfontein, two weeks after leaving home.[89] Various aspects of this narrative recur in other descriptions of families deported to the camps: the lack of consideration; the inordinate delays, alternating with reckless racing; the exposure to the elements; the illness of children. This may be illustrated with other examples from the Winburg district. Ella Cronjé's married sister was removed from the farm though only partially dressed; Wilhelmina Bester experienced days of trekking in convoy, including a stage from 4 A.M. till 1 A.M. the following day; Maria de Jager provides a graphic description of pell-mell flight over rocks and through gullies to escape Boer pursuit; Rachel Scott was with women and children who sat huddled on an open wagon for a day and

Women and children arrive at the Bloemfontein concentration camp in open railway trucks. (Free State Provincial Archives)

a night in teeming rain. Afterward one child after another died. Magdalena Potgieter also attributed the death of a thirteen-year-old child to the privations endured on the journey to the camp.[90]

P. J. du Toit writes, "The poor females and children must have had a hard time of it as they were taken from comfortable homes and literally thrown upon ammunition wagons and carted away to the English camp."[91] If transport was not available, women and children had to walk into Winburg, as happened to Ella Cronjé's sister and her five children. It is said that women were, on occasion, driven on foot before men on horseback. Hester van der Hoven was allegedly herded to the Winburg camp in this way by Bergh's black scouts. [92] Before the Winburg camp was opened in January 1901, people from the Winburg district were transported to Bloemfontein sixty-five miles away in open railway trucks.

Women and children arrived at the camps emotionally and physically spent and vulnerable to infection. Because large numbers were dropped off at the camps without prior notification, many ended up sleeping on the ground in old frayed tents that provided inadequate shelter. Letters from the camps frequently mentioned the bitter cold.[93]

The Famed Militancy of Boer Women

In spite of all they endured, Boer women encouraged their husbands to persevere. When the Du Buisson women of the Winburg district thought they were going to be brought in, one of them was caught trying to pass a note to a messenger to take to her brother: "Dear Brother, the English have taken us, so now you must fight, not only for your country, but for me, fight to the end and God will preserve you."[94] Certainly, some inmates of the camps collaborated with the British and some encouraged their menfolk to surrender,[95] but the general pattern was one of fierce resistance. Emily Hobhouse told of a woman she interviewed in a camp who had lost her only two little children and had suffered much, but when her husband came in, instead of welcoming him, she burst into tears, exclaiming, "Oh this is the hardest blow of all."[96]

Hobhouse says that the women in the camps were often pressed to sign petitions calling on the fighting burghers to give in but that no one would sign. On his arrival at Green Point, the Winburg storekeeper Wilhelm Tripmacker told of such a document that would circulate in the Winburg camp and said that those who refused to sign would be put in the Showyard, which served as a punishment camp.[97] Another strategy employed was that members of the Peace Committee were posted to different camps to influence the inmates in favor of peace, but in April 1901 Kitchener had already been informed that the wives of burghers in the field were proof against these attempts at conciliation.[98]

According to the women's testimonies, the almost universal reaction of the women in the camps to the news of the peace terms was an outpouring of grief.[99] This reflected the incredulity of those who believed the war could still be won. It was not the peace they wanted. They left the camps to pick up the pieces of their devastated lives with profound embitterment, and their autobiographical accounts of their war experiences are redolent with outraged sensibilities, anger, and a desire to be avenged.

Because of the limitations of the archival record and of the women's testimonies, which were all compiled by Boer loyalists, the bittereinder image of the women is not unproblematic. One must also allow for a large measure of bravado on the part of women who, in retrospect, represented themselves as having occupied the moral high ground in relation to their menfolk.[100]

Yet it is unimaginable that the wholesale destruction of their homes and lives would not produce deep anger and aggression. Olive Schreiner's argument that women give birth to males and therefore cannot countenance the killing of males is disposed of by another pacifist, Helen Swanwick, who pointed out that "although men made war, they could not have done so had women not been so adoring of their efforts."[101] Women are generally the custodians of societal values and therefore show more enduring ideological commitment (as is evident in the preponderance of women in shrinking church congregations), and as we have seen, Boer women often surprised outsiders with their forthright manner and boldly stated opinions. The convictions they felt were not always restrained by European notions of becoming modesty.

Commenting on the "white feather" phenomenon (of women accusing men of cowardice), the historian Bill Nasson draws attention to the gap between the men's experience of the enemy and the women's. The former knew the fear of the battlefield—for example, of a cavalry charge, the despair of not being able to muster enough men to put a plan into action, even the admiration compelled by astute or courageous action on the part of the enemy; the latter had "the single perspective of contempt for men who make war on women."[102] Early in the war, Alie Badenhorst's brother-in-law reprimanded her: "Hush, sister, you don't know what you're talking about. You're living here in peace; we're in the midst of war. You've seen nothing, but I've heard and seen it all—men dead and dying, homes waste and desolate, fleeing women and wailing children, the thunder of guns, the crash of rifles. In short, you don't know anything yet."[103] But the accusation of ignorance lost its force when the home front became the battlefront. There, as Elsa Leviseur put it, the Boer woman's experience of the British soldier was overwhelmingly that of "a marauder, a brigand, and a brigand of the worst type."[104] The general retreat before the British army alarmed the women, who found themselves in the no-man's-land between their fleeing protectors and the advance of an army intent on violating their domestic space. As in other wars, the fear of the invaders ran before them. One soldier noted "a look of perpetual alarm" on the faces of women, who were "scared stiff by our presence."[105]

To the fear of violation by British soldiers, both physical and emotional, was added humiliation by black men. In terms of the gender norms of Victorian times, women were subordinate to men, but in terms of colonial presuppositions, they were superior to black men. As farm managers they had asserted this superiority; now black men under arms were empowered to assert their male dominance. Whether or not it was accompanied by any physical threat, this overturning of what seemed to Boer women the natural order of things had a traumatic impact on them, making them all the more determined in defense of a state that safeguarded their racial dignity against a foreign power that degraded them by arming black men against them. The threat to their established values that many women perceived in the changed attitude of previously subservient black people is perhaps the most compelling explanation for their militancy. Their husbands in the field could shoot hostile blacks, while the women felt vulnerable and unprotected and yearned for a restoration of Republican norms.

To this perception Alie Badenhorst gave crude but passionate expression after Prinsloo's surrender: "Our burghers ought to have let themselves be shot to the last man, sooner than surrender to the English; we have lost our freedom and now must do the bidding of [blacks]."[106] The war reminiscences of Boer women, which are redolent with these inflamed passions, played a major role in postwar myth formation, ethnic mobilization, and consequent policy formulation.

The patriarchal Boer's demand of women was that they must endure. This was their proper role, a bittereinder told Margaret Marquard, this and prayer, and De Wet and Steyn were in accord with this opinion. De Wet defined the role of women as active and passive: active in prayer, as prayer was a weapon of offense in their armory ("the lyddite bomb of a Christian woman"), and passive, as they had to endure affliction. When Roberts threatened to send the Boer women to the commandos, President Steyn saw the women's role in the same light: "We will endure this as well and our women will also endure it. Those who must die will die. We men will fight on to the end."[107]

Boer women met this expectation and went beyond it. They endured but did not merely endure, responding actively to the challenges confronting them. Victimhood and agency, compliance and aggression, suffering and rising above suffering exemplified their varied responses to the oppressive reality of alien occupation.

5 In Captivity

THIS CHAPTER ATTEMPTS to capture something of the sense of being cast adrift resulting from life in tents on ill-chosen terrain with improvised facilities, imposed behavior patterns, and conflict among the ever changing camp personnel. Consideration is given to the inmates' grievances relating to water, meat, clothing, work, and lack of freedom. A review of the medical staff leads into the central issue of disease and death in the camps. Ritualized narratives of victimhood are silent on the subject of everyday life and imply a uniformity of political behavior. Accounts of the POW camps, on the other hand, reflect busy and varied conditions. The freedom that POWs had to make existential choices is elucidated with reference to the suborning of prisoners by the British and the prisoners' efforts to maintain group solidarity.

Lifestyle

On 26 December 1900, three months after the establishment of the first concentration camps in the Free State, some 250 men, women, and children were herded together in Winburg's unfinished church building. From as early as September 1900, families in the district had been removed from their farms and transported to the Bloemfontein concentration camp. Now it was proposed to house "refugees" in Winburg too, but there was still no camp to receive them. Conditions in the unfinished building were appalling as a result of exposure to the elements, the reduced rations they received, ill health, and the disconsolate crying of children.[1]

In January 1901 a permanent camp opened at the foot of a range of hills about a mile east of the town. The site was unsuitable because after rain, especially the heavy downpours in summer, the clayey ground was churned up into a quagmire. Because all the cooking was done over fires in paraffin tins at some distance from the tents, this contributed greatly to the discomfort of the inmates. When Maria de Jager arrived at the camp, this was one of her first impressions. It was drizzling and women were battling to keep their fires going to get some food cooked. Even the daughters of wealthy people were barefoot on account of the mud.[2]

The camp comprised 54 canvas-covered "frame houses," 4 marquees, and 525 bell tents. A second camp followed in July, when 48 huts were erected on the showgrounds (referred to as the Showyard). This camp, surrounded by a six-foot-high galvanized iron fence, was initially designated for "undesirables" (women whose husbands were on commando), but later it was used as a segregation camp for more troublesome inmates and accommodated up to four hundred people. This is where Maria van den Heever found herself imprisoned for three months for, as she put it, talking too much politics.[3] By October 1901 the number of inmates in the tented terrain and the fenced showyard had grown to more than three thousand.

Camp Personnel

The first superintendent of the camp was the district commissioner, Lt. Trafford Lewes. The next superintendent, Lt. L. W. Graham-Clarke, was appointed in May but dismissed in October, following an investigation by the chief superintendent of refugee camps, who had visited the camp in order to probe desertions, irregularities in the running of the camp, and complaints by the inmates. Caleb Schnehage, the camp doctor, wrote to defend Graham-Clarke against what he regarded as unmerited charges. It would be unfair, he said, "to remove a Superintendent who had expended so much energy in getting the camp in order." But it was to no avail and Graham-Clarke lamented his fate: "I cannot refrain from saying that I consider the course now adopted rather unjust, as my worst enemy cannot say that I have not conscientiously done my work for Government and the improvement of my camp. Had I studied the Refugees more than the Government, there would probably have been no complaints." He declined the position of assistant superintendent at Norvals Pont, preferring to return to his regiment.[4]

Edward Alexander took over from 24 November until January 1902. Next came Lt. C. W. Adamson, appointed on 15 January 1902 and replaced on 4 March when Alexander took over once more. Alexander was clearly perceived to be solicitous for the inmates' welfare, because when they heard a rumor the following month that he might be superseded, they addressed a petition with

114 signatures (at this stage nearly all the men in the camp) to the deputy administrator. They asked if Alexander might possibly remain and went on to explain: "We have in the past had our experience of an indifferent chief; and now that we have at last obtained a really good officer, and one moreover under whose care this Camp has vastly improved, we are very much concerned to hear that there is a chance of losing him." The rumor obviously related to the escape of eight men from the camp on the night of 2 April under cover of intense darkness and heavy rain. Fourteen hours elapsed before the Intelligence Department was informed and this, according to the camp commandant, Jacob du Plessis, was due to the fact that he could not report the matter to Alexander because the latter was drunk. An inquiry cast serious doubt on Du Plessis's testimony, but Alexander had his work cut out to defend himself against his superiors' perception that there was laxity in the administration of the camp. In his defense, Alexander complained about Bergh's Scouts and men from other irregular units strolling about the camp to visit friends on any sort of pass, "generally a scrap of paper torn from a pocket book"; he drew attention to the practice of recruiting men for the ORC Volunteers and other bodies in the camps, which meant a superintendent could never be sure whether an inmate had escaped or been recruited; and he asserted his conviction that the "wholesale and indiscriminate" imprisonment of men and the crowding of women into cages was no deterrent to escape. Alexander was exonerated on the present charges against him, but the deputy administrator felt that, in the light of other information received, he should be permanently removed or placed under a superintendent. Accordingly, Alexander's letter of dismissal, dated 12 April 1902, referred to unfavorable reports on the condition of the camp. He was offered a month's salary in lieu of notice and informed that his successor, Capt. Cyril Hamilton, would take over on 14 April.[5]

The transfer to Hamilton did not go smoothly. Alexander was offered the post of assistant superintendent at Uitenhage, and on arrival there he submitted an acerbic letter of resignation: "Had I been treated with the courtesy generally accorded to the ordinary criminal in being allowed to say a word in my defence I would not have been unjustly deprived of my position in Winburg. My reason for resigning is that I do not care to remain in a service holding no other prospect but injustice and discourtesy."[6] A month later Hamilton was succeeded by Lt. Arthur Bradley, who lasted until December 1902, when W.M.S. Hope, the last superintendent of the camp, took over.[7]

Although the camps were nominally under civilian control, the entire administration was in the hands of military men. Most of the superintendents of the Winburg camp were army officers, and they reported to senior military officers, who imposed an alien military culture, including a hierarchy of camp officials, bugle calls, rations, a stringent daily routine, regulations, and punishments. Perhaps it was a temporary expedient, but Maria de Jager claims that there were three roll calls a day in the Winburg camp.[8] Military standards were applied in the running of the camps. A bell tent housed fifteen soldiers, therefore it could house fifteen civilians; ration scales were drawn up on the basis of soldiers' requirements, paid work was provided for men and organized games for boys.[9] In an alien environment regulated by authoritarian males, women were deprived of the right to manage their own lives.

The official displeasure incurred by so many superintendents reflects the low level of competence of men who were called upon to perform a complex role of human administration without any training and under difficult circumstances. In the view of the Ladies Commission, sent out by the British government to report on the camps, the caliber of the superintendent was the primary factor in the success of a camp: "Each camp bears the impress of the character and capacity of the superintendent, and in going through a camp one could almost see what sort of man had been placed at its head."[10] The brief incumbency of the superintendents of the Winburg camp—just three and a half months on average—was not conducive to stability, and the constant conflict that marked their tenure, although no doubt largely unknown to the inmates, would inevitably have had a deleterious effect on the general well-being of the camp.

The instability that marked the tenure of the camp superintendents was not limited to them but was characteristic of all the staff in all the camps. In Winburg this is clearly reflected in the unhappiness of the teachers and nurses, who had been recruited not only to render a specific service but also to serve as agents of empire and "models of genteel womanhood."[11]

The assistant director of education had to take Superintendent Bradley to task for the hostile reception accorded four British teachers in May 1902. The teachers complained that they were starving, protesting that "mealie meal [cornmeal porridge] might be a good thing in its way but required getting used to." Bradley defended himself by listing the extra rations they were drawing and by pronouncing on their class status, which, in his view, was the source of the discord between him and them. "I would add," he wrote, "that these females do not appear to belong to that class that one has the pleasure of meeting amongst one's usual acquaintances, and I attribute [their] lack of courtesy to that defect."[12] Most of the teachers were from a lower middle-class background,[13] so the disdain of an officer and a gentleman for "these females" transposes the British class struggle to the African veld.

Six nurses from England, who had arrived the month before, did not have an easy time of it either. They endured much discomfort and had difficulty in overcoming the language barrier, with the result that their intentions were often misunderstood. Stress led to quarrels among themselves and with the local nurses.[14] The newcomers to the Winburg camp reasoned: "We were now six English sisters and if we all pulled together we could raise the tone of the place." Not surprisingly, their superior attitude alienated the locally trained nurses. On 7 May the English sisters all applied for transfer, complaining about the food, the lack of comforts, and the "undercurrent of opposition" that made for a "most unpleasant existence." The doctor "abused his position by making disparaging remarks . . . of 'the English sisters.'" The other nurses ignored them, and Sister Hamilton, one of the local nurses, was "allowed to make disgusting remarks about the conduct of English sisters out here comparing them with Colonials. Her deliberate pro-Boer opinions [were] allowed to pass too." Furthermore, because "the maids took their tone from the mistress," the cooks burned their food, the orderlies failed to clean their tents, saucepans were unwashed, no food was left out for them when they were on night duty, staff laughed at them if they tried to impose some discipline, and they were "described to the town in general as mischief makers." Later that year, when these nurses were all gone, Dr. Theodore Molesworth felt the urgent need to dispense with the services of Sister Oliver, identified as "a source of trouble," lamenting that "there has been quite enough of that sort of thing in this camp."[15]

Grievances

The grievances voiced by the inmates of the Winburg camp during Graham Clarke's incumbency relate to perennial problems that successive superintendents had to contend with and that occurred, to a greater or lesser degree, in other camps as well. These grievances related to water, meat, clothing, being overworked, and the lack of freedom.

One inmate characterized the shortage of water—a quarter of a small pail per day for an entire family—as the "greatest disaster" of the camp. A medical report dated 22 August 1901 described the supply as "absolutely insufficient" and called for urgent attention, because the inmates of the camp were unable to wash. The main supply came from a "not very copious" spring in a nearby ravine. It was insufficient at the best of times, and when columns were in Winburg it was almost impossible for civilians to obtain any water, because, as Schnehage put it, "the military always goes first." A woman recalled in later years that there were times when the camp was without water because a column was watering its horses and mules.[16] At first, water was pumped into water carts to be conveyed to the camp. With more than three thousand inmates, the seven trips daily were inadequate, and the problem was exacerbated when one or the other of the two pumps broke down. Later the water was piped and augmented from a camp borehole. In January 1902 the superintendent reported that the water scheme was nearing completion and the following month that the camp was "now well supplied with water." Pipes from the ravine supplied three thousand gallons to storage tanks installed in the camp, and pumping from the town fountain delivered no less than four thousand gallons per hour.[17]

Meat had always figured prominently in the Boer diet, so it is not surprising that it became a focus of dissatisfaction with the food provided in the camps, which was deficient both in quality and in quantity. This was acutely felt in the Winburg camp, where, the Ladies Commission noted, "the people grumbled more about food, and especially meat, than at any other place."[18]

In theory, wealthier inmates could supplement the official ration by purchases from the three stores in the Winburg camp, but sometimes the stores had hardly any foodstuffs on their shelves, so rich and poor alike suffered hunger. There was at first no differentiation between adults and children, and the rations were inappropriate to small children's needs. The lack of fresh milk was an especially serious deficiency, and the children's emaciated condition made them vulnerable to infection. A letter written by Hester van der Hoven in the Winburg camp on 6 October 1901 rings with indignation: "I am a prisoner in the Showyard. We cannot . . . [manage on] ½ lb. meat and ¾ lb. flour per day without any vegetables or rice. We will all die or get sick." Everdina Cilliers wrote: "Here in the camp hunger and misery are in store for us all." Maria de Jager, on the other hand, was in the fortunate position of being able to supplement the camp diet, so she never suffered hunger, though she felt run-down because of the wretched food. After the tour of inspection by the Ladies Commission, the diet was vastly improved with the addition of potatoes and onions, corn starch and jam for the children, and soup and, sometimes, milk for the sick.[19]

The meat supplied to all the camps was notoriously objectionable, "often inedible, lacking in fat, sometimes diseased, occasionally bad."[20] This is amply borne out by the camp diary of Jacob Kirchner, whose negative descriptions of the meat ration include the epithets "suspect," "frightfully scrawny," "inedible," "lamentable," "horrifically bad," and "revolting in appearance." As late as October 1902 the report on the Winburg camp indicated that "the ORC Cold Storage Co. still give a good deal of trouble with their supplies, which in several cases have had to be returned, being reported upon by the Senior Medical Officer as unfit for consumption." Maria de Jager recorded that on one occasion a woman presented the superintendent with her meat ration. When he said, "Bah! Take it away!" she thrust it under his nose and invited him to eat it, which caused much hilarity among the bystanders.[21]

Not only did the quality of the meat cause offense; the manner of its distribution did so too. In the Winburg camp the issuing was poorly carried out,

Coping with primitive conditions in the Winburg camp. Note the gendered roles. (War Museum of the Boer Republics)

with the handing out of the meat and grocery rations taking an entire day, so the Boer women had additional cause for frustration, and the issuers, being compatriots, were handy and emotionally satisfying targets for their pent-up hostility and aggression. The bywoner responsible for distributing rations in the Winburg camp allegedly threw a piece of meat at Anna Bosman, who picked it up from the ground and beat him about the head with it. According to another informant, women in the Winburg camp who were dissatisfied with the meat commonly threw it back at the issuer.[22]

Food was cooked outside over perforated paraffin tins holding burning fuel. If it rained, no food could be prepared, and the same applied if there was no fuel to be had. Children under the age of twelve were allowed to leave the camp to collect dry bushes at a stream some five miles away.[23] On 28 October 1901 the Kirchner family barely managed to cook their food with bits of wood begged from others. On 1 November they found enough wood to boil a kettle but not to cook. On 4 November they were still without fuel. On 6 December Kirchner's diary records that they had been without wood since 30 November. He could afford to buy coal, but poor people had to make do with dried cow dung as fuel.[24]

Because the soldiers who rounded up the women to take them to the camps were often in a hurry and there was limited space on the wagons they used for this purpose, women were prevented from taking any more than the barest minimum of bedding and clothing with them. Even as late as February 1902, the provision of beds in the Winburg camp could be described as "deplorably deficient." Tents offered little shelter against the harshness of a Free State winter—the winter of 1901 was particularly severe—and inmates complained of the bitter cold. Moreover, the tents were frequently threadbare, and in January 1902, when Winburg experienced nightly storms, the superintendent had to resort to using empty sacks as an outer covering on the tents, which did not improve their appearance but reduced ill health in the camp. "What a deluge we've had this week," Kirchner wrote on 16 March 1902. "Here in the camp we may pray for drought because rain makes life hard for the inmates, even harder than when the weather is normal. The tents leak and all around is mud."[25]

The provision of clothing was dependent on authorities whose attitude to economy bordered on the pusillanimous. When the Winburg superintendent requisitioned articles of clothing in March 1901, he was told: "No boots will be supplied, but you can make out an indent on the Ordnance Department, and send me, for one chest shoemaker's tools, hides, etc. and the refugees will then be able to make their own *veldschoenen* [homemade shoes]. Please bear in mind that clothing will only be issued free to persons who are quite destitute. . . . Kindly pay more careful attention to economy and only indent for persons who are destitute." A year later an inspection of the camp revealed that "the whole of the people are very badly shod and boots are urgently required."[26]

Another complaint was that the men were overworked. This came at a time when drains were being constructed and there was some pressure to get them completed before the rains set in. The problem may have arisen from the choice of overseers and how the necessity and urgency of the task was communicated. Generally only light chores were performed in the camps, because the men objected to doing what they regarded as demeaning work, and digging would certainly fall in this category.[27]

Another possibility is that the men in the camps claimed the "patriarchal dividend" that Bob Connell speaks about in the male prerogative of laziness. When Dr. Thomas Hime saw little girls working the pumps in the Bloemfontein camp and asked why the work was not being done by men, he was told that the men were too lazy.[28] Although there is probably some truth in this allegation, one must also allow for the animosity between the women, many of whom were the wives of fighting burghers, and the men, many of whom may have been in British service.

Coming from inmates of a concentration camp, a complaint about a lack of freedom is either sublime or ridiculous. If they were refugees, as the British said, they should be free to come and go; if they were prisoners, it was simply absurd to chafe against the restrictions imposed on them. Schnehage saw it as a frivolous complaint of people who "want to go where they like, for instance to town." But, then, Schnehage was a townsman and did not live in the camp. Accustomed to living isolated lives, camp inmates found it intolerable to be cooped up in a confined space. This, a contemporary said, "is in itself the greatest hardship that they had to endure."[29] They were captives, cut off from the world, serving an indeterminate sentence.

And yet there was an oddity about the Winburg camp, because toward the end of the war some of them were apparently set free. In October 1901 the British colonial secretary, Joseph Chamberlain, had suggested that inmates of the concentration camps should have the option of leaving them. Milner could see no advantage in the proposal. The Ladies Commission pointed out that allowing inmates to leave would mean "turning them out to starvation," and Milner was conscious of the fact that even after the conclusion of peace, "it would not be possible to let the people in the concentration camps go back at once to their former homes. They would starve there."[30] In December 1901 Kitchener came up with his proposal, to which Milner agreed, to send camp inmates who were willing to go to the Boer commandos. In an impassioned response, Steyn wrote:

> Your Excellency makes a proposal which you know, if accepted by us, would result in making the lives of those poor innocent victims intolerable. For Your Excellency knows and His Majesty's Government knows, or ought to know, that there is hardly a single house in the Orange Free State that is not burnt or destroyed, that all the furniture and especially the bedding and clothing of the women and children have been burnt or have been looted by His Majesty's troops.[31]

There were therefore two proposals relating to people leaving the camps, but both were rejected for precisely the same reason: that the suffering of the women would be aggravated. It is generally assumed that neither proposal was acted upon, but in a report dated 3 February 1902 the superintendent of the Winburg camp advised the chief superintendent in Bloemfontein that a number of women had left the camp to return to their farms.[32] He listed those who had indicated a wish to go, mentioned the provision made for them in terms of fourteen days' rations and an armed escort of burgher scouts, and revealed that some of the women had had second thoughts and did not leave camp with the rest. In Kirchner's account there is also mention of some people being "offered the chance of leaving . . . with seven days' rations at own risk with regard to the future" and of one who declined to accept these conditions.[33]

From this we gain the strong impression of a voluntary exercise in line with Chamberlain's proposal. This is how Elizabeth van Heyningen interprets it. She comments that they all "seem to have been the wives of burgher scouts" and quotes an instruction to the superintendent: "Don't send any woman whose husband is a prisoner of war unless her mother or other near relation with authority goes with her. Choose who you like otherwise."[34]

However, annotations in the Winburg camp register paint a totally different picture. According to these notes, five of the women who left the camp—Rosina Dreyer, Martha du Preez, Sarah Engelbrecht, Anna Malan, and Susanna van der Merwe—were deported to the Boer commandos on 27 January 1902 by order of the district commandant. The others who left at the same time were Elizabeth du Buisson, whose husband was an irreconcilable in India, and Sarah Kleynhans, whose husband was a POW on St. Helena. A month later, Johanna Fouché and Maria Haasbroek, two women who had declined to go, were removed to the Norvals Pont camp, which suggests punitive action.[35]

From the available evidence it seems possible that Superintendent Alexander complied with the orders of the military authorities but misrepresented the situation to his superior. If this interpretation is correct, it provides an interesting insight into the complexities of civil-military relations in an occupied territory.

Medical Staff

In spite of discord among the nurses, which impaired their morale and efficiency and became the talk of the camp and the town, Winburg camp enjoyed great advantages from a medical point of view. Emily Hobhouse held that the attitude of foreign medical staff had a lot to do with the aversion of Boer women to the medicine practiced in the camps. Winburg camp was fortunate in being served by the local practitioners, Caleb Schnehage and Victor Werdmüller, and sympathetic foreign doctors. Dr. Conrad Kops was a German, but he had already been in South Africa for a number of years on account of his wife's health, and he understood Dutch. Although Dr. Molesworth, who arrived in Winburg in July 1901, came out from England to work in the camp, he was sensitive to the cultural aspect of medical practice, believing that someone who could speak the language and take a personal interest in the inmates was best suited to nursing in the camp, and this could contribute greatly, as Molesworth put it, "to reconciling the people and reconciling them to our Government." He was also clearly committed to his work. During the first seven months of his contract, he was the only doctor resident in a camp that grew to three thousand inmates with epidemics raging, and on completion of a year's service he had not taken a single day's leave.[36]

In particular, the camp was blessed in the person of Sister Maria Bakkes, one of four volunteer nurses from the Netherlands. Emily Hobhouse quotes a "Mr. Koenbrink" (Henderik Koenderink, the Boer camp commandant) as saying, "She is like a ray of light for the camp and does some noble work; she is heartily beloved by all the women and children in the camp." Dr. Molesworth said of her, "In the early days of this camp she was quite alone and the amount of work she got through was wonderful. Besides she has worked in the Camp now for nearly two years without leaving it for a single night. She has always shown great tact and fairness and it has always been a pleasure for me to work with her." Dr. A. Pierce-Green concurred: "She works night and day and never asks for anything but to do her work." When Annie Champley, a qualified nurse sent to South Africa by the Society of Friends, was appointed as hospital matron in June 1902, Maria Bakkes assumed the role of camp matron with equal diligence. After the war she was given a free passage back to the Netherlands and was appointed an Honorary Nursing Sister of the Order of St. John of Jerusalem in recognition of her services.[37]

Disease and Death

In the early months of the camp's existence, the mortality rate in the Winburg camp was consistently lower than that in other camps. Yet this is not to say that medical and nursing care was adequate. In June 1901 there was only one doctor, one trained nurse, and three nursing assistants to 1,738 inmates in the Winburg camp. Capt. A. G. Trollope, the chief superintendent of concentration camps in the ORC, claimed that the ratio of doctors and trained nurses to inmates in the camps under his control was 1:1,000 and of nursing assistants to inmates 3:1,000. Even if this ratio had existed, it still would have been too low to provide the attention called for in the adverse circumstances of the camps.[38]

In August 1901 the medical staff at Winburg voiced their concern about weaknesses in current procedures and inadequacies in equipment, and in August disaster struck. Up to now the doctors had made a daily round to examine the sick in their tents. This was not only time-consuming; it also made it easier for patients to leave their tents on the approach of the doctor for fear of being taken to hospital. At this stage the hospital already had fourteen typhoid patients and was not equipped to deal with any more. If all the sick were moved from their tents to the hospital, its thirty-nine beds would be filled. They therefore requested one hundred more beds and other hospital equipment in order to be able to cope with "any sudden outbreak of infectious diseases." They also reported a case of scurvy. Because no fresh vegetables were issued in the camp, they asked for lime juice to be administered twice a week to avoid an epidemic of this disease.[39]

In the same month, Captain Trollope had noted in his report "the heavy death rate in some Camps due to the recrudescence of the epidemic of measles, complicated with pneumonia, and the destitute and ill-fed condition of some of the refugees when brought in."[40] Measles was the largest single cause of death in the concentration camps, accounting for 42–43 percent of all deaths, while pneumonia, in many cases linked with measles, was the cause of a further 13–18 percent. In the period June to December 1901, 61 percent of camp deaths were attributable to these two conditions. The virulence of the measles epidemics that racked the camps was due to four causes: the Boers' lack of immunity to infection, malnutrition, overcrowding, and the transfer of infected people from one camp to another.[41]

The low-density dispersal of the Boer population over the previous two centuries had resulted in a loss of immunity to the disease, so deaths in the camps stemming from loss of immunity were not limited to children but also affected the older age groups. People were brought to the camps in a debilitated condition that heightened their vulnerability to infection. The eight hundred members of the women's laager captured at Graspan were "worn out in constitution from constantly moving about in order to get out of the way of the columns." The ill-fed condition of these people was not helped by the minimal rations they received in the camps, and malnutrition was conducive to the secondary complications of pneumonia and bronchial infections.[42] The trauma of experiences such as seeing their homes destroyed and their animals slaughtered added to their debilitation.

In the Winburg camp the problem of overcrowding became a serious one as early as April 1901 when 250 people who were brought in from Senekal had to be accommodated in the church. In June 1901 a medical report drew attention to "the indiscriminate massing together of people of all sorts from different parts of the Colony in a large camp, whereby no doubt contagion is bound to assert itself." In spite of this the Winburg camp nearly doubled in size—from 1,700 to 3,178—between June and October 1901. In August the medical officers had warned that the camp was overcrowded and could not be enlarged to the west because of an adjoining rifle range. In September the camp had to be extended to the east, despite the rocky terrain.[43] In January 1902 the military authorities deposited no fewer than a hundred unfortunate people at the Winburg camp without any prior notification. In February, with people still being brought in by the troops—despite Kitchener's order to the contrary—the possibility of demolishing the rifle range in order to allow for expansion westwards was raised, but the commandant, Col. H. Crosbie, was adamant that it was impossible to relinquish the rifle range. Other ground was cleared and twelve marquees were erected but, as they were immediately filled, there was again no margin for any emergency.[44]

In October 1901 the mortality rate of the camp leaped from 9 per thousand inhabitants to 23 per thousand. At the end of August 720 people had been transferred from Bloemfontein, when Winburg could accommodate only 250, and they brought measles and whooping cough with them. The ill health in the camp was exacerbated not only by overcrowding but also by the malnutrition of its inmates, as the lime juice ordered in August had still not been received by the end of September. Although isolation was at first successful, the diseases raged through the camp,[45] and by November the mortality rate in the Winburg camp was almost on par with the average for the ORC camps.

In addition to the four major etiological factors, micro-factors such as the choice of the campsite, ventilation, standards of hygiene, and the level of treatment also came into play. The poor drainage of the Winburg campsite was conducive to the survival of typhoid bacilli with which the soil became contaminated, either as a result of the fouling of the ground in the environs of tents by inmates who were reluctant or unable to visit the latrines in the icy cold and inky dark at night,[46] or as a result of the careless handling of buckets collected for emptying. Contaminated soil was tracked into tents, where some inmates slept on the ground.[47]

Flies were also a source of vector contamination. The camp authorities made something of a fetish of ventilation and were vociferous in their complaints about the inmates' poor hygiene.[48] This, Paula Krebs notes, was part of the stock in trade of British sanitary inspectors visiting working-class homes, and it meant that because of the "degeneracy" of the Boers, Britain's civilizing mission could be added to her other motives for the war.[49] That Boer women were sensitive to this accusation is demonstrated by an inmate of the Winburg camp who wrote in her diary that the Boers were accused of dying of dirt, but whose fault was it when there was not even enough water to drink?[50] The scarcity of water in the Winburg camp was often referred to,[51] and Trollope urged "strict economy" in the issuing of soap.[52]

The British Blue Books made much of the application of bizarre home remedies as a contributory cause of death. Elizabeth van Heyningen is more sensitive to the disempowering effect that the clash of medical cultures had on women in the camps. On the farms women were normally the sole caregivers; in the camp their children were removed from them and isolated in an alien institution.[53] On the one hand, one must repudiate the generalization that women were responsible for the death of their children; on the other, one cannot deny that a child treated for measles with a decoction of goat's dung and wormwood was denied the medical attention needed to survive. Furthermore, it is disturbing to read of the ingenuity with which mothers contrived to outwit the medical personnel by finding hiding places for their rampantly infectious children. This practice would have been a major factor in the spread of diseases in the camps.[54]

There is no doubting the depth of the fear that women had of hospitalization. One must not exaggerate the perversity of this fear. In England, too, working-class mothers were unwilling to admit their children to a hospital where they might die alone in an alien environment.[55] Liz Stanley quotes statistics from the hospital records of two camps on the basis of which she demonstrates that sick children were more liable to die in their tents than in the hospitals.[56] One can safely assume that these conclusions would also hold good for Winburg, with its sympathetic doctors, yet the perception of the inmates of the camp was that there was no returning from the camp hospital. In the Winburg camp, Maria de Jager, who readily consulted doctors when she and her children were ill, regarded it as miraculous if someone returned from the camp hospital, and a fellow inmate wrote: "When a child is taken to the hospital, it is just like a funeral with the whole Showyard in tears, because there is no difference between a child being carried to the hospital or to the grave."[57]

When everything possible has been said in contextualization, extenuation, or exoneration of medical practice in the camps, one has still said nothing about the way inhabitants of the camps experienced it. It is the trauma of experience that blighted the lives of mothers and children in the camps and continued to affect the lives of generations to come, those who grew up with the postmemory of the camps, "dominated by narratives that preceded their birth."[58] There are hundreds of these narratives. One inmate of the Winburg camp told of spending six weeks on her knees watching over three children on one bedstead, one of whom had measles and another had whooping cough. Another account refers to the bitter experience of Rachel (Hannie) Scott, who arrived at the camp with seven children. One of them fell ill and was taken to the Showyard hospital outside the camp, but the mother was not allowed to accompany her. When the child was dying, the mother was refused permission to go to the hospital, and the child died without seeing her mother again. Others of her children fell ill and were taken to the hospital, and in the space of two months she lost four children.[59]

The concentration camps have achieved a deserved notoriety on account of the four thousand women and twenty-two thousand children who died in them. Yet the recurrence of claims of poison being administered to inmates and of babies being murdered by the medical staff of the camps points to a climate of opinion in which such things could be believed rather than to the veracity of the reports.[60] Responsibility for the unprecedented disaster of the camps and the opinion the women consequently formed of camp personnel rests squarely on the military authorities. The army was incapable of ensuring a healthy environment, even for a concentration of its own men, and it is notorious that during the South African War more British soldiers died of disease than as a result of enemy action. How, then, were untrained officers seconded as superintendents supposed to cope with concentrations of men, women, and children in unsanitary camps?[61] The description "concentration camps" is appropriate because it was the concentration of people that killed them; however, as Liz Stanley and Helen Dampier point out, in the post-Nazi era the term "concentration camp" has all too often functioned as a prism through which the camps have been perceived.[62]

For almost all inmates the ever present reality of death precluded any possibility of seeking healthy diversions. Profound weariness produced indifference to preventive measures, and predestinarian religion fed into a stoicism bordering on apathy. Perhaps one could speak of a melancholic predisposition in this regard. An observation by Dr. Thomas Hime, who carried out a medical inspection of the camps in January 1902, rings true:

> All the Medical Officers of the Camps have noticed the want of resisting power, the despondency and tendency to take a gloomy view of the most trifling ailment, which prevails among the Refugees. On feeling in the least unwell it is no uncommon thing to see a Boer take to bed, and declare that he feels his end has come. . . . I have been informed by Medical men who have been practicing many years in the country, this morbid condition was no less wide-spread among the Boers when resident on their own farms.[63]

In the camps at large, a focus on life was replaced by a culture of death. All that was left was to make a "good death," and deathbeds became the object of morbid fascination and prurient curiosity. The chaplain of the Bethulie camp insisted that "friends and relatives abstain from all long-faced despondency, with total absence of any cheer and hopefulness; this [has a] bad effect on patients; if anyone [is] seriously ill, they 'hands up' and cluster around to await the end, lest perchance they miss seeing '*zoo 'n prachtige sterfbed*' [such a beautiful deathbed]."[64] Of course, one must not prescind from what happened at Bethulie camp, probably the worst run and most demoralized of all the camps. This was the failing of traditional camp historiography that aggregated the worst elements of each camp to arrive at a totality of misery, without regard to the fact that—as Emily Hobhouse emphasized—the camps varied greatly.[65] Yet it is interesting to note that Henrietta Armstrong also deprecated the practice of clustering around a dying patient in the Irene camp in order to witness—and precisely the same words are used—"such a beautiful deathbed."[66]

Based on the figures provided in the official British Blue Books,[67] the mortality rate per thousand inhabitants for the period May 1901 to April 1902 was as follows, with "ORC Camps" representing the average rate for the camps controlled by the ORC Burgher Camps Department:

	ORC Camps	Winburg
May 1901	13	9
June 1901	12	6
July 1901	18	6
August 1901	28	6
September 1901	25	9
October 1901	33	23
November 1901	30	29
December 1901	29	27
January 1902	18	14
February 1902	7	12
March 1902	3	9
April 1902	3	3

In the estimation of Sir Hamilton Goold-Adams, the deputy administrator of the ORC, it was only in April 1902, a month before peace, that it could be claimed that a "practically normal death-rate" was sustained in the camps,[68] but, as this table shows, in Winburg such near normality was, at last, attained rather than sustained.

The figures presented here are useful in providing a comparison between Winburg and the other camps, but as statistical entities they have an air of unreality about them. They represent mortality rates rather than deaths. The raw figures tell a different story. Altogether some 545 people—the vast majority of them Winburgers—died in the Winburg camp; in addition, about 575 Winburgers died in other camps [69] It is not surprising that the trauma of more than 1,000 deaths in a community of only about 2,000 families endured beyond the generation that bore its immediate impact.[70]

Everyday Life

The trauma of disease and death entirely displaces the "everyday" in women's camp testimonies. Recent scholarship has drawn attention to the problematic provenance of these testimonies.[71] For the most part they served a nationalist agenda, and evil and even genocidal motives were freely attributed to the enemy. They operated with stereotypical tropes and rhetorical devices, and anything pleasurable was automatically excluded from the narrative.

Yet daily life in the camps would have brought its share of pleasurable experiences to relieve the burden of monotony and to lift the pall of depression. Such experiences might include shopping, religious observances, doing chores together, visiting friends and relations, seeing children at play, and talking in the tents after lights-out.[72]

Prisoners of war were disturbed by reports of unfaithfulness on the part of the women they had left behind, and one censorious patriarch, Josias de Klerk, writing from Ceylon to his wife in the Winburg camp, described the death and disasters in the concentration camps as an admonition to righteousness, since immorality, according to him, was rampant in so many camps.[73] Clearly the erotic interests of all camp inmates would not have disappeared with their incarceration. The superintendent of the Winburg camp complained of young officers coming into the camp after women.[74] A nearby ravine was a place of assignation, and one young woman was confined for twenty-four hours (her father asked that it should be for a month) because a soldier was found standing in the doorway of her tent.[75] There were four illegitimate births in the Winburg camp,[76] but as almost every church council meeting in the wake of the war probed untoward pregnancies, this hardly constitutes evidence of rampant immorality.

Part of the problem has always been that we have had only the women's testimonies to go by. This is what makes Jacob Kirchner's concentration camp diary such a significant document, for it provides an unvarnished account of the ordinary experiences of an educated, more affluent male detainee, who "greatly enjoyed domestic life" and engaged in leisure activities with other inmates.[77] While in the camp, Kirchner read, wrote a poem about camp life, corresponded, played chess and tennis, exercised regularly, baked bread, attended and conducted religious services, started a Sunday school and ran a choir, and served on the health committee and as a dispenser and administrative assistant. Other camp activities he mentions include knitting, crochet work, making brooches, playing soccer, and courtship!

Such a life of purposeful activity is reminiscent of many descriptions of daily life in the prisoner-of-war camps, where the men were well fed, well housed, in good health, not responsible for the care of children, and not constantly preoccupied with death and dying. Perhaps such activity was also exceptional in the concentration camps, where, it would seem, many men preferred not to exert themselves but sat around drinking coffee and reading newspapers.[78]

Defiance and Compliance

While the women's testimonies represent the women as uniformly passive in their victimhood, they are also portrayed as uniformly active in their defiant protests. The political agenda of proto-nationalist Boer writers obscures the fact that camp life could be experienced very differently by different inmates. They provide the perspective of politicized or even retrospectively politicized resistance, not of those for whom, according to one informant, life in the camps was "paradise."[79]

Clearly the camp authorities had rebellious inmates to contend with. In their report on the Winburg camp, the Ladies Commission recommended the discontinuation of the practice of segregating the more troublesome women in the Showyard, remarking that they "found the women in this camp to be exceedingly violent and bitter in their language." In time, this recommendation was complied with because it was found that according the Showyard camp this status actually enhanced the power of the Van der Hoven family—Helena van der Hoven; her husband, Antonie; and their daughter, Hester—who, with the Wessels and Theron families, were held to be the main cause of insubordination. In the future, Superintendent Alexander proposed to put recalcitrants into a recently constructed wire cage, although he did not anticipate much need for this form of coercion. In January 1902 it was reported that it was no longer considered necessary to segregate the hostile element in the camp and that the practice was being discontinued.[80]

In later life, Helena van der Hoven boasted of the fact that "she was such a fire-brand in the camp that she was sent to East London where the English had a special camp for women who were beyond control. Kubusie [*sic*] the old-timers called it or just plain Double Hell." In actual fact, Kabusie was intended as a model camp and was "infinitely more comfortable for the residents" than the camps they came from. But apart from the fact that sending women away from their home districts suggests punitive action, there is the categorical evidence of a telegram dated 5 April 1902 asking the superintendent of the Winburg camp to supply the names of persons he considered "absolutely undesirable to retain" in his camp and his response indicating the removal to East London of between 100 and 150 "undesirables."[81]

There were also male offenders who were put on trial and deported. The most general category was that of "troublemakers." Some were accused of conspiring or attempting to escape; the tent mates of those who succeeded in escaping were charged with failing to report deserters. George Norris and Gerrit Cooper were found guilty of "mutinous and seditious conduct" for intimidating men who were about to take the oath of allegiance; Willem N. Pienaar of abusing the policemen and guards; and Frederik Goossens of dissuading others from taking the oath; while Frans Heyman was designated "leader of a rebellious clique" and Antonie van der Hoven "a notorious bad character."[82]

According to Superintendent Alexander there was a serious act of defiance when a military funeral passing the gate "was greeted by various indecorous noises and remarks and some stones were thrown." Jacob Kirchner was clearly unaware of any disturbance, recording in his diary entry for 2 November 1901 that there was dismay among the camp inmates when five men were arrested for standing at the gate and watching the procession. The men were released the following day.[83] Despite "most pressing inquiries," reads the official report, "the instigators and perpetrators of this outrage could not be identified," and Alexander had to resort to threats that in the event of any repetition of such behavior the children would be removed to the care of a matron and the camp put on a ration of biscuits and water "for a period commensurate with the offence."[84] The reference to the children is interesting because, according to a recent informant, his father, who was a youngster in the camp, recalled that some children playing *kleilat*—a game in which flexible sticks are used to propel clay pellets—were distracted from their customary internecine warfare and, whether accidentally or deliberately, one of their missiles struck the coffin.[85]

In February 1901 the central Burgher Peace Committee suggested to Milner that pro-peace prisoners of war should be sent to the concentration camps to try to allay the women's bitter feelings and get them to win over their husbands on commando. The attempts of these men were largely in vain, stirring up many altercations.[86] The solidarity of the women in the camps has often been commented on, but "many altercations" implies many dissenters. Indeed, one gains the impression that, despite multitudinous stories of acts of defiance, rebellious behavior was the exception rather than the rule. So agency is restored to the camp inmates: some chose to defy the authorities, others chose compliance or cooperation. Although nonmilitant women are absent from the narrative, their presence in the camp becomes evident once we move away from the distorted picture of the camps accommodating women and children and a few old men.

At the beginning of 1902 there were about 500 men in the tented camp and the Showyard, no fewer than 317 of whom were in the twenty to sixty age range. In spite of this very large number of able-bodied men, Superintendent Bradley complained that so many men in the camp were in British service that there were not enough left to perform the day-to-day chores, and efforts were made to persuade volunteers from other camps to transfer to Winburg.[87] If one considers that of the 311 married men in the camp, fully 83 percent of them were living with their wives, one must imagine, as Elizabeth van Heyningen has pointed out, the absurd situation of a large number of male collaborators living in harmony with their supposedly militant wives.[88]

The rational conclusion that very many women were as dissentient as their husbands is supported by the fact that the possibility of a second camp at Winburg to accommodate one thousand "loyalists" was a sufficiently serious one for a suitable site at Mompeling to be identified. However, it was decided that such a move would be inadvisable, as "those against whom the Boers would be most bitter . . . would be most unprotected" at the new site.[89]

Daily Life in the POW Camps

The superior conditions that prevailed in the POW camps must not blunt one to the reality of the suffering experienced by many of these prisoners. A number of factors were conducive to radical disorientation: Prisoners were isolated from their familiar environment, family, occupation, and ordinary lifestyle; they were deprived of their freedom and subjected to enforced confinement; they experienced loss of dignity, recognition, and social status. The indeterminacy of their confinement had a deleterious effect, and beyond their present circumstances they had no idea what life held in store for them.[90]

The Senekaller Jan Brink describes the torpidity that was common among prisoners: "Many, if not most, do nothing but sleep, eat, laze about and talk about their experiences on the battlefield. These stories might interest someone who has not himself fought in the war; for a fellow-fighter they eventually become unbearably boring."[91]

Leisure activities served as a palliative. Athletics meetings were held in celebration of special occasions, specifically the presidents' birthdays, the birthday of Queen Wilhelmina, Boxing Day, and New Year's Day. Sports engaged in included rugby, soccer, cricket, boxing, swimming, angling, tennis, quoits, and even croquet. Board and card games were checkers, chess, dominoes, whist, and an immensely popular card game called *klawerjas*, and as a pastime, wood and bone carving enjoyed great prominence. Cultural and religious societies flourished, and education classes were provided by fellow exiles for young and old alike. The head teacher at Diyatalawa in Ceylon was the Winburger Schalk Pienaar, and Hugo van Niekerk was the "superintendent" of a school of seven hundred at Broadbottom in St. Helena. Van Niekerk also played a leading role in organizing sporting and cultural activities. He participated in Christian Endeavor, a debating society, and the sports union, of which he was president for a long time, and he established and headed a camp library.[92]

The Christian Endeavor Society made tremendous headway in the POW camps, with branches numbering from 170 to 800 members. Johannes du Buisson was secretary in the Diyatalawa camp and, using an old Eagle hand press, produced a biweekly called *De Strever* from 19 December 1901 until 9 August 1902. Bible study and prayer meetings fortified many prisoners, but some became obsessive in their religious preoccupation. Discord arose from the fact that many inmates—in particular, members of Christian Endeavor—regarded games and even the activities of debating societies as sinful, and the hall that was built at Broadbottom to promote these activities was scathingly referred to as "the Devil's House." Theatrical performances, one old Boer said, were "a very good way to pass a sinful evening." In India, too, the "sporty" were distinguished from the "ultra-religious."[93] Inevitably the censorious attitude of some members of the Christian Endeavor Society alienated their fellow prisoners.

There was also discord between Free Staters and Transvaalers, who thus had to be accommodated in separate camps in St. Helena. More fundamentally, those inclined to take the oath of loyalty and irreconcilables had to be kept apart. In the Bermudas, "agitators," prisoners on parole, and "pro-British" lived on different islands, and similar gradations applied in Ceylon (Sri Lanka) and India (including present-day Pakistan).[94]

The Peace Movement

Captivity provided the British with the opportunity of systematically suborning their prisoners. From the diarist Rocco de Villiers we know that all captured officers were invited to meet with officers of the British Intelligence Department. His experience of being plied with whisky and soda, cigarettes and friendly persuasion may well have been standard procedure. Certainly, the prisoner F.C. Charles von Maltitz was also wined and dined by Col. M. H. Lambert.[95] Green Point was the primary clearinghouse, with pliant prisoners going from there to Simonstown or rejoining their families in the concentration camps, while those who proved more obdurate were deported.

Even if a burgher did not succumb to the threat of deportation, the pressure to apostatize was kept up in the camps and in exile. How assiduously this policy of subversion was carried out is evident from an instruction addressed to the chief superintendent of refugee camps. The superintendents of Springfontein and Norvals Pont were to meet former commandant Stephanus Vilonel, now in British service, at their military stations, bringing with them "some of their leading refugees." Vilonel would be accompanied by another Winburger, Anton Muller, who had recently been captured and was "a man of great influence." He would live in the Bloemfontein camp with his family and would later return to Winburg with them. "It is particularly desired," Capt. H. L. Reid wrote, "that he should be shown every attention and well treated as he has influence with the Burghers in the field and wishes to see for himself exactly how matters stand."[96]

As burgher commandant of Green Point, it would seem that the former Winburg commandant Helgaardt Theunissen played a key role in these machinations. Meetings with the peace envoys Christiaan Botha and Piet de Wet were arranged, and Gerrie van der Merwe, one of Christiaan de Wet's favorite officers, was one of those who succumbed to recruitment and was dispatched to Bloemfontein "for a certain political purpose."[97]

It is in this political context that the case of Comdt. Mattheus Wessels begins to make sense. When Jacob de Villiers arrived at Green Point, he was warned, "Be careful what you say, the place is swarming with spies," and on his arrival at the transit camp known as Tin Town in Ladysmith, Rocco de Villiers was told the same thing. Distrust also permeated the overseas camps. How widely the net of suspicion was cast is demonstrated by the fact that in the Diyatalawa camp a notice was posted warning prisoners that Wessels was an enemy agent.[98] Given Wessels's family background, his war record, and his postwar activities, this is difficult to believe—but nothing is impossible. The other men listed with Wessels in the warning notice were Laurens Botha, Marius Zylstra, Ruth [*sic*] de Vries, and a certain Holtzhuisen. The role of Zylstra is not clear, but Botha was supposedly a commandant who was transferred from Durban to Green Point and who, within days of his arrival, proposed to hold a meeting of officers with a view to sending a peace deputation to Christiaan de Wet. De Vries penned requests to go home at sixpence a piece and was the secretary of a committee that organized a petition regretting that the Transvaal had made war on Britain; Holtzhuizen was the chairman of this committee.[99]

In January 1901 Wessels was apparently moved from Ceylon to Green Point, where he had a meeting with Goold-Adams and from where he successfully petitioned the British authorities on behalf of two sons, one sentenced to death and the other in need of an artificial leg. This may help to elucidate an enigmatic passage in Margaret Marquard's letters that suggests Mattheus Wessels and his wife in Winburg enjoyed the favor of the British authorities. On 20 November 1900, three weeks after the warning notice incident, Margaret Marquard had a long visit from Susanna Wessels, of which she reports: "She can only tell of kindness from the officers,—had written to her husband at Green Point of horses & oxen taken away, and—so she says—a letter from Sir Alf. Milner (!) has been consequently received by the Asst. Commissioner taking him to task!" In what sounds like a typically gentle rebuke, the author impressed on Mrs.

Wessels "the responsibility there would be for those who like her have hardly lost anything, to help to their feet those who are so bitterly impoverished."[100]

Attempts to subvert Republican loyalty were not limited to the officers, neither were they abandoned once prisoners were deported to overseas camps. Winburgers were among the ordinary burghers who succumbed, and Winburgers were among those who strenuously opposed the attempts to suborn them.

From time to time Winburgers who were being held in Simonstown and the overseas camps offered to serve against their compatriots. From the start, the British tried to separate the pacific sheep from the recalcitrant goats. Those who passed the test were transferred to Simonstown, where virtually everyone in the camp, including ten out of eleven officers, adopted a resolution calling on the Boer leaders to cease hostilities.[101] In the Bermudas, as has been shown, the more malleable were isolated on a separate island, and on St. Helena a second camp was established. Those who moved from one camp to the other were booed and mocked. Unsurprisingly, therefore, these changes were made by night, and so uncertain were men's dispositions that twelve might go to bed in a hut at night and only one be left in the morning. With regard to these defectors, the governor of St. Helena wrote to Lord Milner: "These are men who proved themselves loyal by steadfastly adhering to their convictions in spite of the jeers and abuse and at times maltreatment of the irreconcilables since their segregation eight months ago."[102]

Ultimately, however, there was no place to hide, as this poignant account by Francois Brink makes clear:

> While a Prisoner of War at St Helena I was one of the first who applied to Colonel Wright to be allowed to take the oath of allegiance to His Majesty King Edward. In consequence, with others I was removed from the camp on May 15th 1901. Nine months after this the Colonel asked if any of us were willing to serve either as Town Guards or Volunteers and I was one of the first who signed. Though we were not allowed to come to South Africa to serve, yet it became known among the Ex-Burghers that I volunteered to serve against them, and as a consequence, after returning to South Africa after Peace being concluded, the owner of the farm where I used to live would not allow me to live there any longer.[103]

In the circumstances of constant defections, the primary preoccupation of many prisoners seems to have been the maintenance of group solidarity. To consolidate group identity among prisoners of war, the national anthems were constantly sung, and anyone suspected of being in danger of breaking ranks was required to sing the anthems. All kinds of stratagems were employed to find out who had signed peace petitions. When it became known that Alwyn

Rautenbach was one of the more than two hundred prisoners in Green Point who had signed an antiwar petition, an investigating committee including fellow Winburgers Philippus Snyman and Jacobus de Villiers surreptitiously got hold of the document in order to see who had signed. Even more assiduously, such "investigators" sought to uncover the identity of instigators of peace petitions, and those who were found out were dunked in the latrine troughs. There were also more violent assaults. At Ahmednagar in India, for example, up to one hundred lashes were administered to "traitors," some of whom had to be hospitalized.[104]

Being a prisoner of war was an alienating experience, but for those who filled their time with meaningful activities, it could also be an enriching one, the benefits of which would have been carried over into postwar communities. By contrast, the concentration camp experience was so dominated by deprivation, disease, and death that its negative legacy was one of enduring bitterness.

6 White Man's War

THE TITLE OF THIS CHAPTER serves as a reminder of the long cherished but now totally discredited myth that the South African War was an "Anglo-Boer" war in which, as in all ethnocentric narratives, black people were no more than a shadowy background presence. They were indeed integrally involved, whether responding creatively to new situations, serving either the Boers or the British, or entirely overwhelmed by circumstances not of their making.

This chapter, which seeks to deal with their involvement, labors under the profound difficulty of an almost total absence of firsthand written evidence and the passage of more than a century, which would severely limit the value of any oral tradition that might still be traced. The Free State government made no provision for black education, and the 1904 census revealed that only 8 percent of blacks in the Free State could read and write, as opposed to 73 percent of whites.[1] Apart from widespread illiteracy, the subordinate status of blacks militated against their being represented in the archival record. Only one letter from a black man in Winburg has been found that has any bearing on the issue of black-white relationships and only one brief statement from a black man who enlisted in British service. There were black concentration camps in the district, but the records relating to the individual camps have been lost or destroyed, and very little direct evidence on the Winburg camps can be found in the surviving documents. The Winburg district was notorious as the scene of operations of Bergh's Scouts, a black military unit in British service under Boer officers, but all we know of its activities comes from hostile white witnesses.

This chapter deals with Boer-black relations; blacks in Boer service; black resistance to Boer hegemony fostered by Ethiopianism and manifested in the activities of armed gangs; service with the British troops, particularly Bergh's

Scouts; the black concentration camps; and recurrent claims of blacks murdering and mutilating whites contextualized in the colonial mythology of black savagery and recontextualized in terms of a general descent into murderous brutality.

Boer-Black Relations

The Boers' attitude toward blacks before and during the South African War has been described as highly racist. Although this is certainly true, it is too unnuanced. The racist attitudes that prevailed among the Boers, and that were typical, in varying degree, of other white nations, developed over time into a unique brand of South African racism that earned the opprobrium of the world community. But to conflate the two is to overlook the crucial difference that, while the harshness of the former could be mitigated by experiences of co-humanity, the latter was premised on social segregation, designed to remove all points of meaningful personal contact. Discussing the "otherness" of the past, John Tosh describes anachronism as particularly blameworthy, and the worst kind of anachronism, Lucien Febvre said, is psychological anachronism. To avoid these pitfalls, the historian needs to consider changes not only in material conditions but also in *mentalité*.[2]

What characterized many Boer-black interactions was the paternalistic element of quasi-kinship,[3] an ethos that could develop where mutual dependence was accompanied by submission on the part of the blacks to superordinate white males, who, in turn, accepted a measure of responsibility for the welfare of their clients, and where the cultural isolation of the farm promoted some commonality of material culture. As Eugene Genovese put it in his analysis of slave society: "Paternalism's insistence upon mutual obligations . . . implicitly recognized the slave's humanity."[4]

Some commonality of culture may be associated with a subaltern class comprising various groups: Griquas and other people of mixed descent, descendants of former slaves who had accompanied the Voortrekkers on their northward migration, "apprentices," as well as other blacks whose cultural bonds had been loosened in the *mfecane* period and who were in the process of achieving a new identity through long association with white people. During the war, Free State blacks who were culturally unconquered could seek refuge with their kinsmen in Basutoland, but those who had lost their ancestral language and traditional attributes were rendered subordinate to the dominant white culture and therefore amenable to loyal farm labor or commando service. Although the vast majority of *agterryers* (mounted colored retainers) on commando would have been Africans, a disproportionate number appear to have been of mixed extraction.[5]

This mitigation is not to deny that for whites in South Africa blacks were for centuries the "other"—not merely in the sense of being different but also excluded from consideration, in the manner of colonial discourse, as ontologically inferior and fit only for tutelage. The epistemic violence of reducing fellow human beings to the status of *skepsels* (creatures) was reflected in physical violence and in the symbolic violence of imposing often hurtful names on them and of excluding their voice from the historical record. Yet the genealogy of the racism of apartheid is not in seamless continuity with the racism of colonial domination. In that situation the racism was certainly cruder in its basic assumptions, but it was mitigated by daily interaction.

However, this mitigation was itself gendered. White and black boys played together; white and black men worked together, and during the war they were on commando together. For white women left on the farms, the intersection of race and gender was a fraught one. In their unaccustomed dealings with black men, the horror stories they had heard from their mothers already predisposed them to the hate, fear, and abhorrence that is such a striking feature of their testimonies.[6] It is astonishing that early in the war Sarah Raal feared being attacked by an employee called Andries who had been in her father's service for twenty-seven years.[7]

Yet, in contrast to these women's writings that subserved a nationalist agenda, Maria de Jager's memoir, which was specifically intended for her children, presents a picture of relaxed and more humane relationships. When one of her farmworkers first sees the multitudes of British soldiers and says they must be machine-made, she enjoys the joke with him. She speaks civilly to black scouts who come to her farm. When she is on the way to captivity and the convoy halts for the night, she encourages her black workers to avail themselves of the chance to make good their escape. She also provides a fascinating account of a chance meeting with a group of black women. Some Boer women from the Winburg camp obtained permission to accompany the boys who went out to collect firewood so that they could do their laundry at a nearby stream. There they encountered a group of black women captives, who looked really wretched. One of them, we are told, had also (and that "also" is significant) already lost five children. The Boer women agreed to employ the black women to do their laundry and subsequently shared food with them.[8]

It served the purposes of British propaganda to present the Boers as particularly brutal in their treatment of black people, the alleviation of whose lot could then be added to the reasons for waging the war. However, the Russian nurse Sophia Izedinowa contends "that really inhumane treatment of the blacks is not found among the Boers, who are even-tempered and just."[9] A photograph in Tabitha Jackson's *The Boer War* is captioned: "Blacks loyal to the British faced appalling brutality at the hands of Boers, like this man tied to a wagon wheel to be flogged."[10] However, the British use of precisely the same method is illustrated by a photograph in the KwaZulu-Natal archives that shows a black man in British service similarly immobilized in order to be "thrashed to within an inch of his life." Blacks in the Winburg district were also subject to the exercise of such arbitrary power. In his diary entries for both 15 and 16 August 1900, Major Pine-Coffin, the British commandant at Ventersburg Road, records quite casually: "Had some niggers flogged."[11]

Given the common context of the racial attitudes that prevailed among whites, the lack of social distance between Boers and their black agterryers, to which both anecdotal and iconographic evidence points, is all the more noteworthy. In January 1901 the regimental paper *Highland Light Infantry Chronicle* commented on the easy relationship between burghers and their servants. The following year an intelligence officer recorded his surprise at Boers' "familiarity with their black comrades. . . . They laugh, talk, eat and joke with them like equals." In his diary, Lt. E. G. Spencer Churchill remarked on the "fellowship" between burgher captives and their black servants, who shared food, drink, eating utensils, and items of clothing and sang hymns together.[12] Sophia Izedinova noticed the close personal relations and strong attachments that often subsisted between Boers and black people.[13] As Bill Nasson put it: "With agterryers and burghers enmeshed in a common culture, there was little visible distance between them; social distinctions between masters and dependents often appeared blurred, with the latter intimately assimilated into the guerrilla bands in which they lived and fought."[14] Pieter Labuschagne's *Ghost Riders of the Anglo-Boer War* is replete with examples of the leveling effect of coexistence on commandos, and this is confirmed by the evidence of photographs in his book.[15]

The records of claims for compensation in the Winburg district yield very scant evidence regarding relationships between whites and blacks. Countless witnesses, whose names—Klaas, Kleinbooi, or Piet—contribute to their invisibility, testify to the number of sheep or cattle their employers previously possessed, but give no hint as to their personal feelings. A letter from Doorn River Camp, however, provides a nice mix of cordiality and epistolary convention. Writing to his employer, Johannes Schnehage, on 12 September 1901, Stephen Kgabale says:

> My dear Master,
>
> Here I take the greatest pleasure as to write to you these few short lines, hoping to hear the same from you, Sir.
>
> My dear Master, I must let you know about my health that I am well

at present, yet everything is right as far as I can tell, but the sheep, horses and cattle I haven't got. The Government took it all away from me when they had shifted me away from the farm, Sir. Nothing in my care. Everything is in the Camp.

Best love to all. I am yours

Stephen Kgabale

Complement from me and all my children. Please ascuse me for bad writing.[16]

However, the cordiality of a paternalistic relationship is dependent on the dominance of one party and the acquiescence of the other. Not clearly recognizing this, a book like *Ghost Riders* is too sweeping in its favorable account of white-black relationships.

As the tide of war turned in favor of the British, black people in vast numbers deserted the Boer farms and the Boer commandos to ally themselves with the British. One of the few statements by a black employee encountered in the Winburg records in which a personal voice is discernible gives notice of this change. A man identified only as Serra, who worked for Marthinus Venter on the farm Vlaklaagte, deposed: "I was present on the farm when the British came to our huts where the claimant's wagon was standing and burnt it. This was in May 1901. Captain Bergh burnt it. I was one of Bergh's Scouts at the time. Captain Bergh had a lot of White and Native scouts in Winburg."[17]

In Boer Service

In the early stages of the war, black workers assisted the Boer women in carrying on farming operations. The commandos made use of labor levies, employed, for example, as drivers and diggers of trenches, and, in a different category, some trusted workers accompanied their employers as agterryers. In addition to the burghers who had personal retainers, black men were commandeered as communal servants. At this stage, according to Pretorius's estimate, there was a ratio of one agterryer for every four burghers.[18] Later in the war, the agterryers largely disappeared from the ranks of the Boer forces, both as a result of desertion and because the guerrilla band was a more focused fighting machine.

Agterryers performed a multitude of roles, from the grooming of horses to the preparation of food. Given the Boer style of fighting, a simple duty like holding a horse could assume military significance. When a Boer took cover and fired on the enemy, it was essential that his horse was held in readiness close at hand but out of danger in order to ensure a speedy departure when this became necessary. Agterryers also became involved in military encounters. On one occasion, when the Winburg commando was under pressure, it was

David Botes's agterryer, Duimpie, who defied heavy rifle fire to replenish their ammunition supply.[19]

The Boers also made use of blacks' intimate knowledge of the terrain, employing them as spies. Commenting on the early stages of the conflict, an Australian war correspondent claimed that blacks were "all in the pay of the Boers, no matter how loyal they may pretend to be to the British."[20] In the Winburg district a certain Jonas van Tonder, who lived in the Korannaberg, was a valuable source of intelligence. He had been orphaned in the wake of Blood River and was brought to the Free State as an apprentice by a Boer named Van Tonder, whose surname he assumed. He is alleged to have taken service with the British forces in order to keep the Boers informed. The loyalty to be found among such agents of the Boer cause is exemplified by Alfred Malapi, who was shot in the northeastern Cape toward the end of 1900 for infiltrating a British unit.[21]

Although it was vehemently denied at the time and there was ideological resistance to referring to the matter in official documents, the Boers were pragmatic about the possibility of recruiting black allies, and there were occasions when blacks were armed by them. Blacks were used as armed guards both at Mafeking and at Ladysmith. General French reported the presence of armed blacks in the Boer units he encountered in October 1900, and Col. H. M. Lawson claimed there were some fifty armed blacks in a commando that raided the Upper Tugela in July 1901. In their operations in the Cape, J.A.J. Bezuidenhout, Jan Smuts, and Manie Maritz also used blacks as sharpshooters.[22] In addition to the systematic but limited arming of blacks, there were probably also sporadic occurrences of agterryers adding marksmanship to their other duties. This was something that grew out of the shared joys and tribulations of men involved in what was perceived by many as a common cause. Gabriel Setiloane tells us that when the Jordaans of Kroonstad went on commando, four of his maternal uncles, members of the Mosebi family, accompanied them "to go and thrash the Red-necks."[23] Two died from British bullets. When a Winburg patrol was attacked and one of them, Pincus Scott, was wounded, an agterryer named Harry took over his rifle: "He didn't hesitate . . . but fired with a will at the English and their henchmen."[24]

The arming of blacks by the Boers is of interest more for being largely omitted from the historical record than for its military importance. Furthermore, the limited voluntary participation of blacks on the Boer side pales in significance when compared with their subsequent rapid mass desertion of the Boer cause. The Boers were not only taken by surprise but also outraged when vast numbers of blacks shook off their subject status. Boer survival depended on the subordination of blacks, and now, all of a sudden, they were losing control and their social world was tumbling about their ears.[25] The shock and outrage is evident not only in violent overreaction but also in the pained memory of the mockery experienced by men and women on their way to internment. Most searing of all was the taunt: "Where are your passes?" This triumphing of blacks over whites has entrenched itself in Afrikaner folklore.[26] In the stories told, the nature of the abuse hurled at the Boers may vary, along with the projectiles sometimes hurled by the Boers in retaliation, yet the salient features are invariable, suggesting that these stories reflect not only actual occurrences but also deep anxieties within Boer society, defused by such narratives.

In British Service

The British army established labor depots to service its insatiable needs, and in the course of time, anything from 70,000 to 120,000 black men were employed in one way or another on the British side.[27] And as more and more men were employed, more and more were armed.

Kitchener was evasive when pressed for the number of blacks under arms but eventually, in March 1902, admitted to ten thousand. David Lloyd George claimed that it was more like 30,000, and in Peter Warwick's view this figure "may not be wildly exaggerated." André Wessels believes it could have been in excess of 50,000.[28] He points out that if there were that many blacks under arms by the end of the war, their number actually exceeded that of the 15,000 to 17,000 Boers still in the field. When blacks were disarmed after the war, no fewer than 50,488 firearms were handed in in the Transvaal alone.[29]

Because of the tacit understanding that it was a "white man's war," the Colonial Office refused to allow Maoris to embark for service in South Africa.[30] However, tribesmen on the borders of the republics were armed for self-defense; then black spies, scouts, and guides serving on an ad hoc basis were replaced with armed corps. Each of Kitchener's columns was accompanied by at least fifty such auxiliaries. Increasing use was also made of black soldiers, and Lt. Col. J. S. Barker's column, which operated in the Free State, comprised some twenty-five hundred whites and one thousand blacks.[31] Many of these blacks, as well as some whites, formed a subunit under Capt. Oloff Bergh.

Black Resistance

It is a commonplace of South African history that subterranean black labor resistance occurred from the time when whites first appeared on the scene. This manifested itself in sullenness, insolence, theft, desertion, laziness, or deliberate damage to farm implements, but it needed the intrusion of new factors for such resistance to take on a more overt form that shattered the mold of subservience.

Black auxiliaries attached to a British column.
(War Museum of the Boer Republics)

The war itself, and, more specifically, the arming of black men by the British, was clearly the predominant influence in this regard and was identified by Smuts as the principal political factor in ultimately bringing the war to an end.[32] The British, for their part, had not intended to arm black people, for they shared the racial presuppositions of the Boers,[33] but increasingly they resorted to this expedient to accomplish their ultimate aim.

The war achieved the British objective of destroying the obdurate oligarchy that constituted the leadership of the Transvaal and replacing it with a more compliant class of progressive farmers and professional men. This was the "revolution from above" of which Jeremy Krikler speaks, but this aim could be achieved only at the cost of permitting and even fostering a "rebellion from below."[34] With British concurrence, if not encouragement, blacks refused to work for the Boers, were armed and fought against the Boers, harassed their wives, looted their cattle, destroyed their possessions, and occupied their farms. Once the British aim of "regime change" was achieved, however, the black people they had empowered were very speedily disempowered once more. Krikler's focus is on the Transvaal, but events followed a similar course in the Free State. When Bloemfontein was occupied, black people thought their deliverance was at hand. However, strict control over them was exercised by the British military authorities. To this end, a police force was immediately created, followed by the South African Constabulary in May 1901, and Republican laws were applied with greater severity than before. Blacks were disarmed; they had to return the Boer cattle that had fallen into their hands. They were obliged to leave the urban locations, the camps in which they had been interned, and the farms they had occupied,[35] and they were coerced into returning to the employ of their prewar masters.[36]

Although politically conscious blacks supported the British cause from an idealized perception of British nonracialism that would be to their future benefit, the masses were, in large measure, motivated by more basic considerations, such as wages and provisions. Yet the degree of politicization among ordinary black people has generally been underestimated by whites. Krikler argues that, in contrast to Edward Thompson's view that class consciousness is the touchstone of class, a class struggle does not necessitate class analysis.[37] The Boers did not credit their black employees with any understanding that they were oppressed by insecurity of tenure and labor exploitation and were therefore very surprised when those blacks turned against them.

Ethiopianism

The "Ethiopian" movement that swept the country in the years immediately before the war was a powerful agent of conscientization. The Ethiopian Church had been founded by Mangena Mokone in Pretoria in 1892. Mokone heard about the American-based African Methodist Episcopal (AME) Church from his cousin's daughter, Charlotte Maxeke, the founder of the Bantu Women's League (now the Women's League of the African National Congress).[38] In 1898 the Ethiopian Church merged with the AME Church. "Ethiopianism" speedily became a dreaded word in white South Africa because of the political awareness of these churches. Officialdom associated it with insurrection, while the disquiet and distaste of whites is evident in a number of early South African novels.[39]

Although the AME Church was apolitical in the narrower sense of the word, it offered a vision of hope and restored human dignity by providing opportunities for leadership, independent action, social reintegration, and upward mobility in a structured community free of white control. Such a vision is profoundly political and could inspire resistance. A minimalist estimate of the political impact of the church is adopted in James Campbell's appraisal of the role of the church; however, André Odendaal concludes that the religious and political movements "evolved in tandem," while Tim Keegan goes further, contending that the AME Church "was born out of black nationalist ideals."[40]

As a minister of the church, the Rev. Jacob Morapedi of Winburg felt enabled to offer resistance to the Boer authorities, even before the British appeared on the Free State scene. In 1899 Rev. Samuel Mabote of the AME Church (Ethiopia) wrote to the landdrost of Winburg claiming that the church enjoyed state recognition and that Morapedi could therefore not be commandeered for service in terms of the Commando Law, which empowered landdrosts to place a vagrant or unemployed person of color at the disposal of any burgher who applied for his services. Landdrost Jacobus van Zyl disdainfully referred the matter to the government secretary:

> I don't know whether this new church is recognized or tolerated. What I do know about it is that the aforementioned Jacob J. Morapedi (better known as drunken April) causes dissension amongst the members of existing churches. April (whom I do not and will not recognize as a minister of religion) was commandeered to take a wagon to Harrismith for Dr. Schnehage along with another black. . . . The sooner an end is put to this church in this country the better. I have no intention of replying to Mr. Samuel J. Mabote.[41]

In addition to the Winburg congregation of the AME Church, there was probably one at Senekal, as a researcher has drawn attention to the existence of no fewer than five African Independent Churches in the area in 1900, and there was certainly one in Ventersburg under Rev. John Kubedi. Other Free State congregations were to be found at Kroonstad, where the church "virtually swept the location"; Ladybrand, with several hundred adherents; Springfontein, where the missionary Christof Sandrock regarded the church's activities as political and fueled by the conviction that Britain was winning the war; and at least ten other locations.[42] When Jacobus Xaba, who was head of the church in the Free State, applied for exemption from carrying a pass in March 1903, the commissioner of police advised that Xaba was "a big man in his own sect" and that if his request was refused, "his Church which is politically active will probably make a fuss."[43]

Armed Gangs

Following the British invasion of the Free State, some black men availed themselves of the unsettled condition of the country to band together in armed gangs that posed a serious threat to the Boers. However criminal their intentions or actions, the solidarity of such gangs was also conducive to political conscientization. These gangs were sometimes alleged to be under white control, but this claim could not be substantiated. It may have been a back-projection of the Bergh's Scouts phenomenon, reinforced by the familiar colonial trope of contented indigenes stirred up by outside agitators. The available evidence regarding the gangs is sadly riddled with contradictions, inconsistencies, and improbabilities.

As early as June 1900 there was such a gang occupying cave hideouts near the border between the Winburg and Bethlehem districts. According to Christiaan de Wet, this gang was led by "a certain Grobler, a Free State subject." De Wet does not say that he was a white man, but this is perhaps implied by saying that he "used 50 or 60 armed natives." M. H. (Tewie) Wessels concurs that the gang, known as the "Klaasbende" (or Klaas gang), was led by Gert Grobbelaar, as he spells the name.[44] The leader of the gang was believed to have guided the Imperial Light Horse when Lt. Col. C. J. Briggs made an attack on Reitz in an attempt to capture De Wet. De Wet believed that the column was guided by the son of a member of the Volksraad, whom he does not identify, but the regimental historian says that it was "a native named Klaas."[45]

In the most circumstantial account of the gang's activities, that of H.C.J. Mostert,[46] the gang leader was a black man and his name was Klaas. According to this version, Mostert's father, Jacobus Mostert, and a policeman named Jan Fourie were killed by gang members in June 1900. On 21 September the Winburg commando launched a protracted attack on their fortified caves. However, the approach of British troops from Senekal obliged the Winburgers to withdraw. That night two black men and two British soldiers burned down the Mostert farmhouse. The next afternoon two burghers, Frik Heymans and a certain McCarthy, were murdered. Possibly that same night, Everdina Cilliers, wife of Daniel Cilliers of the farm Fraaiuitzicht, managed to hold members of the gang at bay with a hand axe as she, her mother, two sisters, and their children escaped to the farm of her brother-in-law, Hendrik Pienaar.[47] When two members of the Bethlehem commando, Frans van Wyk and Steven van Deventer, were set on and killed, Comdt. A. M. Prinsloo resolved to deal decisively with the gang. After a night-long fight (28–29 September) the gang surrendered, although Johannes van Wyk, brother of Frans van Wyk, had to enter the caves to bring the leader out. The men under Prinsloo's command were obviously Winburgers, because Tewie Wessels mentions the involvement of Frederik Cronjé, and Hendrik van der Walt provides what is clearly a firsthand description of the captured gang leader's distress.[48]

The gang's fate is instructive in revealing how past events are recontextualized in subsequent memory. According to accounts written by M. J. Grobler, Tewie Wessels, and others in the 1930s and 1940s, twelve blacks were killed in the battle and forty-three prisoners were taken, twenty-five of them minors. In pursuance of a krygsraad decision, the adults were sentenced to death and the juveniles to twenty-five lashes, and these sentences were immediately carried out. According to Tewie Wessels, the gang leader was interrogated by Frederik Cronjé. The death sentence pronounced on him was confirmed by Gen. J.B.M. Hertzog and was carried out the night after the latter's departure for the Cape Colony. However, both Grobler's and Wessels's versions of events are substantially incorrect, because in a letter to Gen. W. B. Knox dated 6 October 1900, Christiaan de Wet says the gang was "dispersed" while the leader was "caught and shot."[49] Furthermore, Grobler has Maj. Gen. Sir Leslie Rundle protesting against the executions "a day or two later" in a letter dated 12 September 1900,[50] while Hertzog's departure for the Cape followed only three months later. Significantly, according to the contemporary report, only one person was killed, although the later narratives speak of some thirty killed and twenty-five beaten. This would be in conformity with the subsequent "horizon of expectation" as to the appropriate treatment their conduct merited.

A reminiscence of Catharina van den Berg, recorded in 1952, corresponds in some respects with the above account but differs in others. It also tells of a black gang that took refuge in a cave and agrees that twelve of them were shot in an engagement with a Boer force, that a brave burgher entered the cave to bring the leader out, and that eighteen adult survivors were executed. However, the encounter is located in the Kroonstad district; the small commando, which was led by Dolf Brits, a Cape rebel, appears to have consisted of members of the Kroonstad commando; and the eighteen black men were sentenced to death by a recently constituted court and were, implausibly, executed by hanging. Dot Serfontein also reports on a black "commando" led by a certain Croucamp, presumably a white man, at Holfontein, south of Kroonstad. In this narrative the mythological accretion is so substantial that the factual substratum is hard to discern. Two burghers are said to have attacked the black commando. Severely wounded, the burghers surrendered and, in the manner of a gothic novel, were tied to horses' tails and torn asunder. When a white commando "exterminated" the gang, a survivor reported that they had acted under orders of Croucamp. This alleged atrocity so enraged the Boers that every black person found in British service from then on was doomed to death.[51]

Bergh's Scouts

The ultimate armed band organized in resistance to the Free State Boers was Bergh's Scouts. Oloff Bergh was born in the Cape Colony on 1 November 1865.[52] He joined the Cape Railway service and was transferred to the Free State in 1889. He was pensioned from the railway service in March 1900 and became a storekeeper in the Winburg district. In August he was attached to Military Intelligence, managing the four thousand blacks employed by the department. Bergh's Scouts must have been in existence by January 1901, because Frederik Gouws became a member of the unit in that month. Although many of the white members moved on to Vilonel's ORC Volunteers when that body was formed at the end of 1901, some whites continued to serve in Bergh's Scouts. Members were not only spies but also helped to round up the civilian Boer population, raided livestock, looted farmhouses, and clashed with Boer guerrillas operating in small bands in the Winburg district, and, in the course of doing so, they achieved enduring notoriety.

Used by the British for such tasks as conducting Boer women to the camps, the Scouts were able to assert themselves, so on every side the "insolence" of previously docile blacks was remarked upon.[53] "Insolence" is, of course, a common trope of colonialist discourse. It can be deconstructed as self-assurance. Self-assured black scouts treated white women with disdain in the presence of British officers and were allowed to take loot as remuneration. They shook off subservience and gloried in the dignity, assurance, and self-importance of independent men, uniformed and under arms and associated with the winning side.[54] They were, in the words of Sarah Wilson, "proud men [who] stalked the streets with their precious rifles, evidently feeling such a sense of security as they had never experienced before."[55] It was a proud black man who could reprimand a Boer woman for addressing him in what he regarded as a derogatory manner and self-assertive black men who on occasion manhandled or sexually abused Boer women.[56]

In all of this, blacks felt they had the support of their British superiors. When blacks raided the farm Morgenzon in the Winburg district, their spokesman said that they were fighting for land, having been promised a redistribution of white farms when the war was over.[57] Mrs. J. H. van der Merwe, raped on or about 26 November 1901 by a black man with Rimington's column, reports him as saying that his officer had authorized the black members of the force to do with the women as they pleased. Catharina Koen, wife of Comdt. J. J. Koen, testified that Colonel Pilcher had told her that if her husband harmed the eighteen blacks he had captured the previous day, Pilcher would allow the other thousand under his control to do what they wished with Boer women. This threat was repeated in a letter from Pilcher to Koen dated 21 January 1902.[58]

Killings Contextualized—and Recontextualized

In examining the black rejection of Boer authority we are confronted by the double jeopardy not only of what has been called "the tyranny of available evidence,"[59] since the provenance of the archive is almost exclusively white, but also the hidden agenda of those from whom it derives, for, as Michel Foucault points out, history functions as a legitimating mechanism for exercising power in society.[60] There are numerous accounts of white people who were murdered by blacks in the Free State, but in spite of the fact that murder is a heinous human interaction seldom perpetrated without a motive, the sources are not concerned with the motives that may have given rise to such extreme actions. Instead the killings are contextualized in terms of colonialist perceptions of the colonized as brutal and barbarous. In order to explore this theme, it is helpful to look more closely at nineteen murders said to have been perpetrated in the Winburg district.

The first victims recorded were Pieter du Plessis and Dirk Kotze, who were allegedly murdered by blacks at Schoemanskop, about six miles northeast of Winburg on 25 September 1900. However, we are told that their bodies were never found,[61] so it is not clear how it can be established that they were murdered, when and where they were murdered, or by whom. Information is also lacking in regard to the murder of the seventy-nine-year-old mother-in-law of a Mrs. Reineke, which Jacob Kirchner learned about on 11 September.[62] This was a time of turmoil in the Winburg district when the bonds of control were loosened and criminality not directly connected with the war may have peaked.

Almost all the other alleged murders appear to have been at the hands of Bergh's Scouts or other blacks in British service, with most of them occurring in the course of a military encounter. Being killed by blacks in the employ of the British army was therefore simply equated with murder. In a number of cases, extreme brutality is alleged, but often the evidence is contradictory. The stereotyping of blacks in the historical record is redolent with tales of barbarity, and such historical habituation made for greater credibility. When an intelligent Boer woman heard of eight Boers who had been mutilated with knives and their eyes cut out or of thirty Boer families exterminated by blacks, she took these reports at face value because of all the stories she had heard over the years of the terrible wars against blacks.[63]

On 28 March 1901, Hendrik Bresler and Matthijs van Wyk were killed when Bergh's Scouts trapped some Boers at the Vet River, near Smaldeel. According to the sworn testimony of Willem and Jeremias Cronjé, their bodies were horribly mutilated.[64] Sometime after the war the remains of Bresler and Van Wyk were reinterred in Theunissen (previously Smaldeel) at a memorial to the 1838 battle of Blood River.[65] This battle avenged the killing of Piet Retief and his followers by the Zulu king Dingane. The fate of Bresler and Van Wyk was thus contextualized in the metahistory of the barbaric killing of whites.

A cause célèbre in the district was the encounter between blacks and Boers on the farm Welgevonden, near Tabaksberg, about fifteen miles southwest of Winburg. A group of Boers led by F.C. William Marthinus Scott had spent the night of 25 May 1901 within the perimeter wall of the farmyard, when at dawn the next day they were surprised by a patrol of Bergh's Scouts, comprising approximately two hundred blacks under a white officer.[66] The attackers ensconced themselves in a seasonal stream two hundred yards to the east of the house, from where a withering fire was directed at the defenders. William Edward Scott, a nephew of William Marthinus, was killed, and Johannes Scott, a younger brother, was wounded. At about ten o'clock the defenders ran out of ammunition and fell back on the wagon house. At this stage the Scouts charged them, and Izak Vivier, a son-in-law, was killed, allegedly with a white flag in his hands. Tobias Singleton, two burghers surnamed Jooste and Greyling, and Jan Koen made good their escape, but Koen was killed by blacks on a nearby farm that night.[67] The inscription on William Scott's tombstone, "Died at the hands of traitors,"[68] might imply that he was killed by surrendered Boers serving in Bergh's Scouts rather than by blacks. The presence of Jan Viviers, Stoffel Heinecke, Carl Tempelhof, and other white members of Bergh's Scouts is mentioned in connection with the death of Josephus du Plessis on his farm sometime in 1901.[69]

On 17 August 1901 a section of Haasbroek's commando was surrounded by Bergh's Scouts at Doornberg. Four burghers died—Johannes du Preez, Philippus Potgieter, Abraham (Ampie) Botha, and his uncle Ampie van Schalkwyk—the last three so hacked or bludgeoned, according to Gert van den Heever, who saw their bodies, that their death was described as murder.[70] How such a story grew in the telling is evident from the version recorded by G. D. Scholtz in 1973: "Somehow it was discovered that a small number of Boers was again taking refuge in the Doornberg. Early one morning, while they were still asleep, they were attacked by a commando of non-whites and killed to a man. Most of their bodies were horribly mutilated."[71] However, in Anna Barry's version, which was apparently also based on the testimony of Gert van den Heever, there is no mention of blacks, and Ampie van Schalkwyk suffered five bullet wounds.[72] Ampie Botha's brother, D. W. Botha, confirms that seventy men of Haasbroek's commando were surrounded by a "gang" and that the fleeing Ampie Botha and Ampie van Schalkwyk were shot, "one could almost say murdered," the former suffering two wounds and the latter three.[73]

On 16 September 1901 Bergh's Scouts visited the farm Morgenzon, about twenty-four miles southeast of Winburg, which was occupied by Johanna Mynhardt and her three daughters, Stoffelina, Johanna Elizabeth (Bettie), and Cornelia. The scouts, who had come looking for Boers, hid in the garden and ambushed Bettie's husband, David, and his brother, Daniel Janse van Rensburg. David's horse was killed under him, and he himself was shot in the head at close range. This would suggest instantaneous death, contradicting another version of the story that says he was tortured.[74] There is no mention of Daniel's death, but his name appears on the war memorial in Winburg. According to another source, a certain Erasmus Janse van Rensburg also died on this occasion.[75] We have no further information about the killing of Leendert Haasbroek on his farm in December 1901 or of Jan Maartens at Bloemhoek near Ventersburg some time in 1902.[76]

Finally, we consider the mysterious death of Assistant F.C. David Pretorius. Before dawn on 4 January 1902, about 130 Boers encamped at the confluence of the Vet and Sand rivers were surrounded by 600–700 soldiers. Many got away, but 50 to 60 Boer prisoners were taken, including Pretorius.[77] According to the sworn testimony of Johannes Erasmus, some of the prisoners informed him that Pretorius had been led away by his captors, that shots were heard, and that his body was later found by Comdt. Jacobus Theron.[78] With typical verbal economy, the diarist F.C. Hendrik van der Walt merely records that Pretorius "was shot by the enemy."[79] However, in P. J. Marx's account, we are told that when Pretorius's body was found, it bore no bullet wounds, but his arms and legs had been broken as a result of his having been "treacherously beaten to death by the blacks."[80]

Two disparate observations are necessary to recontextualize these killings. The first is that black violence against the Boers was the exception rather than the rule.[81] Attacks that were feared from the Basotho never materialized, and although Hintrager's comment on the peaceable behavior of blacks was made before the scorched-earth policy was fully implemented, General Froneman could claim as late as May 1902 that in the districts of Winburg and Ladybrand, blacks were "well-disposed and . . . of great service to the burghers." [82]

The second observation is that the killings must be seen in the context of a brutalizing war, for, as one Boer writer observed, "very few men are proof against the demoralizing influence of war."[83] The British records list 235 incidents of unarmed blacks being killed by Boers in the field as early in the war as November or December 1900, including the shooting near Virginia station of two men accused of showing British troops the road to Ventersburg.[84] As a result of the British policy of clearing the land, any black man encountered was assumed to be a spy, and if he was armed, the evidence was regarded as conclusive. As one burgher wrote, no meeting of the krygsraad was necessary; if an armed black was caught, he was summarily shot. On 29 June 1901 Haasbroek reported to De Wet that his Winburgers were shooting blacks on a weekly basis.[85] In July 1901 Gen. Piet Kritzinger served notice that any black in the service of the British army who was caught by the Boers would be executed, whether or not he was armed, and toward the end of the war there was little chance of a black prisoner being spared.[86]

On 27 July 1901 a British patrol led by Lt. G. Fraser of the 85th Company, Imperial Yeomanry, was surrounded on the farm Dankbaarheid in the Winburg district. One of the Boers present—said to have been Comdt. Jacobus (Tollie) de Beer—shot eight black guides, who had their hands in the air, as well as a wounded British soldier, Trooper W. Finch, possibly in the mistaken belief that he was a person of color.[87]

The Black Concentration Camps

Black resistance to Boer hegemony proved futile not only because of these savage reprisals but also because, in the long term, nothing came of British blandishments and blacks' hopes. British victory over the Boers meant a reassertion of their common racism. As a result of the scorched-earth policy, thousands of blacks were sucked into a vortex of destitution and misery.

Since the purpose of the scorched-earth policy was to deprive Boers still in the field of any possible aid or sustenance, it was directed not only against whites but also against blacks who might, voluntarily or involuntarily, provide them with food, shelter, or information. In addition to being driven from the farms, blacks were forced from reserves and mission stations as well.[88] At first those who were displaced by the war were simply abandoned to their fate. Some escaped to neighboring Basutoland, where, by the end of the war, 12,000–15,000 refugees were accommodated. However, not all who set off for Basutoland reached their destination. A group of 130 from Winburg got only as far as Brandfort, where 50 of them were siphoned off for military work.[89] Some moved into already overcrowded locations; others established informal settlements clustered around the army camps or the white concentration camps, desperate for jobs in order to feed themselves. Limited employment opportunities were available doing menial work in the white camps, so the superintendents of the white camps assumed some responsibility for the settlements adjacent to them.[90] These satellite settlements developed into black concentration camps, which the inmates were not free to leave except to work in the white camps or for the British army.

Conditions in these first, informal camps were grim. Inmates had to provide their own shelter, which in the Edenburg camp was described as "scattered in slightly built wigwams covered with sacking." The Brandfort camp had no latrines. Free rations, consisting exclusively of ground corn, sorghum, and salt, were issued only to the indigent. These were budgeted for at the rate of 4½ pence per person per day, compared with 9 pence for white camp inmates and 1shilling and 5 pence in Free State prisons.[91]

Flimsy structures in a black concentration camp.
(War Museum of the Boer Republics)

In June 1901 the newly established Native Refugee Department under Capt. H.G.J. de Lotbinière took over responsibility for the town camps in the Transvaal and in August for those in the Free State as well. In outlining the genesis of the department, De Lotbinière explained that when the British occupied Johannesburg, some fifteen thousand black men were employed on the gold mines. About four thousand of them were absorbed into the Army Labour Depot and made available to various army departments with the understanding that they had to be returned to their previous employment when the mines became operational again. Now he was instructed to return them to the Chamber of Mines and replace them with black refugees. "Thus the Native Refugee Department came into existence, and our first consideration was the supply of native labourers to the Army."[92]

When the Native Refugee Department assumed responsibility at the beginning of August 1901, there were about 22,700 black civilians in camps in the bigger Free State towns. In that same month, De Lisle's column brought about 130 blacks into Winburg and the superintendent of the white camp had to telegraph the chief superintendent to ask what he was to do with them. Capt. A. G. Trollope passed the query on to the chief superintendent of native locations in Bloemfontein, noting that "a native camp has never been formed at Winburg and the Military should not have landed them there."[93]

But it was a time of rapid change, because just a month later there was evidence of such a camp.[94] We know from Colonel Hamilton's subsequent report that there had been a black camp to the east of the white camp in Winburg. The black servants of the camp inmates Pieter Karemaker and Antonie van der Hoven would have been accommodated there, as well as a woman who sold milk and cow dung for fuel to the women of the white camp. When it was discovered that this woman was helping the Boers, Maria de Jager tells us, she was removed from the camp and sent far away. From the same source we learn about some black women employed to do laundry work. As mentioned previously, the white women in the camp shared their food with them. But, she says, when the guards found out, the black women were prevented from returning. Possibly both actions, interpreted as retaliatory, relate to the removal of black refugees from the area and the burning of their huts, as their makeshift settlement was considered unsanitary and a danger to the health of the white camp.[95]

Within the space of one month, all black civilians in camps adjoining white camps were moved to new locations along the railway line, where the blockhouses created a "protected area." The burning of black homes had become standard practice, so thousands more were being swept from the farms, villages, and mission stations. By September 1901, twenty-three black camps falling under the ORC had been established, and by the end of war there would seem to have been twenty-nine of them.[96] These camps accommodated some sixty thousand people, about 50 percent of whom were children, more than 25 percent women, and fewer than 20 percent men.[97]

With its head office under Capt. F. Wilson Fox at Bloemfontein, the ORC Native Refugee Department was organized into seven districts. District No. 1, under H. S. Bradshaw—with seven superintendents, two assistant superintendents, five dispensers, and three clerks—comprised seven camps strung out along the railway line from Alleman in the Bloemfontein district to Doorn River in the Winburg district, while District No. 2, under P. H. Gresson, covered the northern part of the Winburg district up to Serfontein in the Kroonstad district. There were six district inspectors, who were supposed to visit the camps at least twice a month, and, at least on paper, medical officers carried out weekly inspections.[98]

Black camps in the Winburg district comprised the following: Houtenbeck camp on the farms Geluk, Rietgat, Goliathshoogte, and Houtenbeck accommodated 3,900 people. Eensgevonden, with 1,020 residents, was situated on another portion of Goliathshoogte. Vet River camp, which had 1,350 inmates, was on Paardevlei and Goedgedacht. The Winburg camp was on Woolwash, while Smaldeel camp, with 1,020 residents, was on the farm Tweefontein. The Doorn River (or Virginia) camp, with some 815 people, was situated on three farms, Leeuwarden, Leeuwfontein, and Welgelegen; and Rietspruit camp was on the farm Rietgat. Finally, there was the Ventersburg Road camp, home to 1,244 people, on Zwartpan and Bloemkruin.[99]

De Lotbinière saw his task as twofold: to supply laborers to the army and to the Rand mines and to promote self-sufficiency. All able-bodied men were compelled to work, those in receipt of wages had to pay for their rations, and the inmates, mostly women and children, had to cultivate crops to feed themselves and their families—as well as the army departments. Those who refused to work for the army or participate in cultivation had to pay double for food; those who cooperated still had to pay for ground corn and sorghum, though at half price.[100] Stowell Kessler describes the policy as "forced removal, forced confinement, forced labour," but De Lotbinière saw it in a more benevolent light. "What we are doing now," he wrote, "viz. part payment system, together with our cultivation plan, might be held as a partial compensation for the destruction of their grain and food by the Columns."[101] The compound system protected blacks against speculators and helped to safeguard community life, while the stores in the camps provided luxuries, such as sugar, candles, tobacco, lard, and corned beef at cost and clothing at near cost. In any case we may be sure that in De Lotbinière's view the imperial ends justified the necessary means. Apart from the first priority of channeling labor to the military, he was inspired by a wider vision. The refugees were "all farm boys and as such a valuable asset to be held in trust for the civil administration," and the colonial farmers and "some twenty yeomen" who superintended them were equally a valuable asset for a future land settlement program.[102]

By the end of April 1902 there were more than 13,000 blacks on the army's payroll. The disruption of the migrant labor system as a result of the war left many blacks with little option but to work for the army. The wage was a shilling a day, but certain categories of workers—for example, drivers, leaders, scouts, and blacksmiths—could command double this amount. By contrast, service with the Boers was commandeered and unpaid, and the penalty for refusing to serve was a fine of five pounds, imprisonment, or twenty-five lashes.[103] Other benefits of army enlistment were the novelty of the experience, a sense of belonging, the possibility of loot, the acquisition of firearms, and, in some cases, daily rations of meat. The downside included harsh discipline, ambivalent relations with British soldiers, and poor working conditions.[104] Those who were employed at a distance from the camps were engaged for three months at a time so that they could visit their families. Black men whose labor was not required by the army, as well as women and children, could be contracted to the civil administration, to the white camps, or to private employers. In the ORC camps, 11.6 percent of the camp population—comprising 6,382 men, 310 women, and 242 children—were thus employed, 5,312 of whom were in government service, 1,248 in white camps, and 374 in private employment.[105]

Self-sufficiency was vigorously promoted, and in time the cost of running the camps was brought down to two pence per head per diem.[106] Employment and rationing were therefore related issues, and the following figures for the Winburg camps were submitted to the government secretary for November 1901:[107]

	Men	Women	Children
In government employ	2,055	3	1
Rationed on payment	1,347	3,903	7,181
Rationed free	2,694	6,455	9,930
Not rationed	1,680	3,204	7,119
In private employ	92	95	32

For the cultivation of crops, each family was allocated three acres of land. A few plows were supplied, but most of the cultivation was done with picks and hoes. Potatoes, pumpkins, and fodder crops were grown for the army, and corn and sorghum were raised for domestic use.[108]

The farms chosen were close to railway lines to facilitate the supply of labor to army bases and other centers as well as the distribution of surplus produce and to allow the inmates to cultivate in safety. Deserted farms might be used, but a circular from Maj. Gen. W. F. Kelly directed that it should be made clear that the blacks who settled on these farms had no claim to the land. This caveat was evidently necessary in the light of frequent promises that blacks would be rewarded for their loyalty by being given Boer farms once the war came to an end.[109]

In early September 1901 there was a food crisis as a result of British troops destroying blacks' grain, which had become routine by then. This prompted a plea for help from Abner Sethabela and Solomon Pitso on behalf of the black population of Winburg, because the people were starving.[110] Furthermore, rinderpest had broken out in Winburg and was spreading rapidly. There were also logistical problems in providing the new camps with agricultural implements. The inmates of the camps had to subsist on a monotonous and nutritionally inadequate diet of one and a half pounds of ground corn and half an ounce of salt for adults and one pound of ground corn and half an ounce of salt for children. It is really not surprising that from September to December of that year, 3,961 black people died in the Free State camps, 3,102 of whom were children.[111]

Although reports on the individual camps have been lost or destroyed, a protest by Daniel Marome and Gert Oliphant, inmates of one of the Kroonstad camps, has survived: "We have to work hard all day long but the only food we can get is mealies [corn] and mealie meal [corn meal], and this is not supplied to us free, but we have to purchase same with our own money. . . . We humbly request Your Honour to do something for us, otherwise we will all perish of hunger for we have no money to keep on buying food." The resident magistrate of Kroonstad dismissed Oliphant as "one of those highly educated Natives who evidently does not use his advantages in the right direction, but is a source of trouble and annoyance to all who have dealings with him."[112]

We have very little knowledge of how black people experienced their lives in the camps, and little reliance can be placed on the overoptimistic assessment of Wilson Fox that "the natives seem generally contented." Desertion was one of the few alternatives to docility, but this was not easy in view of the barbed-wire fences that enclosed them, the armed guards, and the exposure to grave risk in a militarized countryside. In spite of these hazards, 522 desertions were recorded from ORC camps.[113]

The nonagenarian Emelia Pooe, who was a young girl in a Vredefort camp, remembered life there as a constant struggle for survival. The memory of having to grow wheat to supplement their rations stayed with her, especially as she saw women cultivating large areas with their bare hands and hoes. The inmates of the camp were not allowed to eat green mealies (corn on the cob, picked young for eating), because it would bring down the production targets. Like the white women in the Winburg camp, Emelia experienced the bitter cold of winter and the struggle to get fuel to cook food over an open fire. Her father was away serving with the British, and she was very conscious of the disruption of family life and societal norms. A couple had to marry without the payment of *lobola* (a dowry), and she recalled the birth of some mixed-race children in the camp.[114]

It requires little empathetic imagination to draw on the copious accounts of life in the white camps to form some idea of how these black camps were experienced. There would have been the same anguish of separation from family members, the same bewilderment caused by the disruption of the ordinary course of daily life, the same apathy engendered by the deprivation of personal initiative, the same helplessness in the face of illness, the same grief in bereavement.

Unlike the camps for whites, the black camps experienced a steady increase in numbers during the final phase of the war. In September 1901 there were already 37,098 inmates in the Orange River Colony camps; by December the number had grown to 45,987, and by May 1902 to 51,648. And if conditions were bad but improving in the white camps, they were even worse and with less evidence of amelioration in the black camps. Medical care was virtually nonexistent. The medical officer of health in the ORC, Dr. G. Pratt Yule, visited some of the black camps in August 1901 and in his report was able to indulge the current obsession with the beneficial effects of ventilation, a source of much contention in the white camps,[115] and other fantasies as well. "The health of the camps," he wrote, "is exceedingly good when allowance is made for the high birth-rate—better, in fact, than the White Refugee Camps. This is probably due to the imperfect nature of the shelters erected by the natives which allow of a perfect ventilation by numerous crevices and holes in the walls."[116]

The annual mortality rates per one thousand inhabitants for these camps—even compared with the shocking figures for the white camps—tell a different story:[117]

	White ORC Camps	Black ORC Camps
May 1901	13	
June 1901	12	
July 1901	18	135
August 1901	28	170
September 1901	25	93
October 1901	33	175
November 1901	30	355
December 1901	29	436
January 1902	18	377
February 1902	7	228
March 1902	3	137
April 1902	3	72

Neither does Yule's reference to the high birth rate reflect the true state of affairs. In January 1902 there were 1,542 deaths in the ORC camps compared to only 50 births, a ratio of 30:1; up to the end of the war 7,328 deaths and 534 births were recorded, a ratio of about 14:1.[118] The excessively high ratio of children's deaths is also a striking feature of the black camps. In November 1901, 1,518 deaths were recorded in the Winburg camps: 104 men, 160 women, and 1,254 children. This means that men made up 6.85 percent, women 10.54 percent, and children no less than 82.6 percent of the total. One is further struck by the variation from one camp to another. In November 1901 children's deaths in the Smaldeel camp made up 59 percent of the total; in the Ventersburg Road camp the figure reached 90 percent.[119] This was, no doubt, related to the prevalence of epidemics.

According to the official returns, altogether 14,154 blacks died in the camps, but the records are defective and the number of deaths may have been in excess of 20,000—some 80 percent of them children. Kessler has indeed come to the conclusion that there were as many as 25,000 deaths or even more. Again, one notes the cavalier attitude of officialdom, for Wilson Fox says of the November figures in the ORC: "The Death rate appears high, but, under the circumstances, I think it can scarcely be called excessive."[120]

De Lotbinière acknowledged that the death rate was high and adduced four reasons for this: having lost their stock, black people no longer had access to milk; their huts, which were positioned for protection and supervision, were too close together from a health point of view; their huts were not up to the normal standard (which Pratt Yule regarded as an advantage); and "natives do not stand change of soil, water, variations of climate, and shelters well."[121]

More horrifying than the bare statistics is Kessler's conclusion that most of the deaths from measles as well as typhoid and other water-borne diseases in both the black and white camps could have been avoided. "It is an irrefutable fact," he contends, "that the British Army medical system had the knowledge, medical equipment and technology to have significantly reduced the death rate in the black and white camps. It is also clear that since the black camps, as well as the white camps, were deliberately located along the railway they could have provided the supplies and equipment necessary to provide adequate medical service . . . in a much better fashion."[122]

The British army, Kessler points out, lost more men from disease than in battles. While 3,671 (15.36 percent) of those invalided home suffered from wounds, 20,240 (84.65 percent) were victims of illness. His scathing conclusion is that "a nation that did not care about the suffering and welfare of its own soldiers cannot be expected to care about the families of the enemy." However, this blanket condemnation is an emotive overstatement. The British people were unaware of what was happening, the House of Commons was starved of information, and although the army and, ultimately, the War Office cannot escape culpability, Kessler makes no allowance for the complexity of the situation on the ground and therefore the extent to which the army was overwhelmed by medical disaster.[123] To the condemnation of the British nation as uncaring, Kessler adds a further twist of the knife, for it was standard British colonial medical policy, he says, "to only provide medical care for indigenous people when failure to do so would induce epidemic diseases and thereby pose a threat to the health of the military and white population or disrupt the labor supply."[124]

Clearly, black people suffered in the war, and, clearly, their suffering was to no avail. Sol Plaatje's complete identification with the British cause is evident from a sentence on the first page of his *Mafeking Diary*: "No music is as thrilling and immensely captivating as to listen to the firing of the guns on your own side."[125] John Tengo Jabavu was opposed to the war, but he believed that British victory would result in an extension of the franchise and an amelioration of the condition of blacks in the Republics. In this belief he was strengthened by statements by Salisbury, Chamberlain, and Milner, both before and during the war. When a deputation consisting of Rev. D. P. Matsepe; A. P. Pitso, a Winburg doctor;[126] J. B. Twayi; Jan Mocher; and E. Slamat waited on the military governor of the Orange River Colony, Sir George Pretyman, he assured them that a new dispensation would result from the war.[127] These men articulated the hopes and aspirations of black people; those who were inarticulate were not therefore devoid of hope.

In the circumstances of a humiliating defeat, the Boers' impotent rage against the British conquerors was all too easily displaced onto their helpers, and it is not surprising that the concentration camp writings display more negative sentiments toward blacks than toward the British.[128] It is as Heathcliff says in Emily Brontë's *Wuthering Heights*: "The tyrant grinds down the slaves and they don't turn against him, they crush those beneath them." Blacks believed that the British reneged on their assurances at the behest of the Boers, and a mutual sense of betrayal bedeviled race relations in the wake of the war.[129]

In sum, as Silas Molema lamented in 1920, "The position of the Bantu after the South African War was worse than before it. . . . Their condition has grown worse and worse every year, their rights, never many, nor mighty, have been curtailed systematically from then to now; and the future is dark and dreary."[130]

7 The Aftermath of War

THIS CHAPTER COVERS the period from the conclusion of peace, when Kitchener solemnly shook hands with the somber Boer delegates and pledged, "We are good friends now," to the establishment of the National Party with its anti-British and anti-black bias. It outlines the painful material and social reconstruction, the reintegration of hendsoppers and joiners, and the consolidation of Afrikaner national identity. It then notes the suffering of blacks, their political marginalization, and the establishment of the African National Congress.

Reconstruction

After the Peace of Vereeniging was signed on 31 May 1902, the first requirement facing the colonial administration was to bring the displaced conquered people back to their homes. To this end, an Orange River Colony Repatriation Department under Col. H. McLaughlin was established to supervise the return of prisoners of war, who were reunited with their families in the concentration camps before being transported to their homes. The task of repatriating 24,000 prisoners from St. Helena, Bermuda, Ceylon, and India and 7,000 more imprisoned or paroled in South Africa, in addition to 116,000 white and 115,000 black inmates of concentration camps,[1] was a highly complex one, which took many months to complete. While this population movement was in progress, another was necessitated by the departure of the bulk of the British troops. As the latter clogged up the railways, emaciated mules or oxen drew the repatriation wagons, piled high with people, their meager possessions, and the first month's rations, bedding, and tents with which they were

Going home: internees leaving the Winburg camp.
(War Museum of the Boer Republics)

supplied on departure from the concentration camps. The rations comprised one pound of meal, flour, or biscuit and one pound of tinned meat daily per adult, with children under twelve receiving half rations. Of this spartan fare, Colonel McLaughlin said, "We try to keep them alive; we do *not* try to make them comfortable."[2]

The return to the devastated farms was heartbreaking. In the words of Ramsay MacDonald, future prime minister of Britain: "The country was as waste as the edge of the Sahara; about the only cattle we saw were carcasses rotting on the wayside; we passed only one farmhouse that was intact; we stopped at two villages, about one-fifth of one was destroyed, and of the other not a single roof remained."[3]

In those first few months of 1902, the Boers limping back to their burned-out homes were too exhausted for anything but the business of bare survival; the need to survive imposed priorities. Rebuilding one's house was not a priority; a tent or some sheets of corrugated iron forming a lean-to against a wall that was left standing served as shelter against the bitter winter cold. Government teams assisted with plowing, to safeguard the people against pauperization. By September 1902 more than six hundred oxen had been distributed in the Winburg district, together with wagons, drivers, and seed in expectation of a quarter of the crop. But the country was in the grip of a drought, and both the wheat and the corn crops failed. The following year the severity of the drought was unequaled since 1862. From January to September the Free State received only nine inches of rain, compared with an annual average of twenty-four inches for the period 1879–1901. It was only in the closing weeks of 1903 that plentiful rain held out some hope of recovery.[4]

In some districts the promise was fulfilled, but in Winburg distress continued to prevail. Farmers looked to government agencies for assistance in anticipation of payment of compensation for their war losses, but the more resourceful among them sought ways to help themselves. Maria de Jager tells us that before she was removed from the farm, she hid bags of wool, and although they had been found and emptied out, she and her husband were able to gather up enough wool to sell at a good price. This enabled them to buy their first cow "from the cowards who hid in Basutoland." They were also able to recover a small portion of the wheat she had hidden in the mountains. Her husband, Johan, and Maurits Bobbert bought corn in Kroonstad at two pounds per bag, which they then traded for livestock in Basutoland, and her brother, Lourens Frylinck, went to family in the Cape Colony to obtain sheep and cattle with which they farmed on shares.[5]

Ironically, as a result of the war, not only the poor were poor. Farmers who normally lived from their own produce now had to buy their food. Money in ready cash was in short supply, so they had to resort to promissory notes.[6] For most landowners, their only resource was their land, and in the circumstances of drought the only way it could provide a livelihood was if some or all of it was mortgaged or sold. Their black workers were dependent on them, and their poor relations and neighbors looked to them for help. Rev. Christoffel Snyman of Ventersburg reported that of the four hundred families in his congregation, three hundred could not support themselves, and one hundred could just manage to do so but could not go on giving food to their neighbors.[7] Many landowners were obliged to sell land in order to stave off foreclosure on mortgages after three years of nonpayment. In the Winburg district, farmland was burdened on average with a debt of one pound per acre. Subdivision of land among heirs in terms of Roman Dutch law often produced uneconomical units. The legal obligation to subdivide was rescinded in 1901, but the practice gained impetus as a result of deaths of landowners during the war and was also used as an expedient for the sake of liquidity.[8]

During the war, inmates of the camps seemed a captive market for agents seeking rights to or options on their farms. In the Green Point POW camp, Maj. Robert Lys of the Transvaal Horse Artillery, a prospector in civilian life, tried to obtain prospecting rights on prisoners' farms in exchange for getting them returned to their home districts. So, too, a Mr. Bishop of Smaldeel visited the Winburg concentration camp to secure options "for his various syndicates." With the advent of peace, a notice circulated among the prisoners of war in St. Helena cautioning against the activities of speculators.[9] How necessary this warning was is evident from the proliferation of such speculators and syndicates.

There was a general depression in trade, as the farmers did not have the money to buy, and traders could not compete with the military, who sold off

Though stripped of doors, window frames, floorboards, and roof timbers, this Winburg farmhouse still witnessed prewar prosperity. (War Museum of the Boer Republics)

surplus stock cheaply. A. H. Gudath complained of the special hardships of Senekal shopkeepers who had lost their homes and their businesses and now had to contend with the demands of merchants in Port Elizabeth. In his case he faced ruin after twenty years of honest labor. Although the government could offer no relief, in the opinion of the legal adviser to the ORC administration, the "self-interest of creditors will probably prevent the indiscriminate crushing of debtors." [10]

Packs of up to thirty wild dogs roamed the countryside around Senekal, attacking livestock, while the farmers, deprived of firearms, looked on helplessly. The South African Constabulary reported that these dogs, which were difficult to approach, were causing a good deal of damage.[11] The towns, too, were despoiled. Senekal, evacuated in April 1901, was a picture of dereliction. "There is no furniture anywhere," the magistrate reported. "The streets are overgrown with grass. The whole place presents a sufficiently desolate appearance." In Ventersburg, which had been destroyed during the war, the streets and yards were in a filthy condition, there were no sanitary arrangements, and the stench of dead animals hung in the air. [12]

Although everyone struggled, it was the bywoners who were particularly hard hit. Farmers who were previously able to accommodate them now lacked the means to do so, especially since there was little work for a bywoner to do. Furthermore, many bywoners were no longer welcome because of their actions during the war. The brothers Joachim and Arnold Koekemoer understood that because they had served with the British they would not be able to turn to their neighbors for any assistance.[13] Or the political pretext might serve a landowner to suit his economic convenience. Before the war, Basotho agriculturalists had demonstrated their success in the corn and wheat markets, and white farmers had started employing rent-paying or sharecropping blacks in preference to inefficient bywoners. After the war, Tim Keegan says, Basotho streamed across the Caledon River with the stock and equipment for plowing and sowing and were warmly received by white farmers, particularly in the arable eastern areas.[14] Soon more than 10 percent of the farms in the Winburg district were managed by black people.[15] Frans Schimper, a wealthy local farmer, was alarmed by the increase in sharecropping. According to him, the "poor farmer hires a peice [*sic*] of ground the rent of which is paid by the native and the farmer lives with the native as Bywoner."[16]

Lord Kitchener had played an active role in the recruitment of Boers to serve with the British and, in the process, had made promises not only of material rewards but also of their future role in public affairs. Major Leggett, who had been staff officer for the ORC Volunteers, said of these promises that they "have not and indeed could not have been carried out."[17] He requested that the Winburg Repatriation Committee should include Boers who had fought on the British side, remarking that "they were so often promised by Lord Kitchener that their views should be heard at the end." Lord Milner concurred with this request, but it was too late; the positions had already been filled.[18]

A separate body, the Volunteer Repatriation Organisation, was called into being, with Capt. P.H.J. Blakemore as chief superintendent and Capt. Oloff Bergh as divisional superintendent for the district. Blakemore identified 1,584 "ex-military burghers," including 316 from the Winburg district. In addition to the general repatriation benefits, burghers who had served on the British side received a month's pay after peace; a pony, saddle, and bridle; interest-free loans; and help in securing employment,[19] whether in the South African Constabulary, the railways, or some other government department.

Because of the Boers' passionate attachment to land, an attempt was made at providing displaced bywoners with farms of their own. However, the purchase of land for this purpose was open to abuse. A lawyer involved in filing claims for compensation had knowledge of farmers' financial affairs and was able to influence their actions. In Senekal, Vilonel claimed that he had the permission of Maj. K. P. Apthorp of the Land Settlement Board in Bloemfontein to make the necessary purchases. Having taken out options on 3,000 *morgen* (6,350 acres) at thirty shillings per morgen, he proposed selling the land to the Volunteer Repatriation Organisation at two pounds per morgen. However, since neither Apthorp nor Blakemore had authorized the scheme, which would increase the rental to be paid by the bywoners, Blakemore blocked it with the strong concurrence of Leggett, in whose opinion "the man mentioned is not a desirable agent in matters of this sort."[20]

The board purchased land, and families were settled on it. In contrast to other parts of the country, Leggett advised Milner, "In the Winburg district the 'Tame' Boers have been comfortably settled and seem to be doing well."[21] In the long term, however, the attempt to make bywoners "sharecroppers of the state" achieved no lasting effect.[22] The drought cycle of 1902–04 seriously impeded resettlement and many people were forced off the land. Some found work on the roads at five shillings a day. They took their families with them, subjecting them to an itinerant lifestyle in moving road camps.[23] Others found work as laborers in the towns; some were even drawn to Kimberley or Johannesburg. Gilles and Henry van de Wall, sons of the former Winburg clergyman, worked as guards for the De Beers diamond mine. "It is a monotonous job," Gilles wrote to his sister, "sitting for twelve hours watching a fence."[24]

It had been intended to disband the Repatriation Department once everyone was resettled and the first crops were harvested. Indeed, on 21 December 1902 Milner wrote in a personal letter of his conviction "that the bulk of the 'repatriated' Boers will be off our hands by March or April."[25] Instead, in April 1903 the Repatriation Department was reconstituted as the ORC Government Relief Department. "Relief works" were established to help impoverished burghers to survive. Aimed primarily at bywoners whose repatriation was made impossible by the refusal of landowners to allow them to return to the farms where they had previously lived, the net was extended to bywoners who had returned to the farms but had become indigent following the failure of their crops. Because those who had assisted the British suffered considerable social ostracism, the idea was to create a more congenial social environment for them. However, in the prevailing economic situation, applications were received from people of all political persuasions, and the fact of living side by side at the relief works helped to allay the hostility that was felt.[26]

In the Winburg district, a dam covering one thousand acres to be built at Mushroom Valley on the Vet River would make it possible to put some two thousand acres under irrigation. At this project, a hutted camp eventually housing about one thousand people was established in September 1902. Men were paid four shillings and sixpence per day, though gangers and those with specialized skills earned more, and boys earned between one shilling and sixpence and two shillings. Some of the residents owned chickens, goats, and cattle.[27]

Emily Hobhouse was critical of relief work for bywoners because it was unsustainable, with the result that a touchy administration issued strict instructions debarring her from admission to government relief projects.[28] She was proved right because while Milner was concerned to find sustainable solutions in the Transvaal, he accorded the Free State a lower priority. To assuage the immediate problem, he resorted to relief works, all of which collapsed between 1904 and 1906.[29] Traveling through the Free State from June to August 1903, Emily Hobhouse encountered searing instances of people who were face-to-face with starvation.[30] The funds she raised in Britain provided help in numerous dire emergencies, but she also invested money in spinning and weaving schools. Of the twelve she established in the Free State, three were in Winburg.[31]

The payment of military receipts brought some relief, but the army paid only for what they had requisitioned, not for what they had destroyed. Claims for damage were referred to the civil authority, who would have to compensate the property owners from the £3,000,000 promised in Article 10 of the peace accord. The interpretation of this article was contested. Who precisely were "the people" who were the intended beneficiaries? In the end the British government added £2,000,000 to meet the claims of British subjects, foreigners, and blacks, of which blacks would receive £300,000—£171,000 in the Free State[32]—and the War Office contributed £2,000,000 to indemnify "protected burghers."[33] A claimant under this heading was debarred if, even after his deportation, his wife fled with livestock or a son was forced to go on commando, leading the resident magistrate of Bethlehem to protest that the instructions governing the classification of claimants "are almost daily becoming more stringent."[34] As repatriation costs were offset against their £3,000,000 "free grant," bittereinder claimants' hopes of meaningful compensation dwindled. The assessment of losses was a laborious process, and the bureaucratic measures that accompanied it were a cause of despair to people who were strapped for cash. Articles were valued according to a fixed tariff, regardless of actual cost: forty pounds for small wagons, twenty pounds for carts, ten shillings for slaughter sheep. No payments could be made until all claims had been submitted, assessed, and then scaled down to be covered by the money actually available.[35]

Because there were far more claims against the ex-burgher fund than against the protected burgher fund, claimants against the latter were likely to benefit disproportionately. Based on representations of Comdt. Gerrie van der Merwe of Senekal, Gen. Jan Crowther of Ladybrand, and Comdt. Paul de Villiers of Ficksburg, their followers who surrendered with Marthinus Prinsloo were also accorded the status of protected burghers. This brought the percentage of protected burghers in the Winburg district to 28 percent of those claiming compensation (832 out of 2,948), Ladybrand to 30 percent, and Ficksburg to a massive 60 percent.[36]

At last, thanks to "the unresting expedition of your Commissioners,"[37] the claims of protected burghers were paid out in mid-1904 at the rate of 10s (ten shillings) on the pound. From their allocation, British and foreign subjects received 17s 4d (seventeen shillings and four pence) on the pound. Only 15 percent of the £2,000,000 in this fund went to blacks, and they received 10 percent of their claims or 2s on the pound. Bittereinders' claims were not paid till October 1905 to January 1906, and in the end they received only 1s 10.7d on the pound.[38] Both the delay in awarding compensation and the derisory amounts paid out in some cases gave rise to profound dissatisfaction. Emily Hobhouse gives an example of the sort of situation that could arise: "A man claimed £120, a very poor man. Under assessment it dropped to £18. His share may be 18/- [eighteen shillings] and he has to pay the Law Agent three guineas for expenses!"[39]

Trauma

This narrative has spoken of material loss and how it could be addressed. Even more devastating was the human cost of the war. In this regard the emphasis has generally fallen on the men who died in battle and on the suffering of women and children who died in the camps. It is hard to begin to imagine the psychological scarring of the survivors. Concepts such as posttraumatic stress disorder were unknown to contemporary witnesses, and if they recorded some manifestations of extreme mental distress, they lacked the conceptual framework to grasp the implications of their etiology. Danie Theron reported on the despondency and sense of hopelessness that had beset the burghers in the laager at Paardeberg, and Margaret Marquard notes the pervasive depression in Winburg and prays that Klaas Wessels may be delivered from the "the weariness of despair." Later she records his death "by his own act."[40] That act certainly resonates for us today with our greater understanding of depression as a clinical condition.

Letters from the concentration camps tremble on the verge of depression. The lengthy exile of prisoners of war also left its mark, and psychologists noted irascibility in returned Boer prisoners that had not been part of their personality profile before the war.[41] Marriage relationships were bound to suffer as a result of prolonged separation. In the thirteen months that Willem van der Merwe spent in Ceylon, he had no word from his wife, Maria, and in the Winburg camp, Maria de Jager never heard from her husband. Isabella van den Heever reported in 1903 that her husband, who had been ill since December 1899, had fled on the approach of the British troops and that she had not heard of him since. Marital alienation was intensified in a situation where the marriage partners favored different sides, as happened in the case of Abraham Meintjes, who was pro-Boer while his wife was in British service, or of Christian Rabie, who joined the British while his wife took refuge in a Boer laager.[42]

The mental balance of some prisoners of war was seriously disturbed. A report from St. Helena in April 1901 noted "two quite insane and others on the way." Another, the following month, stated that the doctor hoped to "return nine lunatics."[43] Here, a prisoner threw his Bible and hymn book on the rubbish dump, saying there was no God, as the British were winning the war.[44] Another, fearing his young wife had abandoned him, tried to run onto the wires so that the guards would shoot him. A third heard that his father had committed suicide upon returning home and seeing what had happened to his farm. From Bermuda, the Winburger Johannes du Plooy went straight to the Bloemfontein asylum.[45]

There was another source of mental scarring. Ordinary British soldiers were corrupted and brutalized by carrying out the scorched-earth policy, and Canadian troops were so haunted by the anguish of farm burning that they declined to stay in South Africa for a second tour of duty.[46] As the war became increasingly irregular, it was inevitable that young Boers, too, saw things and did things that did not leave them unaffected. British commandants on Bermuda noted that there were young Boer prisoners who had become inured to violence; Smuts and De la Rey were also concerned about this phenomenon.[47] Such young men displaced the discredited patriarchy of the older generation with a masculinity of unfeeling cruelty.

Children who saw their homes burned down and experienced the ubiquity of death in the camps inevitably suffered trauma. The writings produced in the camp schools bear witness to how the very young were affected. In halting English one child wrote: "One day we [were] sitting in the house and there came the Kakies [British] to catch us. It was a very hard day to go from our dear old house. . . . My mought [mouth] was so dry that I can't eat." Another reported that "there was a big fiting [fighting] with cannon and guns and the boars [Boers] have run away and the Englishman take us and bring us here. . . . And at the farm if we is sick we stay in our homes, but here if we sick we goes to the hospital, and there we died all."[48] Traumatic experiences like these left their mark on an entire generation.

National Identity

In the wake of the war the Boer people were disoriented by defeat. One of the most important aspects of the reconstruction process for any nation that has suffered defeat, ignominy, and trauma is a renewed self-conceptualization, which lifts morale and discourages the probing of discreditable aspects of the past. This is achieved by the construction of a set of societal values imposed by the upper class and embraced by the lower classes that legitimates the social order and consolidates the hegemony of the élite.[49] A dominant societal perspective assuages individual discomfiture by the political use of collective memory. National identity is dependent on such collective memory, to which individual identity stands in reciprocal relationship. Collective memory is not simply an aggregate of individual memories, because in return for the security of belonging to a group or nation, the individual unconsciously accommodates his or her experiences of the past to the prevailing meaning system.[50]

The reconceptualization referred to above was facilitated by a group of élite women who were closely linked with the clergy. They were very active during the immediate postwar years in continuing with the project initiated by Elizabeth Neethling and Emily Hobhouse of soliciting, collecting, and distributing women's testimonies. Emily Hobhouse's intentions were pacifist and humanitarian,[51] but her writings served the very different purpose of those who came after her. Their purpose was to use suffering with a view to identity construction by means of selective memory in a history constituted by proto-nationalism. Such ideologized identity construction is strongly characterized by what Eric Hobsbawm calls "negative ethnicity": the self defined in terms of antagonism to the various others.[52] The testimonies are not only virulently anti-British; they are also often crudely and gratuitously antiblack. The work of these women reinforced the strand of aggrievedness that was a hallmark of early attempts at Afrikaner historiography, such as W. J. Leyds's *De Eerste Annexatie van de Transvaal* (1906), in which the author sets out to "provide the Afrikaner people with a *vademecum*, with a collection of documentary items that have reference to the way in which the English have always acted towards the Boers."[53]

This is not to say that the victim discourse enunciated by this élite was somehow extraneous to the experience of ordinary people. On the contrary, its strong purchase derived from its resonance with their traumatized condition. Political myths are harmonizations of the past rather than falsifications; they denude the historical narrative of its complexities and ambiguities.

On the subject of the camps, leaders among the women and the clergy may be said to have spoken the same language, a conflation of religious, political, and mythological discourses that created a haze in which words lost precision while operating at a subconscious level.[54] Thus the cruel fate to which the women and children in the camps fell victim was spoken of as if it were a voluntary sacrifice and was associated with other emotive terms like "blood" and "altar." The primordial meaning of "sacrifice" is well encapsulated in the Latin formula *do ut des* (I give in order that you may give). In other words, human beings operate with a subliminal perception that sacrifice merits reward. So the religious term evoked powerful feelings at a mythological level to achieve a political purpose that bestowed a sense of entitlement.

Sacrifice was but one element in the theological compendium offered by the clergy. God's covenant people were called to go through the fiery furnace in order to emerge purified. Beyond the pain waited the promise. The children of Israel were slaves in Egypt, but God raised up Moses to liberate them; because of their disobedience they had to endure forty years in the wilderness, but, chastened by the experience, they were at last able to enter the promised land. The Assyrians destroyed the Northern Kingdom of Israel, which had lapsed into idolatry, but God defeated their purposes and the siege of Jerusalem was miraculously lifted. The Babylonians carried the Jews into captivity, but in God's good time a faithful remnant was restored.

The clergy continued to hold out the hope of future restoration, though the secular *eschaton* was delayed. This theological perspective contributed a strong teleological strand to Afrikaner historical consciousness. The war was not a disaster, after all, but rather God's saving means of building Afrikaner national unity with a view to the ultimate realization of sovereign independent statehood and rule over all the people of the country.[55]

Reintegrating the Afrikaner People

On the political front, municipal structures offered the Boers a measure of representation, which credible leaders declined to accept. The civic leaders who served on the Winburg town council, reestablished on 31 January 1902; Senekal's Village Management Board, set up in September 1902; and the Ventersburg board, in January of the following year, were, for the most part, either British or men of known pro-British sentiment. The legislative council appointed for the colony in 1903 consisted of six British officials and four nominated members, two with pro-British sentiments and two who inclined more toward the Boers,[56] but again highly regarded Boer leaders declined to serve, avoiding any taint of collaboration.

At Vereeniging the bittereinders under the new generation of Boer leaders were acknowledged as the only collocutors with the British victors in determining the future course of events in South Africa. Those who had withdrawn from the struggle, whether voluntarily or involuntarily, were "civilly dead,"[57] and the nation was reduced to the faithful remnant of the bittereinders. Yet this remnant was imbued with the ardor of ethnic nationalism, defining itself over against "the English," and therefore the redemption, reintegration, and mobilization of those who had been disloyal during the war achieved high priority.

In the Free State, however, the counterweight of "the English" was less keenly felt, and conciliation with them and the redemption of disloyal compatriots in order to countervail English influence were therefore less pressing demands. Here a different tone was set, and policy formulated by Gen. J.B.M. Hertzog and the éminence grise President Steyn. Hertzog was to proclaim, "I am not one of those who always have their mouths full of conciliation and loyalty. . . . I have always said that I do not know what this conciliation means," and Steyn fulminated with patriarchal vehemence: "Contempt for the National Scouts will continue unto children's children, to far-off generations. The curse of their people will weigh on them forever, no honest man may hold out his hand to them, no Afrikaner shall know them. While yet on earth, may they be damned to the deepest hell."[58]

Despite the vituperation of their leaders, the people on the ground had to find means of moving on. If families were divided by the bitter consequences of different choices, they were also united by the perplexity surrounding those choices. It was as Anna Barry said: people resorted freely to name-calling, but it was different if a member of one's own family was involved; then the issues were no longer so clear-cut.[59] The leaders certainly had some harsh things to say, and those who were directly affected by someone else's actions were inevitably embittered, but it would seem that those who chose the path of patriotism could also empathize with those who opted for pragmatism. This may be illustrated with reference to the musings of two prisoners of war.

Hermanus Pretorius, writing a letter from Diyatalawa POW camp in Ceylon to his brother Johannes in the Winburg concentration camp, adopts an almost apologetic tone:

> I hope and trust that you will not hold it against me that I did not listen to you considering that you have always been right in the past. It was bitter for me to be here and even more bitter to bid my country and my people farewell, but in the end that is what I had to do. But let us forgive and forget what is past and try to work for progress in the future since you are free and I am only too glad that you have not had to endure a protracted exile in such a sad manner as I have.[60]

He did what he had to do, but he goes on to ask his brother to use his privileged position to acquire livestock to secure a better future. Because this brother was a wealthy Ficksburg farmer who, in March 1901, became secretary of Winburg's Burgher Peace Committee,[61] he was well placed to make provision for the future.

After the conclusion of peace, August Schulenburg contemplated the prospect of being reunited with his brothers and wrote in his diary: "How will the meeting with my brothers be? Our fate is so very different, they are free while I am a prisoner; they are on the side of the English, I on our side! Yet I know that we've all suffered a great deal and no one knows which of us chose the right path, so I don't mind how I am received. For my part, I'll be happy to meet them again and I'll love them as much as before."[62]

Apart from the actual bonds of kinship between the people of a particular locality, the quasi-kinship of people who used family terms as a form of address also inhibited retaliatory actions. Local ties were stronger than national ties, and the simple fact is that people needed one another. There is a poignant moment in Chris Schoeman's book *Boer Boy* when the Winburger Philip du Preez is returning to his devastated farm after the war. Overtaken by nightfall, he reluctantly turns to his neighbor, Flip Koekemoer, a collaborator during the war, for hospitality, and is received by Koekemoer and his wife with warmth and generosity. Du Preez's own involvement in the war had been minimal,[63] but he stood higher in the hierarchy of esteem than Koekemoer, and thus, in the midst of muddle and ambiguity, hendsoppers might help to bridge the gap between bittereinders and joiners.

Recalling his Free State childhood, Pieter Grobbelaar comments on avoiding of the war as a subject of conversation. "There was apparently too much divided loyalty amongst our forebears," he writes, "and that made it a dangerous topic."[64] Perhaps it would have been better if the problem had been more incisively dealt with in Winburg, as the divisions returned to avenge themselves in the years to come.

The Role of the Church

As the one cohesive structure to survive the war, the Dutch Reformed Church also played a vital ideological role in rebuilding community. Although it had lost its favored position, the Crown Colony administration was well aware of the standing of its ministers and therefore maintained the Republican practice of subsidizing the church.[65] Officials needed the support of influential leaders like Rev. J. J. Marquard but were distrustful of them.[66] Emily Hobhouse noted: "There is a great recrudescence of church feeling, largely owing, I think, to the fact that the church is the one thing left of the old life, and so they cling passionately to it, and the minister has more power than ever. . . . Undoubtedly their political influence is very great and no wonder the Government hates them."[67]

It was therefore natural for Louis Botha to turn to the church in "knitting together the torn fabric of Afrikanerdom."[68] To this end he worked closely with Rev. H. S. Bosman, moderator of the Transvaal Dutch Reformed Church, and in 1903 urged a secret session of the synod of that church to deal gently with those who had aided Britain in the war. The church called on those who had been unfaithful to their government and their nation to repent of their sin so that they could share in the privileges of membership with a clear conscience.[69]

In general the dissidents found themselves out on a limb. The promises made by the British military authorities were not always kept by the civil administration: they were not provided with transport or arms, and the Land Settlement Board "has broken every promise to them, and has never really tried to keep them."[70] Because the British connection was of no avail, they had little alternative but to submit to the generally benevolent ministrations of the church. Although in some cases there was a formal reconciliation of collaborators following on public confession, for the most part, according to Gen. Ben Bouwer, "the agreement to overlook the past, where they as individuals were concerned, was tacit."[71]

In the Free State, Marquard, as moderator of the synod, was successful in averting stern action against those who were regarded as having failed the Boer cause. Rev. C. P. Theron of Bethlehem urged that "we must forget what is past and cover it over and only work for conciliation," and despite sharp disagreements in some congregations, this was the attitude that prevailed. In general one is struck by how quickly the edge of animosity was dulled.[72]

In Winburg, however, the opening shots of a protracted ecclesiastical battle were fired on 2 August 1903 when the Winburg church council was confronted with the resignation of two of its members. Comdt. Jan Kok was not present at the meeting, but Comdt. Jan Maree explained their motivation. He said that he was unwilling to shake hands with National Scouts. The council chairman drew his attention to the wrongfulness of this outlook, and he and other members of the meeting tried to win Maree to a different point of view, but as these attempts were of no avail, the meeting had no alternative but to accept Maree's resignation.[73]

A year later, petitioners, including Jan Maree, protested against Matthys Kritzinger and Jacobus Smit being allowed to serve on the church council, as they had been guilty of high treason during the war.[74] After both sides had put forth their case at a church council meeting on 3 September 1904, Kritzinger and Smit confessed that "they had received grace and heartily lamented the step they had taken during the war. They asked for forgiveness and said that they had decided for the sake of peace in the congregation to decline the positions they had been offered." [75] Some of those present avowed their willingness to forgive the penitents, but others were unmoved by their confession.

The complete ascendancy of the rigorous party can be seen from an examination of the makeup of the Winburg church council just a few years later. In 1907 all but one of the church councilors had impeccable credentials: seven prisoners of war and six bittereinders. The single exception, Jacob Lategan, had surrendered on 14 May 1900. However, because he was never on commando, he may have been too old or otherwise incapacitated.[76]

In Ventersburg the congregation also had to wrestle with issues of reconciliation. When Lourens Erasmus asked at the church council meeting of 28 February 1903 how he should behave toward Frederik Bekker, "who had so persecuted him during the war,"[77] the chairman, Rev. C. J. Snyman, told him he would find the answer in Matthew 5:33–48 (forbidding retaliation and enjoining love of one's neighbor).

In Senekal a combined church council meeting for the election of councilors took place on 9 February 1903. In a noteworthy address, Rev. Paul Roux, the ex-general, laid down the criteria for election. He urged his hearers to distinguish between political and ecclesiastical matters, saying that a good Christian should not be denied election to the church council for political reasons. This is remarkable because it contrasts so strikingly with the implacable attitude Roux adopted on another occasion when he insisted not only on confession of guilt but also on "the exposure of evils that have been committed."[78] It is equally remarkable for its decisive foreclosing of the whole issue of collaboration in relation to church council membership, which allowed for Comdt. Gerrie van der Merwe to serve despite his disloyalty in the dying days of the war.

There was no contention about such membership until 26 November 1904, when it came to light that two women, the wives of David du Buisson and Jan Malan, had objected to the election of Van der Merwe as a deacon. Only Elizabeth du Buisson appeared before the council and testified that during the war she had seen Van der Merwe in the presence of British troops. Van der Merwe did not deny being seen with a column but asked her if she knew why he was there. The chairman then asked her to admit that the Boers had spies among the British. Next he read a letter from Christiaan de Wet, vouching for Van der Merwe's integrity and saying he was convinced that Van der Merwe's presence with British troops indicated that he was planning to escape. Mrs. du Buisson remained unconvinced. Pressed to withdraw her objection, she declined and declared that she would refrain from taking communion if Van der Merwe was confirmed in office. Asked if she desired the evidence of witnesses to Van der Merwe's innocence, she replied, "No, because one can't believe anyone." The church council unanimously concluded that there was no evidence whatsoever of disloyalty on Van der Merwe's part and that his own statement and De Wet's letter demonstrated that his presence with a British column had a totally different purpose from that imputed to him. They accordingly ratified his election.[79]

Reading the minutes it is hard to escape the impression that Mrs. du Buisson was not given a fair hearing. Perhaps her fellow protester failed to attend the meeting precisely because she feared the sort of browbeating Mrs. du Buisson received. Gerrie van der Merwe's only answer to the charge was to ask the witness if she knew why he was with a British column, without himself offering any credible explanation. The chairman, Paul Roux, pressed her to admit the existence of Boer spies without categorically claiming that Van der Merwe was one. De Wet's suggestion—again no categorical claim—that an escape was being planned is absurd in the circumstances of a prisoner of war detained in Green Point being seen with British troops in the Free State. And if the charge against Van der Merwe was preposterous, why, one wonders, had Roux armed himself with a letter from De Wet?

As one peruses the church council minutes of the period, the impression begins to obtrude itself that larger forces were at play. It is as if, in the Winburg district at any rate, there was an awareness that the problem of collaboration was so vast and so sensitive that it might be best to let sleeping dogs lie. The church dealt with cases with which it was confronted, but was clearly reluctant to seek out offenders. In contrast to adultery, which figured prominently in the council minutes, we hear little of "political" offenses. Occasionally there were complaints about neighbors who would not reconcile—for example, Comdt. Jan Maree and Willem Kok in the Winburg congregation, Lourens Erasmus and Frederik Bekker in Ventersburg, and Frederik Senekal and Andries Eksteen in Senekal.[80] Generally a commission was appointed to deal expeditiously with such cases, but sometimes they just trailed off into oblivion. In general, though, "they [the collaborators] just carried on as before, living amongst their fellow citizens as though nothing had happened."[81]

A striking demonstration of the church's greater willingness to confront sexual issues than wartime collaboration is provided by the case of Oloff Bergh. On 16 July 1904 Bergh sought admission to church membership for his wife. The Senekal church council responded that although this could happen, her presentation to the congregation would have to be deferred for a year in order to allow time for them to address the matter of her having had a child within a month of her marriage. At the same time, Bergh would be required to submit his certificate of church membership so that ecclesiastical censure could be imposed on him in this regard. It was reported that "Mr. Oloff Bergh is willing to submit to church discipline and, with regard to his wife's confirmation, to act in accordance with the church's wishes."[82] And nothing more was heard of the matter.

Political Resurgence

At the founding conference of the political party *Het Volk* (meaning The Nation), established in the Transvaal in May 1904, Botha called for forgiveness to be extended to collaborators and the hand of fellowship to English speakers. He further advanced the reintegration of his ostracized compatriots into the mainstream by affording them the opportunity of serving on the recruitment committees of Het Volk.[83]

In the Free State, on the other hand, it was "protected burghers" who, by a curious turn of events, initiated the national movement that led to the political ascendancy of their adversaries. Johannes Vlotman had surrendered in Winburg on 19 May 1900. In spite of the fact that he had not violated his oath of neutrality, he was arrested and sent to the Green Point POW camp. He objected and was paroled to Stellenbosch. On his return to the Free State, Vlotman discovered that he was prejudiced in that his claim for compensation was not being dealt with as that of a protected burgher. Vehemently indignant, he convened a meeting in Brandfort on 17 September 1904, at which nineteen aggrieved Free Staters, whose primary concern was how compensation claims were being handled, gave vent to their dissatisfaction with the colonial administration. The former laager commandant of Winburg, Jan Erwee, for example, was aggrieved about members of the South African Constabulary who spoke only English. A committee under Vlotman was appointed to pursue the matter of the compensation claims. On the advice of Prime Minister Abraham Fischer, this committee included all categories of complainants: N. J. Vermaak, G. H. Erwee, and G. J. van Graan, who were also hendsoppers; J. P. Marais, who had never been on commando; W. H. Maas, a collaborator; and a solitary bittereinder, J. J. van Rensburg.[84] The committee compiled a manifesto, which resonated widely because there was considerable dissatisfaction abroad.

During October and November 1904, meetings were held throughout the colony. At these meetings, grievances about compensation were interspersed with expressions of dissatisfaction from the bittereinder community relating to the language medium in schools, the South African Constabulary, and the delay in implementing responsible government.

The outcome of these moves was a congress held in Brandfort on 1 and 2 December attended by 102 delegates. According to Sir Hamilton Goold-Adams, they were equally representative of the two factions.[85] Christiaan de Wet and J.B.M. Hertzog attended this congress, and the latter was elected chairman—and, in the words of Oswald Pirow, "from that moment for over thirty-five years dictated the policy of the Free State."[86] Hertzog allowed the originators of the initiative ample opportunity to expatiate on their disillusionment with the government, because their alienation from the British authorities left them with nowhere to turn but to their compatriots, and the ensuing rapprochement would strengthen his hand in the more important matters that were his concern. As Goold-Adams put it: "The result of the Congress has been to confirm my anticipation that, as soon as the actual business of the meeting commenced, the management of the proceedings would be taken out of the hands of the original movers of the Compensation question, and would pass into those of the more important politicians."[87]

The congress was characterized by appeals for unity and the healing of socio-economic divisions. De Wet called for hendsoppers and joiners to be forgiven, saying that even though he had hated them and could not endure the sight of them, he now called them brothers; Hertzog demanded self-government, a rejection of alien innovation, and a return to the familiar past. At a second national congress in Bloemfontein on 20 June 1905, a resolution was passed calling for the establishment of a political party to achieve self-government.[88] So, ironically, Vlotman's manifesto was the catalyst of a national movement that led to the establishment of the *Orangia Unie* (or Orangia Union) in May 1906.

The year 1907 was an *annus mirabilis* in the history of the Free State. Not only did it mark the return of the country's prewar prosperity; it was also the year in which self-government was restored. The opening up of overseas markets enabled South Africa to export six hundred thousand bags of corn, and the wheat crop at the end of the year was the first really successful one since the war.[89] The new ORC constitution was little different from that of the Orange Free State Republic. In the elections for the legislative assembly the following year, the Orangia Unie won no fewer than thirty-one of the thirty-eight seats with 66 percent of the votes cast, and credible leaders were elected to office, including Comdt. Frederik Cronjé to represent Winburg South and Comdt. Hans Hattingh for Senekal.

The granting of self-government by the new Liberal government under Sir Henry Campbell-Bannerman was trumpeted as an act of British magnanimity, but in fact it was a realistic British acknowledgment of political miscalculation rather than an altruistic act of restitution.[90] This myth was neatly counterpoised by the myth of Boer conciliation with Britain. Although Lord Selborne, Milner's more flexible successor, said that no one outside a lunatic asylum could believe that Steyn was reconciled,[91] the nurturing of these myths contributed to an atmosphere of optimism that led in 1910 to the unification of the Cape Colony, Natal, the Free State, and the Transvaal, with Louis Botha as the first prime minister.

However, unity in Afrikaner ranks was short-lived. While Botha carefully avoided ethnicity, Hertzog championed the cause of the Afrikaner poor, and ethnicity was grist to his mill. In 1914 the National Party was founded in the Free State and the country was racked by rebellion.

The 1914 Rebellion

Steyn had avoided signing the treaty of Vereeniging by resigning his office to De Wet. The latter, who favored the continuation of the war, signed for the sake of a united front, but later it was claimed that there had been a secret agreement with Botha that hostilities could always be resumed at a later stage. The war against Germany, it was argued, was England's extremity that provided the Boers' opportunity. De Wet embraced rebellion and Steyn adopted an equivocal stance, withholding the support that Botha so desperately implored, pleading with him, "A word from you will go far."[92]

The geographical base of the rebellion indicates to what an extent it represented unfinished business from the South African War. The Free State and the southwestern Transvaal were precisely the areas where the war leaders—Steyn, Hertzog, De Wet, Kemp, De la Rey, Liebenberg, and Beyers—had favored fighting on.[93] The rebellion was also about the alienation resulting from the war. In 1899 only 2.6 percent of the whites who later identified themselves as Afrikaners lived in urban areas; by 1911 the proportion had mounted to 24 percent of the people, who experienced the increasing group anxiety on which nationalism feeds. They were disempowered by a sense of inferiority, which arose from having to do unfamiliar and demeaning work at the behest of English speakers, in whose social discourse they were stigmatized as backward.[94]

For many impoverished, newly urbanized, and alienated Afrikaners, the rebellion offered an opportunity of recovering the feel of the Republican masculinity of horse and rifle, even if the reality seemed irretrievably lost. The leaders of the rebellion were well off—landowners, civil servants, builders, and contractors—but the rank and file were poor whites.[95] Antonie Baumann, a law agent in Winburg, characterized them as people who were in debt and youngsters, "not men of substance and standing,"[96] and J. K. O'Connor spoke of many of the rebels who did not have "an acre of ground or a decent flock of sheep to their names," for whom going on commando meant "a happy time of riding around on horseback from town to town, living on the country as they proceed."[97] In recuperating a sense of identity in devotion to strong leadership, commando camaraderie, and physical freedom, the rebels thus articulated a republican protest against the modernizing state that subverted all the old familiarities.[98]

In Winburg the opposing factions were unable to reconcile and supporters of the rebellion established a separate congregation, leaving the "mother church" with less than half of its original membership.[99] In 1915 Louis Botha called on the Dutch Reformed Church to censure the rebellion, but at the urging of D. F. Malan, future leader of the National Party, the church declined to do so. Instead it affirmed that it was the church's responsibility "to be national in character and to watch over our particular national interests, to teach the people to see in their history and origin the hand of God, and furthermore to cultivate among the Afrikaner people the awareness of a national calling and destiny, in which the spiritual, moral and material progress and strength of a people is laid up."[100] In the parliamentary election in October 1915 the National Party won sixteen of the seventeen Free State seats. In Winburg, which had been solidly South African Party, ex-commandant Frederik Cronjé was roundly defeated.

The Plight of Black People

If reconstruction was difficult for the whites, it was even more painful for the blacks. Emily Hobhouse was fully aware of the desperate straits in which they found themselves. "The Natives are perplexing me much," she wrote. "Many of them are starving all over the country. Missionaries implore me for some food for them, the old and the young. Eleven thousand have crowded into Kroonstad to find work as they can get no food upon the farms."[101] The resident magistrate estimated that there were about seven hundred unemployed blacks in and around Winburg, with many more coming in daily. Some were encamped along the railway line, others were temporarily housed in Winburg's black township, but it was considered necessary to remove them to the black camps, where they could be more effectively controlled.[102]

In October 1902 the Military Compensation Board paid out receipts to blacks in Winburg, the white population complaining of the unpleasant presence of the "hordes" obstructing the streets.[103] As a sample, twenty-one blacks whose names started with the letters *K* or *L* received varying amounts ranging from £1 10s (one pound, ten shillings) to £344, the average being just under £63. The largest payment went to Laak for fourteen horses and forty-four head of cattle. The names in the register tell their own sad story of men who were disparaged and "hidden from history":[104] Kruiwagen (meaning Wheelbarrow), Kleinbooi (Short fellow), Kompas (Compass), Leeuw (Lion), and Lawaai (Noise).[105] Black civil claims were handled by the Native Affairs Department. In the Central Judicial Commission (CJC) records, 412 such claims in the Free State are noted, close to a quarter of them from Wepener, but none at all from the Winburg district. In an undated petition on behalf of the 1,728 black people of Winburg, the signatories request payment of their compensation claims, noting that they were "the poorest of His Majesty's subjects, and have received nothing yet although our wants and needs are great." A second list with black claims was found in the colonial secretary's papers. Most of these were from Kroonstad, but there were also some from Winburg, ranging from £12 claimed by John to £124 under the name of Jafta.[106]

However wretched conditions were in the camps, they provided black people with access to land, and there was an expectation that if they declined to return to their previous employers, the authorities would feel obliged to relocate them to other communal land. Blacks who had been in British service were fearful of returning to their prewar employers, and there was an equal reluctance on the part of the employers to have them back.[107]

The plight of black people in these camps at the end of the war is well articulated by Morakaba Moletsane, who is described as a man of considerable influence in the black camp community temporarily settled on the farm Woolwash. In a petition to the resident magistrate of Winburg he laments the fact that it is the plowing season and that he and his fellows are still in the dark as to how and when the government intends to place them. They are prevented from leaving the camp to go to town to buy food or even visit the doctor. He raises the possibility of their being allocated a government farm because, as the magistrate is aware, blacks who have been in the service of the army are afraid of the Boers, who mock them, saying, "You niggers thought you would get our farms." The situation of black people is changed, for "we can't agree with boers [*sic*] as we used to do." In submitting the petition to the chief superintendent of the Native Refugee Department in Bloemfontein for transmission to the lieutenant governor, the resident magistrate of Winburg says that as "chief of the Basutos in the District of Winburg" Moletsane was asking for a Native Protection Society. Ever since his arrival in the camp he had made trouble, repeatedly refusing to obey orders and using "his influence, which appears to be considerable, to set all natives against the just orders of those in authority." Significantly, the file is titled "Native 'Marokabi' [*sic*] and gang,"[108] which suggests that, like the Boers, the colonial administration was more responsive to the supposed threat posed by black people than to their very real distress.

Even before the war was officially over, blacks settled on unoccupied farms and may have taken the owners' livestock. This is the imputation of a complaint by Carl Schwartz and Michael Terblanche, who wrote to the colonial secretary on 10 May 1902 to complain about the large quantities of wool, skins, and mohair being sold by black people at Vetrivier Siding, "which wools cannot possibly be of their own sheep."[109] An investigation revealed that William Holland had a store at Vetrivier Siding, trading as Barmer & Co., and although he had no license to deal in hides, wools, and skins, these products were bought or bartered at his store and sent by rail to Port Elizabeth. The investigating officer reported that there was a location in the neighborhood, the residents of which owned three thousand to four thousand head of stock, but in his opinion, "this supply cannot keep up the trade."[110]

Farms in the Winburg district not yet allocated under the land settlement scheme also briefly assuaged the land hunger of the black peasantry. On a portion of Ferndale it was reported that blacks who "will not work for anyone and are a continual nuisance to Mr Smedley" (on the neighboring property) were grazing about three hundred sheep as well as one hundred head of cattle and some horses. Accordingly, the secretary of the Land Settlement Board requested the divisional commandant of the South African Constabulary to "have them turned off Government land." Other blacks had sown crops on about forty acres of land on portions of the farm Kookfontein. "Naturally," the secretary of the Land Settlement Board wrote, "if they can squat on land and plough to their hearts content without being responsible to anyone, they will not feel inclined to work for wages."[111]

Republican legislation of 1893 was implemented by the colonial administration in order to force blacks into the labor market. No unemployed black person above the age of sixteen was allowed to live in an urban location. Residential passes had to be paid for at a rate of sixpence per month, but those who wished to work on their own behalf were subject to a charge of five shillings per month.[112]

Ultimately blacks needed the Boers for access to land, the Boers needed blacks for their labor, and the Repatriation Department needed to close down the camps. More important, it was in the British interest to restart the agricultural industry as speedily as possible. The fact that black camp inmates had to pay for their rations and could leave only if they had a farm to go to was a major factor in breaking down their resistance to coming to terms with their prewar masters. Oloff Bergh, who had considerable influence over the blacks in the district, used his persuasive powers to get them to return to their previous employers.[113] Thus the unequal partnership of white landholder and black laborer that prevailed before the war was entrenched.

Some farmers mistreated their workers, a situation that prompted a black man living in the district to submit a petition to the resident magistrate seeking amelioration. The responses to his mild document give us a good idea of the sheer incomprehension with which white officialdom regarded black people. Foremost among the issues E. Mokhethi raised was that farmworkers were "left to the mercies of the farmers." They could not lay a complaint with the police, who could not or would not understand them. They were told to engage a lawyer, but a white lawyer was sympathetic to his fellow whites. Instructed to investigate, P. H. Gresson of the Native Affairs Department reported that he had interviewed a number of farmers, who said they had no complaints. For a time after peace some blacks had been very independent and reluctant to work, because they had been well paid by the military, but they "were now settling down into their proper place and giving no trouble." He added that the farmers wanted squatting abolished and the Republican law distributing farm labor enforced and that the Ethiopian movement should be rigidly checked. The resident magistrate, for his part, confirmed that blacks were not "giving any more trouble than they usually do."[114]

The resettlement of black people on the land was also frustrated by the drought. When the corn crop failed in Winburg and the greater part of the Senekal district, the divisional commander of the South African Constabulary suggested that grain depots should be set up to feed the hungry in order to alleviate difficulties that were anticipated in maintaining a sufficient labor supply. However, the resident magistrate objected, noting: "We do not want either the farmer or the native to think that the Government is for ever going to assist them."[115]

The Origins of the African National Congress

In order to promote white accord, blacks had been left out in the cold. Lord Milner was of the opinion that they were "at best . . . children, needing and appreciating a just paternal government."[116] However, black politicians felt differently about the matter, and as early as 1902, the Orange River Colony Native Vigilance Association petitioned the high commissioner to grant black people in the colony the same political, land, economic, and educational rights as other British subjects. In 1906 the same movement, now renamed the ORC Native Congress, objected to the exclusion of blacks from voting rights in the new Free State constitution.[117] Josiah Gumede took up the cause of two Sotho communities that had been dispossessed before the war and, at the same time, petitioned for the abrogation of the republican law of 1893, reenacted by the new government as an ordinance in 1903, in terms of which no more than five black families were permitted to live on any one farm. When Goold-Adams categorically rejected the relief sought, a deputation went to England in 1907 in an equally vain attempt to petition the British crown.[118]

That these efforts were doomed to failure is evident from the progress of the National Convention, the meeting of the white leaders of the four colonies, where constitutional negotiations for a union were nearing completion. The racism of the Draft Act of Union was attacked by the various black congress movements. Just over a week after the publication of the draft, the ORC Native Congress met in Winburg on 17 and 18 February 1909. Here the suggestion that an African national convention should be held was unanimously approved. This assembly, organized by Thomas Mapikela, took place in Bloemfontein from 24 to 26 March. The demands made by the convention were rejected, Prime Minister Abraham Fischer of the ORC contending that they derived from white agitators, "theorists and faddists and easychair negrophilists," who were fermenting dissatisfaction "amongst the otherwise entirely contented natives of the Colony." In a minute to Goold-Adams, the prime minister advised that any such concession "amounting to a reversal of a policy long and successfully applied would undoubtedly give rise to a grave and practically unanimous feeling of dissatisfaction amongst His Majesty's subjects of European descent in this Colony."[119]

The approval of the South Africa Act and the failure of the objections of its black opponents led to the unification of the organizations representing them in the South African Native National Congress (later the African National Congress) on 8 January 1912. And so the scene was set for decades of repression and resistance.

Conclusion

OCCUPATION HAS THE twofold objective of material reconstruction that will win the hearts and minds of a conquered people and the creation of a new political order by means of which the erstwhile enemy is transformed into a trusted ally. David Edelstein identifies three critical variables that determine the success of any military occupation: the total devastation of a country that compels it to acknowledge its need for help in reconstruction, the perception of a common threat to both parties, and credible guarantees of the occupying power's intention to withdraw.[1] The destitute people of the ravaged Free State were dependent on their victors, for whom reconstruction was both a strategic and a moral imperative; the unsettled condition of the black population was experienced as a common threat to stability; and even before the final peace negotiations, the British had signaled their intention of an early withdrawal. However, if an occupying power adds an ideological element to its primary concern of establishing a dispensation that poses no threat to its interests, occupation is inevitably prolonged and nationalism is stimulated as a result of the conquered people being denied self-determination.[2]

The first of Edelstein's critical variables was clearly met by the vigorous efforts made by the colonial administration to get the former republics on their feet again. In the Winburg district, St. John Cole Bowen, the resident magistrate responsible for the reconstruction program, was trusted and respected.[3]

Both the Boers and the British had employed the services of black men during the war, but this portended no change in race relations on either side. A remarkable cooperative arrangement was in place in the Winburg district, where a Colonial officer surnamed Cooper, stationed at Smaldeel, was openly sympathetic to the local Boer population, visiting the farms to "keep the blacks in check." Later he appointed a surrendered burgher, Gert le Roux, as a policeman, tasked "to put them in their place, which he does very well."[4]

On the eve of the war Joseph Chamberlain had promised that Britain would not agree to "a shameful peace" in which black people were denied civil rights. At the time of the Middelburg peace talks between Kitchener and Botha in February 1901, Chamberlain insisted on the inclusion of a statement relating to the statutory rights of black people, including progress toward enfranchisement. In the peace treaty agreed at Vereeniging in May 1902, however, the assurance that blacks would enjoy the same legal standing as Africans in the Cape Colony was omitted altogether, and the carefully circumscribed clause holding out the possibility of eventual qualified enfranchisement was replaced by Article 8, which dashed all hope of this ever happening.

After the war the material circumstances of black people were pitiable, yet Boers and British were united in seeing them as a threat and were agreed in blocking any suggestion of advance. Milner believed that the essential means of establishing the occupying power's legitimacy was to ensure Boer-British cooperation, and the essential precondition of achieving this was to sacrifice the interests of the blacks.[5] His attitude toward blacks was determined not only by contemporary race theories but also by his driving vision of the preeminent importance of industrial development, requiring capital on the one hand and a compliant black labor force on the other.

In 1903 Milner appointed the South African Native Affairs Commission under Sir Godfrey Lagden to investigate and report on an efficient system of labor recruitment and regulation linked with white supremacy. The commission's report, known as the Lagden Report, was a precursor of the notorious Natives Land Act of 1913 in its severe restriction of African land rights in favor of reserves conceived of as labor reservoirs.[6]

The third critical variable—namely, the promise of early departure—is a bargaining counter to give the occupying power time to achieve its goals. The risk of resistance is reduced if there is a negotiated peace rather than unconditional surrender and if the occupying power accords the conquered people some role in decision making as a token of good faith.[7] The British clearly articulated their intention of evacuation as early as March 1901, when the failed peace proposal at Middelburg included the following assurance: "it is the desire of His Majesty's Government, as soon as circumstances permit, to introduce a representative element, and ultimately to concede to the new Colonies the privilege of self-government."[8]

At Vereeniging the Boer delegates concurred with the British insistence on a peace treaty; only the diehards like Steyn and De Wet pressed for unconditional surrender as a loophole for resuming the struggle at a later date. The new crown colony governments sought to involve Boer leaders in administration, but the latter preferred to lie low to avoid the danger of appearing to be lackeys of Great Britain. Jan Smuts declared "Milnerism" to be the enemy, and the Boer leaders proceeded to consolidate their political power by means of reuniting Afrikanerdom and anti-Milner mobilization.

The assurance of early self-government receded as a result of the Afrikaners' resistance to Milner's vision, while Milner insisted that he would "keep up a system of autocratic rule till their opposition to the new order of things is completely broken."[9] When Milner left South Africa in 1905, he believed his mission had failed. The historians Shula Marks and Stanley Trapido concluded that he succeeded in laying the foundations for a state that "not only reflected the demands of twentieth-century British imperialism but also fulfilled them."[10] In terms of Edelstein's three critical variables, the military occupation proved a success by generating social institutions and a productive economy that subserved British imperial ends for generations to come.

It was at the human level that the occupation failed. Milner's disdain for black people confirmed whites in their entitlement to superiority and left blacks exposed to exploitation. Because the mines were the engine of economic reconstruction, he supported the reduction of black wages and the importation of indentured Chinese, a move that split the English-speaking community and was exploited by the Boer leaders. On the other hand, his endeavor to split Afrikaans speakers united them instead. Milner's Social Darwinist assumptions were applicable not only to blacks but also to Afrikaners, especially the poor, who did not measure up to the role of whites as a labor aristocracy. The future of the country lay with the English speakers; Afrikaners should submit to their superior power ("the thick end of the stick," as Milner put it[11]) and superior culture.

Milner sought to strengthen English political and cultural dominance by means of schemes to attract vast numbers of agricultural settlers who were provided with choice land, resettlement grants, and generous subsidies. The Winburg district saw an infusion of English-speaking farmers, not all of whom were very successful. Capt. Douglas Saunders, for example, was given financial advances and provided with teams of horses for plowing. Although he had a good season and excellent market opportunities and was allowed to occupy more than one farm, he exhausted his capital and in March 1903 applied for government employment.[12] As the scheme attracted only 546 settlers to the Free State (at a cost of more than £1.7 million), it fell far short of its primary political purpose. However, it did not fail to inflame political passions. The flagrant preferential treatment accorded the settlers was raised at the Brandfort congress, and in an article in the *Friend* the success of Boer repatriation was contrasted with the vain expenditure on British settlers.[13]

Second, Milner determined to use education as a means of anglicization. English was the only medium of instruction, the curriculum had an imperialist bias, and six hundred teachers brought in from overseas were required to advance the British cause.[14] This policy also failed in its political purpose, because it was countered by the establishment of Christian National schools subsidized from the Netherlands. These schools were rooted in Calvinism, used Dutch as the teaching medium, and were supportive of Afrikaner aspirations. They struggled to survive, because the poorest parents had to pay fees while the government schools were free,[15] but they mobilized Afrikaner sentiment and gave proof of determined resistance. Furthermore, because education was not compulsory, thousands of children were unaffected by government schooling as a means of advancing the imperial cause.

Third, Milner believed that the question of ultimate political power could be delayed until an electoral majority could be engineered that would ensure English ascendancy. It was this political miscalculation in the service of an ideological delusion that precipitated long-term disaster by fanning an Afrikaner nationalism that fed on aggrievedness, anti-imperialism, ethnicity, economic interventionism, and racial division.[16] Louis Botha and Jan Smuts were among the Boer leaders who acknowledged that they were defeated and saw the promise in a modernizing federation uniting English- and Afrikaans-speaking South Africans. With the concurrence of Botha and Smuts, Britain's occupation goals were capable of achievement. However, the imposition of imperialist ideology played into the hands of Steyn, De Wet, and Hertzog, who were unwilling to acknowledge defeat and formed a conservative nucleus around which nationalist sentiment could coalesce.

In 1910 Louis Botha became the first prime minister of a united South Africa and with his lieutenant, Jan Smuts, embraced the ideals of reconciliation and empire loyalty. Four years later Hertzog founded the National Party. The cultural exclusivism of this party was bound to win out against the compromises forced on their political rivals. When ethnic mobilization eventually led to political ascendancy, the Afrikaner adherents of the National Party—and whites in general—were enabled to make steady material advances, but always at the expense of black people. So a system of racial oppression evolved that was to bedevil the country for much of the twentieth century and that still casts its long shadow in the twenty-first. Assessed in terms of this outcome, the occupation was imperfect indeed.

Notes

Abbreviations

ASAI	Archives of the South African Institute, Amsterdam	
	EM	H. J. Emous Collection
BPL	Bloemfontein Public Library	
Cd.	Parliamentary Papers published by Command of the Government	
DRCA	Dutch Reformed Church Archives, Bloemfontein	
FSPA	Free State Provincial Archives, Bloemfontein	
	A	Accessions
	CO	Colonial Secretary
	DLS	Director of Land Settlement
	GRD	Government Relief Department
	GS	Government Secretary
	MHG	Master of the Supreme Court
	NAB	Native Affairs Branch
	ORC	Orange River Colony Official Publications
	P	Pamphlets
	SRC	Chief Superintendent of Refugee Camps
	VRO	Volunteer Repatriation Organisation
NASA	National Archives of South Africa, Pretoria	
	A	Accessions
	CJC	Central Judicial Commission
	FK	Photocopies
	GOV	Private Secretary of the Governor
	HC	High Commissioner for South Africa
	MGP	Military Governor, Pretoria
	MHG	Master of the Supreme Court

	PMO	Provost Marshal's Office
	RS	Official Concerned with the Recording of Casualties in the Republican Forces and among Civilians
	SNA	Secretary for Native Affairs
	SO/POW	Staff Officer: Prisoners of War, Cape Town
	TKP	Transvaal Colony Official Publications
	W	Accession
NAUK	National Archives of the United Kingdom, London	
	WO	War Office
NLCT	National Library, Cape Town	
	MSB	Marquard Collection
UFS	University of the Free State, Bloemfontein	
UW	University of the Witwatersrand, Johannesburg	
WMBR	War Museum of the Boer Republics, Bloemfontein	

Preface

1. The official name of the southern Boer Republic was the Orange Free State, but it was widely referred to as the Free State. When the country was annexed by the British, they did not care for the "Free" part, so they called it the Orange River Colony. After unification in 1910, it reverted to its previous name. At democratization the "Orange"—referring to the Dutch royal house—was regarded as inappropriate, so it seemed fair to call the country the Free State throughout this book, except when referring specifically to the British colonial administration.

Introduction

1. Van Jaarsveld, "Veldkornet en sy Aandeel," 340.
2. FSPA, GS 2109.6215.
3. Jacques Malan, *Boere-Offisiere,* 125.
4. Venter, "Geskiedenis van Winburg," 48–49.
5. Denoon, *Grand Illusion,* 60; Viljoen, "Virginia," 115–17.
6. Lamprecht, "Ekonomiese Ontwikkeling," 62.
7. A. Grundlingh, "Stigting van Senekal," 47; Krikler, *Revolution from Above,* 73–74; S.J.C. Wessels and S.F.G. Wessels, *Nageslag,* 1:84; NASA, CJC 691.144.
8. Venter, "Geskiedenis van Winburg," 158; NASA, CJC 146.40; 689.105; 696.239.
9. A. Grundlingh, "Stigting van Senekal," 47–48.
10. Keegan, "Restructuring," 235–36.
11. Van Aswegen, "Posisie van die Nie-Blanke," 52.
12. Keegan, "Restructuring," 237.
13. *De Express,* 14 March 1893, quoted by Van Aswegen, "Verhouding," 291.
14. A bywoner might be anything from a valued farm manager to a tolerated hanger-on. For a useful discussion, see De Kiewiet, *History,* 192–94.
15. Quispel and Ross, "Theorie en Mentaliteit"; FSPA, CO 6164/B.

16. Keegan, "Trade, Accumulation, and Impoverishment," 204, 208.

17. WMBR, 6032: "Diary of Elsa Leviseur," 13 Oct. 1899, 14–15. *Rooinek* translates to "red neck," referring to the English because of the effect the African sun had on them.

18. Malan, *Opkoms van 'n Republiek*, 495, translated.

19. FSPA, P730: *Lijst van Stemgerechtigde Burgers, 1899*, 3–5; "Kommanderingslys," in Venter, "Geskiedenis van Winburg."

20. Van Aswegen, "Verhouding," 219, 316.

21. *Volksraadsnotule,* 5 June 1877, 295, quoted in A. Grundlingh, "Stigting van Senekal," 15.

22. A. Grundlingh, "Stigting van Senekal," 66.

23. FSPA, P730: *Lijst van Stemgerechtigde Burgers,* 39–41.

24. A. Grundlingh, "Stigting van Senekal," 19.

25. BPL, *Friend,* 12 Feb. 1890, 342–43.

26. Van Schoor, "Brand, Johannes Henricus," 1:115–16. The official name of the northern republic was the South African Republic, but it was widely known as the Transvaal. The British called it the Transvaal Colony. From 1910 to 1994 it was officially the Transvaal, and I have used this name also with reference to the Boer Republic.

27. S. F. Malan, *Politieke Strominge*, 111, 162–64.

28. Ibid., 166–69.

29. F. J. du T. Spies, "Engelse Gesindhede," 58.

30. Fraser, *Episodes*, 218.

31. Nasson, "War for South Africa," 209.

32. Porter, *Origins of the South African War,* 209, 214.

33. Ibid., 217, 221.

34. Ibid., 241, 246.

35. I. R. Smith, *Origins of the South African War,* 273, 279.

Chapter 1. Occupation and Insurgency

1. Surridge, "British Civil-Military Relations," 19.

2. Avant, "Institutional Sources," 424–25.

3. Farwell, *Great Anglo-Boer War*, 240.

4. Cd. 426, Proclamation XII, 6; NASA, MGP 260, Army Order 19 Nov. 1900; Dyzenhaus, "Puzzle of Martial Law," 12.

5. S. M. Miller, "Duty or Crime," 316; De Bruin, "Regshistoriese Studie," 80–81 and 69; Cd. 261.

6. Cd. 547, 37–38; Kruger, "Militêre Bewind," 37–50.

7. Surridge, "British Civil-Military Relations," 99.

8. Breytenbach, *Geskiedenis,* 5:160–64.

9. NASA, A 717.18, 26 Feb. 1900, quoted in Breytenbach, *Geskiedenis,* 5:205.

10. Breytenbach, *Geskiedenis,* 5:416–26.

11. NASA, CJC 161.397, Confidential report.

12. Creswicke, *South Africa and the Transvaal War,* 5:97–100.

13. WMBR, 5957/1: Dagboek van J.P.T. Theron, 4 May 1900; Churchill, *Boer War,* 291.

14. M. de Villiers, *White Tribe Dreaming*, 226.

15. Milne, J. W., "Diary of No 8080 Private J. W. Milne," 5 May 1900, 9; Plokhooy, *Met den Mauser,* 114–15, translated; Rev. McQueen, an American reporter, quoted in UFS, "Diary of Betty Wessels," 8 May 1900, 2.

16. Brown, *With the Royal Canadians*, 329–30; M. C. Jackson, *Soldier's Diary,* 55.

17. FSPA, ORC 305: *Government Gazette,* 6 July 1900, 27; Kruger, "Militêre Bewind," 28, 144, 142.

18. Colvile, *Work of the Ninth Division*, 138–39; FSPA, CO 289.3697; Cd. 546, 43.

19. FSPA, CO 62.924.

20. NASA, CJC 687.63; Kruger, *Militêre Bewind,* 42–43; Marquard, *Letters,* 8 Nov. 1900, 112–15, translated.

21. Quoted in McLeod, "Psychological Impact," 142.

22. Marquard, *Letters,* 30 May, 1 June 1900, 78, 80; and 26 Oct. 1900, 110; NASA, CJC 1682.322.

23. Kruger, "Militêre Bewind," 48–49; Marquard, *Letters,* 1 Aug. 1900, 100.

24. *Times History,* 4:110; Jones and Jones, *Gazetteer,* 204.

25. Fourteen Streams was the Vaal River crossing 180 miles southwest of Mafeking where Boer commandos tried to stem Lord Methuen's advance on 24 April 1900.

26. Davis, *With Both Armies,* 203–207.

27. Churchill, *Boer War*, 305.

28. NASA, CJC 700.317; 691.148.

29. Breytenbach, *Geskiedenis,* 5:499, 505.

30. Oberholster and Stemmet, *Senekal,* 71; NASA, CJC 686.44.

31. Watt, "Skirmish at Senekal"; *Times History,* 4:249.

32. J. P. Bosman, *Slaan en Vlug*, 19, translated.

33. A. Grundlingh, *Dynamics of Treason*, 327.

34. Nasson, *War for South Africa,* 204.

35. Boldingh, *Hollandsch Officier*, 12n.

36. Breytenbach, *Geskiedenis,* 5:231; Jones and Jones, *Gazetteer*, 235; FSPA, A 119.1056: I. A. Meyer, "Ervaringe van 'n Veldkornet," 17.

37. Van Schoor, *Christiaan Rudolph de Wet*, 110; L. Scholtz, *Generaal Christiaan de Wet as Veldheer*, 118.

38. For "Haasbroek's commando," see Van der Walt, "Oorlogsdagboek," 122, and De Bruin, "Regshistoriese Studie," 154–59.

39. Jones and Jones, *Gazetteer,* 157; J.A.J. de Villiers, "Diaries and Recollections," 97.

40. Brink, *Ceylon en de Bannelingen*, 88–89; *Times History,* 4:342.

41. NAUK, WO 105, CinC 126/144, General Hunter's Despatch, 4 Aug. 1900.

42. L. Scholtz, *Generaal Christiaan de Wet as Veldheer*, 150; De Bruin, "Regshistoriese Studie," 340–41.

43. Henry Kissinger, quoted in Mack, "Why Big Nations Lose Small Wars," 185.

44. Sullivan, "War Aims and War Outcomes," 497; Mack, "Why Big Nations Lose Small Wars," 178–82; André Wessels, "Boer Guerrilla and British Counter-Guerrilla Operations," 8.

45. Jones and Jones, *Gazetteer,* 206.

46. De Wet, *Three Years War*, 157–60; *Times History,* 5:2–3.

47. Barfield, "Royal Wiltshire Yeomanry."

48. NASA, A 1237: Henning Olivier, 12; Uys, "Olivier, Jan Hendrik," 1:601; Kestell, *Met die Boere-Kommando's*, 98.

49. NAUK, WO 105, CinC 126/163, Maj. Gen. Bruce Hamilton's Despatch, 29 Aug. 1900.

50. Van der Walt, "Oorlogsdagboek," 125–26; De Wet, *Three Years War*, 162.

51. *Times History,* 5:33.

52. De Bruin, "Regshistoriese Studie," 83.

53. S. B. Spies, *Methods of Barbarism?* 79.

54. *Times History,* 5:133–35; *History of the War in South Africa,* 4:76.

55. J. W. de Villiers, *C. R. de Wet in Kaapkolonie*, 25, 60–64.

56. Le May, *British Supremacy*, 97–99; A.H.J. Wilson, "Railway War," 141–42.

57. Quoted in Davitt, *Boer Fight for Freedom*, 484.

58. L. Scholtz, *Generaal Christiaan de Wet as Veldheer*, 263.

59. Van der Walt, "Oorlogsdagboek," 136; Prinsloo, "Vroue in die Anglo-Boereoorlog," 59.

60. FSPA, A 119.1060: Marx, "Vryheidsoorlog Herinneringe," 23; Van der Walt, "Oorlogsdagboek," 137.

61. Nasson, *South African War*, 211; *Times History,* 5:331; Grobbelaar, *Kommandeer! Kommandeer!* 53–54.

62. Cf. Riall, *Boer War,* 175–83.

63. Riall, *Boer War*, 187; A.H.J. Wilson, "Railway War," 182.

64. NASA, SO/POW 72; Van der Walt, "Oorlogsdagboek," 132, 149. When the Boers laid down their arms, the British photographed the child and the British officer took the rifle from his hands and gave him half a crown (two shillings and sixpence).

65. NASA, SO/POW 71, 72, 73.

66. FSPA, A 119.1099: "Herinneringe van G. J. S. van den Heever," and A 119.85: Letter from Piet Beukes.

67. FSPA, 119.1060: Marx, "Vryheidsoorlog Herinneringe," [23].

68. Rompel, *Uit den Tweeden Vrijheidsoorlog,* 14, translated.

69. Nasson, *South African War,* 217.

70. Hintrager, "Dagboek," 11 June 1900, 31.

71. Giliomee, *Afrikaners,* 252.

72. Merriman, *Selections from the Correspondence,* 3:352.

73. Hintrager, "Dagboek," 7 June 1900, 28.

74. Hintrager, "Dagboek," 6 Sept. 1900, 142, translated. See also Pretorius, *Life on Commando*, 261.

75. McDonald, *Terugblik,* 61, translated.

76. A. Grundlingh, *Dynamics of Treason,* 38.

77. De Wet, *Three Years War,* 417; Mitchell and Nicholson, "Rational Models and the Ending of Wars," 503.

78. NASA, A 1149: "Toespraak van J. C. Asselbergs," in Pretorius, "Waarom het die 'Bittereinders,'" 63.

79. McLeod, "Psychological Impact," 72.

80. Meintjes, *President Steyn,* 133, 166; For Steyn's reaction, see N. J. van der Merwe, *Marthinus Theunis Steyn,* 2:85.

81. Hancock, *Smuts: The Sanguine Years,* 151–52.

82. Pienaar, *Op Kommando met Steyn en De Wet,* 89; Rompel, *Uit den Tweeden Vrijheidsoorlog,* 24; L. Scholtz, *Christiaan Rudolph de Wet as Veldheer,* 99, 142; cf. Cock, *Colonels and Cadres,* 61–65.

83. Smuts, *Memoirs,* 447.

84. Van den Berg, *Beste Ouders!* 283.

85. Pretorius, "Afrikaner Nationalism," 76. For an example of such misrepresentation, see Childers, *In the Ranks of the CIV*, chapter 8, footnote A.

86. NASA, A 230/2, 48; NASA, GOV 257; Creswicke, *South Africa and the Transvaal War,* 3:38.

87. Lowry, "World's no Bigger," 268.

88. De Kock, "Pres. Marthinus Theunis Steyn," 257.

89. Van Warmelo, *On Commando,* 163; Weber, *Eighteen Months,* 71.

90. Grobbelaar, *Kommandeer! Kommandeer!* 47 and 123.

91. Worsfold, *Lord Milner's Work,* 431.

92. Quoted in S. B. Spies, *Methods of Barbarism?* 285.

93. S. B. Spies, *Methods of Barbarism?* 294–95; Kestell and Van Velden, *Vredesonderhandelinge,* 124.

94. A. Badenhorst, *Tant' Alie of Transvaal,* 131.

95. Pretorius, "Waarom het die 'Bittereinders,'" 71.

96. Cf. Cock, *Colonels and Cadres,* 61.

97. Ver Loren van Themaat, *Twee Jaren in den Boerenoorlog,* 216, quoted by Pretorius, "Waarom het die 'Bittereinders,'" 71, translated.

Chapter 2. The Failure of Protection

1. Cd. 426, Army Proclamation, 2–3.

2. Rompel, *Uit den Tweeden Vrijheidsoorlog,* 13; Brink, *Ceylon en de Bannelingen,* 79.

3. M. de Villiers, *White Tribe,* 213. The Dutch word "*plaats*" underwent a significant semantic narrowing in South Africa from the generalized sense of "place" to the specific meaning "farm." A Boer's farm was his very particular place.

4. NASA, CJC 1702.1219; Pretorius, *Life on Commando,* 244; NASA, CJC 1706.1372; 703.393; FSPA, A 1209; Sternberg, *My Experiences,* 116.

5. NASA, CJC 697.271; A. Grundlingh, *Dynamics of Treason*, 91; NASA, CJC 697.266.

6. NASA, CJC 697.271; 697.273.

7. NASA, CJC 698.288.

8. A. Grundlingh, "Collaborators," 258–59.

9. A. Grundlingh, *Dynamics of Treason,* 51; Le May, *British Supremacy,* 85.

10. NASA, CJC 1714.1708; 1696.984.

11. NASA, CJC 697.257.

12. NASA, CJC 1707.1426; Marquard, *Letters,* 22 July 1901, 98.

13. Cd. 261. 25; Fletcher-Vane, *War and One Year After*, 7.

14. NASA, CJC 698.92; 161.397; 161.394.

15. NASA, CJC 161.397; 161.394; 687.71; 153.208.

16. NASA, CJC 714.828; 702.364; 698.285; 1715.1732; 161.386.

17. Binny, "Letters," 101.

18. Marquard, *Letters,* 30 May 1900, 80; and 1 June 1900, 81. Halm not identified; perhaps Helme.

19. Van Rensburg, "Ekonomiese Herstel," 166; NASA, CJC 690.116.

20. NASA, CJC 1718.1865; FSPA, CO 83.2589/02; BPL, *Friend*, 20 Oct. 1902.

21. Marquard, *Letters,* 30 May, 1 June, 28 July, and 30 May 1900, 78, 80, 100, and 79; NASA, CJC 262.723.

22. BPL, *Friend,* 4 April 1900; FSPA, ORC 305: *Government Gazette,* 10 Aug. 1900, 102; Marquard, *Letters*, 14 June 1900, 87; *Government Gazette,* 28 Sept. 1900, 173; J.A.J. de Villiers, "Diaries and Recollections," 12 Feb. 1901, 52.

23. NASA, CJC 1692.703; Marquard, *Letters,* 14 June 1900, 87; CJC 1692.716; 1698.1068.

24. Wade, Phillips, and Bradley, *Constitutional Law*, 412.

25. Fletcher-Vane, *War and One Year After*, 8.

26. NASA, PMO 47.3169, 16 Oct. 1901; NASA, SO/POW 18: PR/A1455/01.

27. Berger, *Chapters*, 44–45.

28. NASA, CJC 689.102; 692.164; 690.124.

29. NASA, CJC 690.120; 692.151, Resident Magistrate's note.

30. UFS, Wessels, "Diary of Betty Wessels," 8 May 1900, 1; NASA, CJC 692.151.

31. De Wet, *Three Years War*, 242; NASA, CJC 702.365; FSPA, CO 92.3318.

32. NASA, PMO 54.3760; 35:2371. The charge does not appear to have been without substance.

33. NASA, GOV 846 PS 18/243/05.

34. FSPA, CO 7.508; 11.829; NASA, CJC 266.771.

35. FSPA, CO 9.648.

36. FSPA, CO 7.508; 9.648: Letter from Major O'Leary, NASA, A 2030, vol. 45.

37. Rosslyn, *Twice Captured*, 265.

38. NASA, CJC 686.45; 686.44.

39. NASA, CJC 706.534.

40. NASA, CJC 699.144.

41. Cd. 426, 1 Sept. 1900, 16; Kruger, "Militêre Bewind," 87.

42. McDonald, *Terugblik,* 55, translated.

43. NASA, CJC 692.269; 1685.442; 1685.443; 1720.1940; 1683.397; 1684.433; 1690.646; 1684.406; 1688.578; 699.303; 1716.1766; 1687.506.

44. Hobhouse, *Boer War Letters*, undated, 212; Grundlingh, *Dynamics of Treason,* 68.

45. Hobhouse, *Boer War Letters*, 113; NASA, CJC 1706.1387; 1722.1999; 1701.1173; 1722.1999; 1701.1173; FSPA, CO 85.2805; GRD 40.1342; CO 187.4788/03.

46. S. B. Spies, *Methods of Barbarism?* 103–112.

47. Surridge, "British Civil-Military Relations," 139; Bradford, "Gentlemen and Boers," 39.

48. Van Warmelo, *On Commando,* 195; De Wet, *Three Years War*, 215–16.

49. Barry, *Ons Japie,* 22 July 1901, 62, translated.

50. NASA, CJC 1704.1299, translated.

51. NASA, CJC 703.391.

52. NASA, CJC 1691.660; 702.381; 1722.1986.

53. NASA, CJC 689.97; 707.542; 689.97.

54. De Wet, *Three Years War*, 158; Danie Theron, quoted in Grundlingh, *Dynamics of Treason,* 56–57.

55. J.A.J. de Villiers, "Diaries and Recollections," 18 July 1900, 15–16; Hintrager, "Dagboek," 16 July 1900, 86.

56. Van der Walt, "Oorlogsdagboek," 132.

57. NASA, CJC 703.940; 1706.1376; 692.167; 687.56.

58. NASA, CJC 698.280.

59. See NASA, CJC 1719.1893; 686.35; 697.268; 714.816; 1719.1893; 698.279; 687.51; 1720.1952.

60. NASA, CJC 695.228.

61. NASA, CJC 1715.1739.

62. NASA, CJC 690.109; 696.246.

63. NASA, CJC 693.176.

64. NASA, CJC 702.363.

65. NASA, CJC 703.420; 1692.692; 699.301; 712.766; 1718.1860; 1696.1017.

66. NASA, CJC 146.39.

67. NASA, CJC 1693.887.

68. NASA, CJC 699.305; 700.310; 701.339; 696.256.

69. NASA, CJC 701.345.

70. NASA, CJC 703.409.

71. C.C.J. Badenhorst, *Uit den Boeren-Oorlog*, 104–105; Blake, *Boereverraaier,* 158–75; NASA, CJC 689.92; CJC 1690.647, 652, 653; FSPA, 119.1060: Marx, "Vryheidsoorlog Herinneringe," [78].

72. Pienaar, *Op Kommando met Steyn en De Wet,* 113; Brink, *Oorlog en Ballingskap,* 76.

73. De Bruin and Wessels, "Militêre Verhore," 77–79.

74. FSPA, A 119.1099: "Herinneringe van G.J.S. van den Heever," 63–64; A 119.52: Letter from Tewie Wessels, 25 June 1949; Blake, *Boereverraaier,* 193–98.

75. M. C. Jackson, *Soldier's Diary,* 263–64.

76. NASA, CJC 1717.1842.

77. NASA, CJC 1711.1572.

78. NASA, CJC 1717.1830; 696.239.

79. Marquard, *Letters,* 29 Aug. 1900, 106; NASA, CJC 694.206; 693.163; 1719.1894.

80. A. Grundlingh, "Collaborators," 258–59; Bradford, "Gentlemen and Boers," 50; cf. Pretorius, "Waarom het die 'Bittereinders,'" 68–69.

Chapter 3. From Neutrality to Collaboration

1. Bouwer, *Memoirs,* 125; Smuts, *Memoirs,* 5; Schutte, *Boerenoorlog na Honderd Jaar,* 8, translated; Fisk, *Age of the Warrior,* 493.

2. Milner, "Letters," Milner to Kitchener, 14 Feb. 1901, 128.

3. Quoted in A. Grundlingh, *Dynamics of Treason,* 313; Preller, *Ons Parool,* 93–94, translated.

4. Denoon, "Participation," 118.

5. NASA, CJC 709.640; 1699.1113, and 1114; 2329.206; 1682.327.

6. L.W.F. Grundlingh, Review of *Putting a Plough to the Ground,* 125; Lamprecht, "Ekonomiese Ontwikkeling," 89; Weideman, "Geskiedenis van die Ekonomiese Ontwikkeling," 32, 41; De Kiewiet, *History,* 178–207.

7. J. J. Oberholster, *Nederduitse Gereformeerde Kerk,* 126; Van Schoor, *Christiaan Rudolph de Wet,* 55; Van Rensburg, "Ekonomiese Herstel," 14; Taylor, *Doctor to Basuto, Boer, and Briton,* 117–18; NASA, CJC 1353.1253; 1554.1232; 1674.177; 1694.922. Serfontein, *Keurskrif,* 152, 153; Van Niekerk, "Dagboek," 3 Jan. 1901, 152.

8. S. F. Malan, "Openbare Onderwys," 290–91.

9. A. Grundlingh, "Sosiale Geskiedenis," 44–45, 47.

10. FSPA, SRC 90; NASA, SO/POW 73.

11. FSPA, P730: *Lijst van Stemgerechtigde Burgers.*

12. Preller, *Ons Parool,* 93, translated.

13. NASA, CJC 690.121; 1702.1227.

14. NASA, FK 1135: Milner Papers, 254; Swart, "Rebels of 1914," 51; Pansegrouw et al., quoted in Weideman, "Geskiedenis van die Ekonomiese Ontwikkeling," 41; Letters in De Tijd, 25 March and 15 April 1868, referred to in Giliomee, *Afrikaners,* 181; Nasson, *South African War,* 66.

15. FSPA, GS 2113 R6286: P. L. du Preez to OFS Government, 4 Dec. 1899, translated.

16. NASA, CJC 1717.1825.

17. Nasson, *South African War*, 216.

18. Ibid., 47.

19. S. F. Malan, *Politieke Strominge;* F. J. du T. Spies, Review of *Politieke Strominge;* F. J. du T. Spies, "Engelse Gesindhede," 47.

20. FSPA, GS 2113 R6286: Letter of P. L. du Preez, translated; NASA, CJC 1706.1387.

21. For example, Izedinova, *Few Months*, 91n, and Sternberg, *My Experiences*, 86.

22. Leviseur, *Memories*, 69; Lombard, *Uit die Dagboek*, 49; Pretorius, "Caught up in the Cross-Fire," 61 and 67n; Hintrager, "Dagboek," 5 Aug. 1900, 103.

23. Cf. De Wet, *Three Years War*, 197.

24. A. Grundlingh, *Dynamics of Treason*, 275; NASA, CJC 1690.653; 1698.1073; 700.332.

25. Du Toit, *Diary*, 18–25 Nov. 1900, 27 and passim.

26. NASA, CJC 698.292 and 1685.439.

27. K. Schoeman, *Die Laaste Afrikaanse Boek*, 142.

28. Hintrager, "Dagboek," 62, 115, 125; ASAI, EM, Adriani 35 (8 Nov. 1907), Endendijk 4 (undated), Gangel 9 (4 March 1898).

29. NASA, CJC 1718.1851; 1694.948; 1692.710; 700.327; 1692.714; 1686.482; 1722.1998; 703.419.

30. NASA, CJC 1695.983; 688.84; 1698.1096; 1710.1541; 706.531; 700.329.

31. NASA, CJC 709.682; 1694.937; 1695.957; 1695.954; 702.388; 694.213; 1684.434.

32. NASA, CJC 1695.976; 1684.435; 1678.199; 1676.145; 1680.253; 1677.152; 1709.1504; 1710.1547; 1713.1661; 1679.206; 1714.1711.

33. NASA, CJC 703.391; 1695.974; 1676.126; 1685.452.

34. Hintrager, "Dagboek," 7 June 1900, 28; Schikkerling, *Commando Courageous*, 11–13.

35. G. D. Scholtz, *Geskiedenis van Ventersburg*, 12; *Times History*, 5:23.

36. S. M. Miller, "Duty or Crime," 329–30.

37. FSPA, A 119.1060: Marx, "Vryheidsoorlog Herinneringe," [26–27].

38. NASA, A 230/2, 11; Hillegas, *With the Boer Forces*, 100.

39. NASA, CJC 1710.1547; 700.321; 714.832.

40. NASA, CJC 1695.976.

41. Eloff, "Vrystaatse Vlugtelinge," 98.

42. Van Niekerk, "Dagboek," 16 Feb.1900, 18 and 19 Apr. 1900, 61; C. J. de Villiers, *Helpers, Healers*, 2:178–79; NASA, CJC 1684.405.

43. A term coined by the arch-collaborationist Marcel Déat (Littlejohn, *Patriotic Traitors*, 222).

44. Albert Fabre-Luce, quoted by Hirschfeld, "Collaboration and Attentism," 469, translated.

45. Quoted by Nasson, *South African War*, 230.

46. Le May, *British Supremacy*, 85.

47. Pretorius, *Life on Commando*, 191; Stakhovitch and Gurko, "Dépeches," 184; Allum, "Julius Allum's Anglo-Boer War Observations," 49; Van Oostrum, *Bestendige Onbestendigheid*, 28; De Villebois-Mareuil, *War Notes*, 265.

48. Hintrager, "Dagboek," 6 Aug. 1900, 105, translated.

49. Hoffmann, "Collaborationism in France," 376–79; Littlejohn, *Patriotic Traitors*, 210.

50. NASA, CJC 693.196.

51. FSPA, SRC 6.1552; 9.5421; 47.2319; 5.1451, 39.1077.

52. Saron and Hotz, *Jews in South Africa*, 329.

53. Quoted in S. F. Malan, "Rol van J. Geo Fraser," 281.

54. Marquard, *Letters*, 25 June 1900, 91, and 1 Aug. 1900, 100–101; S. F. Malan, "Rol van J. Geo Fraser," 283–84.

55. NASA, CJC 697.272; 693.196.

56. NASA, CJC 691.131.

57. Marquard, *Letters*, 26 Oct. 1901, 110; NASA, CJC 693.182.

58. NASA, CJC 698.280; 1706.1369; 1692.715; 694.213.

59. Marquard, *Letters*, 5 Dec. 1900, 116–18; NASA, CJC 708.603.

60. FSPA, CO 21 1873/01.

61. NASA, CJC 1704.1303; 1676.126; 1695.974; 1701.1174; 701.334.

62. WMBR, 6214/1: De Jager, "Herinneringe," 3, translated.

63. Van Schoor, "Ons Vrystaat," 6; M. de Villiers, *White Tribe*, 212–13.

64. See, for example, Plokhooy, *Met den Mauser*, 60; UFS, "Diary of Betty Wessels," 3, 16, 41.

65. Baumann and Bright, *Lost Republic*, 170.

66. Plokhooy, *Met den Mauser*, 114–15; Marquard, *Letters*, 23 May 1900, 78.

67. UFS, "Diary of Betty Wessels," 29 July 1900, 42; Pine-Coffin, *One Man's Boer War*, 23 Sept. 1900, 138; NASA, CJC 639.195.

68. See Cleaver, *War Letters*, 11.

69. Leviseur, *Memories*, 104. See also Taylor, *Doctor to Basuto, Boer, and Briton*, 173.

70. NASA, CJC 161.397: Assistant Provost Marshal's report on T. Mitchell.

71. Phillips, "Family of an Irish Soldier Settler," 21. According to Cole Bowen, another brother also identified "very strongly from the very first during the war with the British cause" (FSPA, CO 357.9478/04). This would have been Charles Henry Dennis Acton (NASA, MHG 66631).

72. Preller, *Ons Parool*, 98–99, translated.

73. NASA, CJC 1683.396; Venter, "Geskiedenis van Winburg," 176.

74. NASA, CJC 146.41.

75. Taylor, *Doctor to Basuto, Boer, and Briton*, 244–45; NASA, CJC 702.364; SO/POW 28; PMO 35.2428.

76. NASA, CJC 698.285.

77. Saul Dubow comments on the "unconscious disposition of English speaking South Africans, refined over generations" to define other groups in terms of their own supposedly normative identity. See Dubow, "Thoughts," 52.

78. NASA, CJC 699.304; *Times History,* 6:53–54; CJC 686.48; Du Toit, *Diary,* 31 May, 2 and 3 June 1901, 51–53. Capt. Hosler could not be identified, but this is not surprising, as Du Toit has "Higgie" for Hickey.

79. Cf. NASA, PMO 54.375: Governor of St Helena to Lord Milner, 22 Feb. 1902; De Graaf, *Boere op St. Helena,* 82; quoted in Grundlingh, *Dynamics of Treason,* 319.

80. NASA, CJC 1692.700; Pretorius, *Anglo-Boer War,* 36.

81. Higginson, "Hell in Small Places," 108; NASA, SO/POW 70.

82. NASA, CJC 703.414.

83. Quoted in A. Grundlingh, *Dynamics of Treason,* 321–22.

84. Marquard, *Letters,* 9 June 1900, 85; see also 3 June 1900, 83–84.

85. See, for example, Groenewald, *Bannelinge,* 85.

86. Grundlingh, *Dynamics of Treason,* 281–82.

87. Lee, *To the Bitter End,* 122–25.

88. Quoted in A. Grundlingh, *Dynamics of Treason,* 340.

89. Idiomatically modified version of the translation in NASA, FK 660.790 (CO 417/348/2274).

90. Dubow, *Commonwealth of Knowledge,* 139–40, 159.

91. Marquard, *Letters,* 12; Schreiner, *Words in Season,* 124.

92. Phillipps, *With Rimington,* Letter, 16 April 1900, 104–105.

93. Oosterhagen, *Oorlogsdagboekie,* 17–18 May 1902, 57; Van den Berg, *Beste Ouders!* 20 Aug. 1899, 291.

94. NASA, FK 1869 (WO 8960), Comdt. E. R. Grobler to Lord Kitchener, 3 May 1901.

95. Cd. 903, 48; Du Toit, *Diary,* 54–55.

96. Boveri, *Treason in the Twentieth Century* (1961), 62; see also the 1971 edition, 46–47, quoted in A. Grundlingh, *Dynamics of Treason,* 317.

97. NASA, CJC 2514.358; 689.105; 693.181; 694.206.

98. NASA, 705.495; FSPA, MHG C1181.

99. Grobbelaar, *Kommandeer! Kommandeer!* 130; A. Grundlingh, *Dynamics of Treason,* 476; FSPA, VRO 4.1423; NASA, CJC 686.40; 692.167; A. Grundlingh, *Dynamics,* 493; FSPA, VRO 1.995; NASA, CJC 702.358; 704.443; FSPA, VRO 2.1168; 4.1419.

100. Reproduced in St. Leger, *Mounted Infantry,* 271–74.

Chapter 4. War against Women

1. Quoted in Raath, *Boerevrou,* 1:11.

2. Marquard, *Letters,* 5 Nov. 1899, 43.

3. Gräbe, "Writing between the Lines," 50.

4. Connell, *Gender and Power,* 79.

5. Van Heyningen, "Women and Gender," 91; Theron, "Victorian Women," 5.

6. WMBR, 6214/1, De Jager, "Herinneringe," [27]; Lombard, *Uit die Dagboek,* 112.

7. Pretorius, *Life on Commando,* 322–25; Brohier, "Boer Prisoner of War," [11].

8. Marquard, *Letters,* 10 March 1900, 61.

9. Marquard, *Letters,* 5 May 1900, 74.

10. WMBR, 6214/1: De Jager, "Herinneringe," [2, 11].

11. Rompel, *Uit den Tweeden Vrijheidsoorlog,* 55.

12. St. Leger, *Mounted Infantry,* 221, 222, 225.

13. Hales, *Campaign Pictures,* 22–23; NASA, CJC 2514.684.

14. Marquard, *Letters,* 5 May, 3 June, and 19 June 1900, 74, 83, and 89.

15. NASA, CJC 700.323.

16. NASA, CJC 694:198; 693.195; 696.256; 705.510; 713.790; 703.473; WMBR, 6214/1: De Jager, "Herinneringe," [26–27].

17. NASA, CJC 696.256.

18. Harris, "Archival Sliver," 64.

19. WMBR, 6214/1: De Jager, "Herinneringe," 8–9. In fact, the saying occurs in so many sources that it was obviously common currency among the Boers. *Daily News,* 26 Feb. 1901, 2, quoted in Krebs, *Gender, Race, and the Writing of Empire,* 60.

20. Cf. Girouard, *Return to Camelot*; Bannerman, "Manliness," 38.

21. Rice, *From Dolly Gray,* 134.

22. Pine-Coffin, *One Man's Boer War,* 23 Sept. and 23 Nov. 1900, 138 and 172.

23. NASA, CJC 687.69: A. M. Ford.

24. Cd. 819; *Manchester Guardian,* 18 Nov. 1901, quoted in Krebs, *Gender, Race and the Writing of Empire,* 50.

25. Chamberlain, quoted in S. B. Spies, *Methods of Barbarism?* 185.

26. *Times History,* 4:241–42.

27. Quoted in S. M. Miller, *Lord Methuen and the British Army,* 175.

28. Cd. 582.

29. Otto, *Konsentrasiekampe,* 7.

30. *Cape Argus,* 21 June 1900, quoted in Van Rensburg, "Ekonomiese Herstel," 156.

31. Trooper Tuffin, "Personal Diaries."

32. FSPA, CO 204.6164/03B: Report by S. Cole Bowen, 25 Aug. 1903.

33. Hobhouse, *Boer War Letters,* 31 Jan. 1901, 53.

34. Krebs, *Gender, Race, and the Writing of Empire,* 59; S. B. Spies, *Methods of Barbarism?* 261.

35. *Huisgenoot,* 25 Feb. 1938, in *Veg en Vlug,* 131–43 and Raath, *Boerevrou,* 1:154–55; NASA, CJC 690.113; Albertse, "Seun, Hond," 11–13.

36. Wessels and Wessels, *Nageslag,* 1:85.

37. Diary of R. B. Pott, in *Witnesses to War,* 86–87; Kestell, *Met die Boere-Kommando's,* 166.

38. "Camps of Refuge," House of Commons debate, 25 Feb. 1901.

39. WMBR, 6214/1: De Jager, "Herinneringe," [50, 41, 43].

40. Van Heyningen, "British Doctors," 188–89.
41. WMBR, 6214/1: De Jager, "Herinneringe," [41], translated.
42. Bradford, "Gentlemen and Boers," 40–44.
43. Madsen, "Canadian Troops," 55; Pretorius, "Caught up," 52 and 52n.
44. Stakhovitch and Gurko, "Dépeches," 166.
45. NASA, CJC 714.828; Marquard, *Letters,* Appendix, 135–36.
46. Bannerman, "Manliness," 5.
47. T. Jackson, *Boer War*, 131.
48. Gibbs, "Chaplain in the Boer War." Eustace Hill was conspicuous for his courage and lost an arm and gained a Military Cross in the First World War.
49. C. Miller, *Painting the Map Red*, 278.
50. Wilcox, "Australia's Boer War," 2.
51. Marais, *Vrou in die Anglo-Boereoorlog*, 140.
52. Madsen, "Canadian Troops," 56.
53. Phillipps, *With Rimington,* 201.
54. Pine-Coffin, *One Man's Boer War,* 8 Aug. 1900, 108.
55. Cd. 426, no. 26, 14 and no. 31, 17–18; Otto, *Konsentrasiekampe,* 19.
56. Pine-Coffin, *One Man's Boer War,* 26 Oct.1900, 156; S. B. Spies, *Methods of Barbarism?* 119–20; Hobhouse, *Brunt of the War*, 17.
57. Pine-Coffin, *One Man's Boer War,* 1 Nov. 1900, 160.
58. Marquard, *Letters,* 17 Oct. 1900, 106–108.
59. Protest of Boer Officers, 22 Oct. 1900, in Hobhouse, *Brunt of the War,* 43–44.
60. NASA, CJC 1682.346.
61. NASA, CJC 691.144.
62. NASA, CJC 1717.1847.
63. Colvile, *Work of the Ninth Division*, 136–38.
64. NASA, CJC 692.159; 687.161.
65. NASA, CJC 687.71; 1682.343.
66. NASA, CJC 689.92; 692.164.
67. Phillipps, *With Rimington,* Letter 25, 23 Dec. 1900, 213.
68. Cf. Townshend, *Oxford History of Modern War*, 177–83.
69. Kitchener quoted in Nasson, *South African War*, 218.
70. See, for example, NASA, CJC 690.113; 1710.1529; 702.381; CJC 2514.354; 2514.656.
71. Roberts Papers NAUK 48, WO 105/20, T40/30, quoted in S. B. Spies, *Methods of Barbarism?* 122.
72. Phillipps, *With Rimington,* quoted in T. Jackson, *Boer War,* 130.
73. Raath, *British Concentration Camps*, 88–89.
74. Kestell, *Met die Boere-Kommando's*, 171.
75. Rijksen-Van Helsdingen, *Vrouweleed,* 49–50, 76.
76. *Witnesses to War*, 67; Pretorius, "Fate of the Boer Women and Children," 39.
77. Pretorius, "Fate of the Boer Women and Children," 40; NASA, CJC 696.239; C.C.J. Badenhorst, *Uit den Boeren-Oorlog,* 129–31.

78. NASA, CJC 1703.1250; 1706.1387.
79. Pine-Coffin, *One Man's Boer War,* 26 Nov. 1900, 174.
80. NASA, CJC 705.485.
81. Brink, *Ceylon en de Bannelingen*, 147; NASA, CJC 705.485.
82. Marquard, *Letters,* 18 July 1900, 97.
83. S. M. Miller, "Duty or Crime," 322.
84. Marais, *Vrou in die Anglo-Boereoorlog*, 39, with reference to Frederick Tucker, *Private Tucker's Boer War Diary*.
85. S. M. Miller, "Duty or Crime," 322.
86. FSPA, A 69.1. See also Coetzer, *Fire in the Sky,* 227.
87. Rijksen-Van Helsdingen, *Vrouweleed,* 68.
88. Phillipps, *With Rimington*, quoted in Lee, *To the Bitter End*, 165.
89. Marquard, *Letters*, 107–108.
90. Hobhouse, *Brunt of the War,* 60; WMBR, 6214/1: De Jager, "Herinneringe," [24]; Hobhouse, *Brunt of the War,* 255.
91. Du Toit, *Diary*, 47.
92. Hobhouse, *Brunt of the War*, 60; Otto, *Konsentrasiekampe,* 55; J. Grobler, "Haat, Vrees, Afsku," 36; Serfontein, *Deurloop,* 21.
93. Brink, *Ceylon en de Bannelingen*, 137–40.
94. *Witnesses to War*, 87.
95. Nasson, *South African War*, 223.
96. Neethling, *Should We Forget?* 5–6.
97. Hobhouse, *Brunt of the War*, 254; J.A.J. de Villiers, "Diaries and Recollections," 8 and 9 May 1901, 57.
98. S. B. Spies, *Methods of Barbarism?* 257.
99. *Stemme uit die Verlede*, 12, 83, 128; WMBR, 5108/1: "Herinneringe van mev. H. M. Potgieter."
100. Stanley and Dampier, "Cultural Entrepreneurs," 508.
101. Schreiner, *Woman and Labour,* 48–49; Swanwick quoted in Bourke, *Intimate History*, 312.
102. Nasson, *South African War*, 257–58.
103. A. Badenhorst, *Tant' Alie of Transvaal,* 24 Jan. 1900, 114. Hobhouse's archaic translation is updated somewhat.
104. WMBR 6032: "Diary of Elsa Leviseur," 13 March 1900, 79.
105. Nasson, *South African War*, 255.
106. Bradford, "Gentlemen and Boers," 49; A. Badenhorst, *Tant' Alie of Transvaal*, 131.
107. Marquard, *Letters,* 8 Nov. 1900, 114; De Wet quoted in Van Schoor, *Christiaan Rudolph de Wet,* 158; Hintrager, "Dagboek," 139.

Chapter 5. In Captivity

1. NASA, W19/2: Van den Heever, "Herinneringe."
2. WMBR, 6214/1: De Jager, "Herinneringe," [33 and 29].

3. NASA, W 19/2: Van den Heever, "Herinneringe."

4. FSPA, SRC 14.5385; 14.5263; SRC 36.A611; 38.A936; 40.A1153; 21.8040; 40.1153.

5. FSPA SRC 36.A611; 38.A936; 40.A1153; 21.8040.

6. FSPA, SRC 41.1322.

7. FSPA, SRC 23.8298; 23.8301; 31.10543; 47.2448.

8. Van Heyningen, "Women and Gender," 95–96; WMBR, 6214/1: De Jager, "Herinneringe," [37].

9. Van Heyningen, "Women and Gender," 95–96.

10. Cd. 893, 7.

11. Van Heyningen, *Concentration Camps of the Anglo-Boer War*, 258, 215–16.

12. FSPA, SRC 23.8378.

13. Riedi, "Teaching Empire," 1,316.

14. Van Heyningen, "Women and Gender," 97–98.

15. FSPA, SRC 41.1359; 43.A1805.

16. Barry, *Ons Japie*, 21 Aug. 1902, 105; FSPA, SRC 12.4454; 14.5385; A 119.89: Letter from Mrs. A. C. Meyer.

17. NASA, A 2030.110; FSPA, SRC 21.RC7976: Inspector of Works' Report, 15 Feb. 1902.

18. Cd. 893, 85.

19. NASA, A 2030.46; WMBR, 5591/2: "Wel en Wee," 3, translated; WMBR, 6214/1: De Jager, "Herinneringe," [64], [53], [63].

20. Van Heyningen, "Women and Gender," 95.

21. Kirchner, "Kampdagboek," 29 Sept., 19 and 28 Oct., 6 and 30 Dec. 1901; NASA, GOV 276.20, Refugee Camps: ORC Reports.

22. J. Bosman, "Boervrou Looi Hensopper," 130–32; Burger, "Luistervink," 200.

23. FSPA, A 119.89: Letter from Mrs. A. C. Meyer.

24. FSPA, SRC 20.7581: Report of Inspector of Refugee Camps, 19 Feb. 1902; SRC 20.7581; Kirchner, "Kampdagboek," 25, 26, 28.

25. FSPA, SRC 20.7581, 19 Feb. 1902; Searle, *History of the Development of Nursing*, 211; Brink, *Ceylon en de Bannelingen*, 137–40; FSPA, SRC 18.7064; Kirchner, "Kampdagboek," 34, translated.

26. FSPA, SRC 3.666 and 533; 20.7581: Report of the Inspector of Refugee Camps, 19 Feb. 1902.

27. FSPA, SRC 14.5436; 23.8400; 20.7563.

28. Connell, *Gender and Power*, 79; T. W. Hime, quoted in Raath, *British Concentration Camps*, 192.

29. Dr. T. N. Leslie, quoted in Farwell, *Great Anglo-Boer War*, 398.

30. Chamberlain to Milner, 31 Oct. 1901, and Milner to Chamberlain, 15 Nov. 1901, quoted in S. B. Spies, *Methods of Barbarism?* 256–57, 259; Cd. 893, 20; Cd. 903, 135.

31. Quoted in S. B. Spies, *Methods of Barbarism?* 258–59.

32. FSPA, SRC 19.7445.

33. Kirchner, "Kampdagboek," 25 and 27 Jan. 1902, 33, translated.

34. Van Heyningen, "British Concentration Camps . . . Winburg."

35. FSPA, SRC 90, 171 (no. 4), 171 (no. 3), 15, 73, 172, 147, and 19. Elizabeth du Buisson's attitude can be gauged from the fact that she "berated" the British who found her hiding in the mountains (*Witnesses to War*, 86–87) and, after the war, boldly accused one of De Wet's favorite officers of having been in British employ.

36. FSPA, SRC 6.1552; 6.1614; 13.4797; 42.A1522.

37. Hobhouse, *Brunt of the War*, 253; FSPA, CO 417.350: Report on Burgher Camp, 9; SRC 42.A1568; 42.A1585; CO 251.558/04.

38. Searle, *Development of Nursing*, 216–18.

39. FSPA, SRC 12.4454; 12.4503; 12.4454; 12.4538.

40. FSPA, SRC 13.4749.

41. With diarrhea/dysentery at 13 percent, enteric 9 percent, and whooping cough 3 percent. See Low-Beer et al., "Disease and Death," 235, 225.

42. Low-Beer et al., "Disease and Death," 237–38, 241; Van Heyningen, "British Doctors versus Boer Women," 179–81.

43. FSPA, SRC 6.RC1796: Monthly Report: Winburg Refugee Camp; Cd. 819: Report of Dr. Henry Becker (with reference to the Bloemfontein camp), 94; FSPA, SRC 12.4454: Medical report, 3–4; SRC 13.4052.

44. FSPA, SRC 19.7444; 19.7442; 20.7581: Report of Inspector of Refugee Camps.

45. FSPA, SRC 13.5042; CO 417.350: Report on Burgher Camp at Winburg, 8.

46. Searle, *Development of Nursing*, 213.

47. Kessler, "Black Concentration Camps," 331–34.

48. For example, FSPA, SRC 12.RC4454: Medical Report and L. W. Graham-Clarke's response.

49. Krebs, *Gender, Race, and the Writing of Empire*, 75–76.

50. WMBR, 5301/5: Dagboek van J. J. de Klerk.

51. For example, WMBR, 5301/5; WMBR, 6214/1: De Jager, "Herinneringe," [35, 45]; FSPA, SRC 14.5385 and 5436; Ladies Commission (Cd. 893, 83): "perhaps *the* question of the camp."

52. FSPA, SRC 3.533.

53. Van Heyningen, "British Doctors versus Boer Women," 178; "Women and Gender," 99–100.

54. Leviseur, *Memories*, 101.

55. See Strange, "She cried a very little," 146–47.

56. Stanley, *Mourning Becomes*, 154.

57. WMBR, 6214/1: De Jager, "Herinneringe," [50]; NASA, W 19/2: "Herinneringe van mev. Van den Heever."

58. Hirsch, *Family Frames*, 22, quoted in J. Jansen, *Knowledge in the Blood*, 67.

59. WMBR, 5301/5: "Dagboek van J. J. de Klerk"; Hobhouse, *Brunt of the War*, 253.

60. For example, *Stemme uit die Verlede*, 33, 63, 64, 87, 119, 145.

61. Nasson, *South African War*, 223.

62. Stanley and Dampier, "Aftermaths," 91–92.

63. Quoted in Raath, *British Concentration Camps,* 201.

64. ADL, *Woman's Endurance,* 24, 25 and 30 Aug. 1901, 5, 9, 14 (and passim).

65. Van Heyningen, Review of *Woman's Endurance,* 215.

66. Armstrong, *Camp Diary,* 110.

67. Cd. 608, 694, 939, 942, 1161, 330, collated with Coetzer, *Fire in the Sky,* 329.

68. NASA, FK 617, vol. 1.

69. Venter, "Geskiedenis van Winburg," 191–92.

70. FSPA, CO 204.6164.03B.

71. For example, Stanley and Dampier, "Cultural Entrepreneurs," 501–13; Stanley and Dampier, "Simulacrum Diaries," 25–52.

72. See Van Heyningen, "Daily Life," 92–119.

73. C. Schoeman, *Vegter en Balling*, 66; WMBR, 3465/1: Letter from J. J. de Klerk.

74. FSPA, SRC 12.4475, with attached Lines of Communication Order (of Lt. Gen. C. Tucker), No. 296.

75. NASA, A 2030.45: Report on the Burgher Camp, 11.

76. FSPA, SRC 103: Register of Births out of Wedlock, 26, 32, 37.

77. Kirchner, "Kampdagboek," 15.

78. Stanley, *Mourning Becomes*, 163.

79. Thus Mrs. A. C. Meyer of Bloemfontein; FSPA, A 119.89.

80. Cd. 893, 86; FSPA, SRC 15.5998; NASA, FK 1048, 46–50 (CO 224/7, vol. 1.4537), Goold-Adams to High Commissioner, Jan. 1902.

81. Serfontein, *Deurloop,* 21, translated; Van Heyningen, *Concentration Camps of the Anglo-Boer War,* 203; FSPA, SRC 21.RC8040.

82. FSPA, SRC 12.4509; Cd. 981.

83. Kirchner, "Kampdagboek," 2 Nov. 1901, 25.

84. FSPA, SRC 15.5998: Report of Superintendent Alexander, 16 Nov. 1901.

85. J. Wessels, "Ryswater."

86. Cd. 903 and Cd. 853.

87. FSPA, SRC 23.8400.

88. Van Heyningen, *Concentration Camps of the Anglo-Boer War,* 8.

89. FSPA, SRC 23.8308 and 23.8424.

90. F. J. G. van der Merwe, *Sport en Spel*, 87.

91. Brink, *Ceylon en de Bannelingen,* 127, translated.

92. F.J.G. van der Merwe, *Sport en Spel,* 87; Brink, *Ceylon en de Bannelingen*, 156; Van Niekerk, "Dagboek," 7–8.

93. Brohier, "Boer Prisoner," [4]; Van Niekerk, "Dagboek," 21 Aug., 19 Dec., 10 Nov. 1901, 137, 148, 146; Royle, "St. Helena," 63; "Ahmednagarfort," 22.

94. Farwell, *Great Anglo-Boer War*, 421; Groenewald, *Bannelinge,* 58–62.

95. R. de Villiers, "Dagboek," 3, 7 Dec. 1901, 38–39; C. Schoeman, *Vegter en Balling*, 55.

96. FSPA, SRC 19.RC7383: Captain H. L. Reid to Chief Superintendent Refugee Camps, 27 Jan. 1902.

97. J.A.J. de Villiers, "Diaries and Recollections," 3 March 1901, 55; NASA, CJC 407.423; SO/POW 14.PR/A1201/01; FSPA, CO 7.456.

98. J.A.J. de Villiers, "Diaries and Recollections," 45; R. de Villiers, "Dagboek," 23 Dec. 1901, 46; Schikkerling, *Commando Courageous*, 177; Van Niekerk, "Dagboek," 31 Oct. 1900, 98.

99. See A. Grundlingh, *Dynamics of Treason*, 128; Van Niekerk, "Dagboek," 1 July 1900, 31 Oct. 1900, 69, 97–8.

100. J.A.J. de Villiers, "Diaries and Recollections," 2 Feb. 1901, 49; Marquard, *Letters*, 20 Nov. 1900, 116–17.

101. C. Schoeman, *Vegter en Balling*, 96.

102. NASA, CJC 699.305; Solomon, "Hands-Uppers;" NASA, PMO 54.375: Governor of St Helena to Lord Milner, 22 Feb. 1902.

103. NASA, CJC 1697.1030.

104. Van Niekerk, "Dagboek," 20 Aug. 1900, 86–87; 101, 110, 124.

Chapter 6. White Man's War

1. Van Aswegen, "Verhouding," 323.

2. Tosh, *Pursuit of History*, 9, 289.

3. In "Paternalism, Patriarchy and Afrikaans," 42–43, Robert Ross rejects this application of the concept of quasi-kinship.

4. Genovese, *Roll, Jordan, Roll*, 5.

5. For background on this subaltern society, see Delius and Trapido, "Inboekselings and Oorlams," 53–88.

6. Cf. J. Grobler, "Haat, Vrees, Afsku," 31–44.

7. Raal, *Met die Boere*, 7–9.

8. WMBR, 6214/1: De Jager, "Herinneringe," [7, 11, 21, 55–56].

9. Izedinova, *Few Months*, 89; Hintrager, "Dagboek," 118.

10. Tabitha Jackson, *Boer War*, 167.

11. Photograph C 1310.08; cf. A. Malan, *Oorwinning sonder Roem*, 229, quoting Weeber, *Op die Transvaalse Front*, 245; Pine-Coffin, *One Man's Boer War*, 15 and 16 Aug. 1900, 114, 116.

12. Grenadier Guards Archives, AGG/Boer War, Diary of Lt. E. G. Spencer Churchill, 30 June 1902, quoted by Nasson, "Africans at War," 137.

13. Izedinova, *Few Months*, 88.

14. Nasson, *Abraham Esau's War*, 99.

15. See, for example, Labuschagne, *Ghost Riders*, 39, 46, 52.

16. NASA, CJC 688.78.

17. NASA, CJC 703.398.

18. Pretorius, *Life on Commando*, 294.

19. Ibid., 285.

20. Hales, *Campaign Pictures*, 9.

21. A. Scholtz, "Brit Verewig Meisie," 24; Nasson, *Uyadela Wen'osulapho*, 9.

22. Siwundhla, "White Ideologies," 232–33; Warwick, *Black People and the South African War*, 26; Nasson, *Uyadela Wen'osulapho*, 11.

23. Setiloane, "Swart en Bruin Mense," 171, translated.

24. Scott, *Scotte*, 13, translated.

25. Denoon, "Participation," 110.

26. J. Grobler, "Haat, Vrees, Afsku," 37; J.A.J. de Villiers, "Diaries and Recollections," 48; Van Niekerk, "Dagboek," 39.

27. Nasson, *Uyadela Wen'osulapho,* 45; A. Wessels, *Militêre Rol,* 18.

28. Warwick, *Black People,* 25; A. Wessels, *Militêre Rol,* 18.

29. Nasson, *South African War,* 283, 221; S. B. Spies, *Methods of Barbarism?* 279.

30. Warwick, *Black People,* 16.

31. A. Wessels, *Militêre Rol,* 18.

32. Warwick, *Black People,* 194.

33. Siwundhla, "White Ideologies," 225–26.

34. Krikler, *Revolution from Above, Rebellion from Below.*

35. Le Roux, "Verhouding," 11; FSPA, CO 93.3388, Report on South African Constabulary, 22 Aug. 1902; Kessler, "Black Concentration Camps," 381; FSPA, CO 74.1874: Resident Magistrate, Winburg to ORC Colonial Secretary, 20 June 1902. See, for example, FSPA, CO 68.1347: Letters from Carl Schwartz, 10 May 1902, and M. C. Terblanche, 14 May 1902; and DLS 29.2105: Letters from George B. Plumtre and K. P. Apthorp, 21 Oct. 1903.

36. Kessler, "Black Concentration Camps," 419.

37. Krikler, *Revolution from Above,* 2–3.

38. J. M. Jackson, "Charlotte Makgoma Manye Maxeke," 75.

39. Kearney, *Representing Dissension,* chapter 1.

40. Campbell, *Songs of Zion;* Odendaal, *Founders,* 201; Keegan, *Facing the Storm,* 22.

41. FSPA, GS 2113.8699, translated.

42. Van der Spuy, "Profiel," 121; FSPA, GS 2160.R262; Odendaal, *Founders,* 170; Britz, "Life and Times of Christof Sandrock," 239; FSPA CO 150.1726, 1727, 1728; 198.5748; 49.4482; Campbell, *Songs of Zion,*166, 172, 174–76.

43. Odendaal, *Founders,* 170; FSPA, CO 100.3863/03: Note from Commissioner of Police to Colonial Secretary.

44. NASA, FK 1905 (WO 1019): Gen. C. R. de Wet to Gen. W. G. Knox, 6 Oct. 1900; FSPA, A 119.15: Letter from M. H. Wessels, 18 March 1949.

45. *Times History,* 5:393; De Wet, *Three Years' War,* 274; Gibson, *Story of the Imperial Light Horse,* 239.

46. FSPA, A 119. 418: Letter from H. Mostert, 28 Nov. 1951.

47. WMBR, 5591/2: "Wel en Wee."

48. FSPA, A 119.15: Letter from M. H. Wessels; Van der Walt, "Oorlogsdagboek," 126.

49. M. J. Grobler, *Met die Vrystaters,* 68–69; FSPA, A 119.15: Letter from M. H. Wessels; NASA, FK 1905 (WO 1019.C5094).

50. M. J. Grobler, *Met die Vrystaters,* 69, translated.

51. "Ouma se Stories"; Serfontein, *Keurskrif,* 194.

52. FSPA, MHG 28671.

53. For example, Hobhouse, *War without Glamour,* 51; Marquard, *Letters,* 109; Merriman, *Selections,* Merriman to James Bryce, 21 July 1902, III, 354.

54. Cf. Nasson, *Abraham Esau's War*, 61.

55. S. Wilson, *South African Memories*, 61.

56. NASA, CJC 1710.1529; 1711.1572; 1716.1763; 1702.1215; T. Jackson, *Boer War*, 137; FSPA, A 69.

57. Raath, *Boerevrou*, 1:131.

58. FSPA, A 69: Sworn statement, 26 Feb. 1902; Kestell, *Met die Boere-Kommando's*, 202.

59. Ngcongco, "Problems of Southern African Historiography," 17.

60. Munslow, *Deconstructing History*, 12–13.

61. FSPA, A 119.1060: Marx, "Vryheidsoorlog Herinneringe," [11].

62. Kirchner, "Kampdagboek," 11 Sept. 1901, 20.

63. Johanna van Warmelo, referred to in J. Grobler, "Haat, Vrees, Afsku," 38.

64. FSPA, A 119.89: Mrs. A. C. Meyer; Sworn statement, 17 March 1902, in C.C.J. Badenhorst, *Uit den Boeren-Oorlog*, 130–31.

65. FSPA, A 119.1060: Marx, "Vryheidsoorlog Herinneringe," [11].

66. What follows is based on Scott, *Scotte*, 12ff.

67. WMBR, 6166/1: "Herinnering van Wessel Scott se Voorouers."

68. Quoted by Grundlingh, *Dynamics of Treason*, 238.

69. FSPA, A 119.1060: Marx, "Vryheidsoorlog Herinneringe," [23].

70. By De Wet and Nierstrasz; confirmed by the evidence of G.J.S. van den Heever, who saw the bodies, in FSPA, A 119:1099: "Herinneringe," 60–62; Venter, "Geskiedenis van Winburg," 180.

71. G. D. Scholtz, *Geskiedenis van Ventersburg*, 22, translated.

72. Barry, *Ons Japie*, 30 Aug. 1901, 67.

73. FSPA, A 119.419: D. W. Botha, "Geval by Doornberg," translated.

74. Raath, *Boerevrou*, 1:131–34.; FSPA, A 119:75: Letter from Mrs. S. Venter.

75. Van der Bank, *Burgermonumente*, 78.

76. FSPA, A 119.1060: Marx, "Vryheidsoorlog Herinneringe," [23]; NASA, RS 13,191.

77. FSPA, A 119.1060: Marx, "Vryheidsoorlog Herinneringe," [38]ff.

78. C.C.J. Badenhorst, *Uit den Boeren-Oorlog*, 132.

79. Van der Walt, "Oorlogsdagboek," 141, translated.

80. FSPA, A 119.1060: Marx: "Vryheidsoorlog Herinneringe," [45].

81. Le Roux, "Verhouding," 11.

82. Hintrager, "Dagboek," 26 Aug. 1900, 118; De Wet, *Three Years' War*, 345.

83. Van Warmelo, *On Commando*, 10.

84. Cd. 821, 5. See also NASA, FK 1849.

85. WMBR, 5107/1: "Herinnering van H. L. Claasen"; Pretorius, *Life on Commando*, 273.

86. Warwick, *Black People*, 23; McDonald, *Terugblik*, 49.

87. NASA, FK 1831, WO 5094.

88. Mohlamme, "Black People in the Boer Republics," 85.

89. Warwick, *Black People*, 158; FSPA, SRC 49.1695.

90. Kessler, "Black and Coloured Concentration Camps," 139.

91. Kessler, "Black Concentration Camps," 121, 138, 140.

92. Transvaal Administration Reports for 1902, quoted in Mohlamme, "Black People in the Boer Republics," 87.

93. FSPA, SRC 12.4437, 26 Aug. 1901.

94. Van Heyningen, "British Concentration Camps . . . Winburg."

95. FSPA, SRC 20.8281, 1 May 1902; WMBR, 6214/1; Kirchner, "Kampdagboek," 5; WMBR, 6214/1: De Jager, "Herinneringe," [35–36], [55–56].

96. Mongalo and Du Pisani, "Victims of a White Man's War," 155; S. B. Spies, *Methods of Barbarism?* 230.

97. Mongalo and Du Pisani, "Victims," 149.

98. NASA, SNA 20, NA 519/02: Report on the Native Refugee Department in the ORC, 116–18.

99. FSPA, ORC 309: *Government Gazette* 118, 4 July 1902; CO 78.2150/02: Report of the Superintendent of the Native Refugee Department, April 1902. The population figures (for Nov. 1901) are from FSPA, CO 52.15/02.

100. Mohlamme, "African Refugee Camps," 112–19; Kessler, "Black Concentration Camps," 148–49, 159, 168, 170, 173.

101. Kessler, "Black Concentration Camps," 179; NASA, SNA 20, 115.

102. NASA, SNA 20, 114–15; and 20, 127.

103. Mohlamme, "Black People in the Boer Republics," 99.

104. Warwick, *Black People*, 137–40.

105. CO 48.2150/02, quoted by Mongalo and Du Pisani, "Victims," 158.

106. NASA, SNA 20, 120.

107. FSPA, CO 52.15/02.

108. Mongalo and Du Pisani, "Victims," 160–61.

109. Mohlamme, "African Refugee Camps," 113; FSPA, CO 30.2758/01; Kessler, "Black Concentration Camps," 123.

110. Odendaal, *Vukani Bantu!* 69

111. Kessler, "Black Concentration Camps," 173, 185–86, 211–14.

112. FSPA, CO 74.4283: Marome and Oliphant to Goold-Adams, 23 Nov. 1901; CO 74.4283: Resident Magistrate, Kroonstad, to ORC Colonial Secretary, 27 Dec. 1901.

113. FSPA, CO 52.29/02; CO 78.2150/02, in Mongalo and Du Pisani, "Victims," 163.

114. Matsetela, "Life Story of Nkgomo Mma Pooe," 220.

115. Cf. Van Heyningen, "British Doctors versus Boer Women," 188.

116. FSPA, CO 50.2976/01: Report of MOH, G. Pratt Yule, 17 Aug. 1901.

117. Mohlamme, "African Refugee Camps," 120.

118. FSPA, CO 57.586/02: NRD Returns for Jan. 1902, and Ploeger, *Lotgevalle* V, 43:40, quoted in Mongalo and Du Pisani, "Victims," 168.

119. FSPA, CO 52.15/02.

120. Kessler, "Black Concentration Camps," 376; FSPA, CO 50.29/02: Native Refugee Camp Returns for November.

121. NASA, SNA 20, 120–21.

122. Kessler, "Black Concentration Camps," 247.

123. Ibid., 241, 294; C. J. de Villiers, *Helpers, Healers,* 1:102–117.

124. Kessler, "Black Concentration Camps," iii.

125. Plaatje, *Mafeking Diary*, 23.

126. Plaatje, *Selected Writings*, 399.

127. Le Roux, "Verhouding," 10.

128. E. Jansen, "Ek ook het besluit," 8.

129. T. Jackson, *Boer War*, 184–86.

130. Molema, *Bantu Past and Present*, 292.

Chapter 7. The Aftermath of War

1. Brits and Spies, "New South Africa," 224.

2. Beak, *Aftermath of War*, 142–43; Richardson, *Selected Correspondence*, 13 Oct. 1903, 128.

3. Quoted in Barnard, "Afrikaner en die Naweë," 128.

4. Beak, *Aftermath of War*, 153; Richardson, *Selected Correspondence*, 13 Oct. 1903, 128; Van Rensburg, "Ekonomiese Herstel," 306; *Times History,* 5:129.

5. Van Rensburg, "Ekonomiese Herstel," 312; WMBR, 6214/1: De Jager, "Herinneringe," [71–73].

6. FSPA, CO 143.1202/03: Resident Magistrate's Report, 19 Feb.1903.

7. Hobhouse, *Boer War Letters,* 30 Sept. 1903, 297.

8. Keegan, "Restructuring," 239 and 239n; Bottomley, "Orange Free State and the Rebellion," 37.

9. J.A.J. de Villiers, "Diaries and Recollections," 18 May 1901, 58; FSPA, SRC 12.RC4586: Permit, 17 Sept. 1901; Hollenbach, *Briewe,* Letter from Meintjies to De Witt Hamer, 30 May 1901, 281–82.

10. Beak, *Aftermath of War*, 193; FSPA, CO 38.3626, 30 Sept. 1901.

11. FSPA, CO 76.2028/02; Van Rensburg, "Ekonomiese Herstel," 297; CO 93.3388/02: Report of the SAC, 22 Aug. 1902.

12. FSPA, CO 83. 2569/02: Report of Magistrate, 17 July 1902; CO 107.4459/03: Complaint, 13 Oct. 1902

13. Richardson, *Selected Correspondence*, 15 Oct. 1902, 42; NASA, CJC 1697.1030; 707.542.

14. Giliomee, "Beginnings of Afrikaner Ethnic Consciousness," 39; Brits and Spies, "New South Africa," 225.

15. According to FSPA, CO 214.6164B, 165 out of 1,260; thus 13 percent.

16. FSPA, NAB 2.6: F.A.S. Schimper to Thomson, 1 Aug. 1905.

17. NASA, GOV 688.17: Leggett to Milner, 1 July 1904.

18. FSPA, GRD 8.164/02: Telegram Maj. Leggett to Maj. McLaughlin, Repatriation Board, Bloemfontein.

19. FSPA, CO 121.5663; Cd. 1551, 61; *Times History,* 5:54.

20. FSPA, DLS 8.A957: Blakemore to Apthorp.

21. Milner, "Letters," 19 Aug. 1902, 139.

22. Brits and Spies, "New South Africa," 226.

23. Hobhouse, *Boer War Letters*, 6 July 1903, 225.

24. WMBR, 5583: Letter, 8 May 1903.

25. Milner, *Milner Papers*, 2:375.

26. Beak, *Aftermath*, 187–89; Cd. 1551, 8.

27. Cd. 1551, 92–93; Richardson, *Selected Correspondence*, 18 Oct. 1903, 133.

28. Richardson, *Selected Correspondence*, 14 and 18 Oct. 1903, 130 and 134n; Hobhouse, *Boer War Letters*, undated, 215.

29. UW: Bottomley, "Political Resurgence," 7–8.

30. See, for example, Hobhouse, *Boer War Letters*, Letter 73, 2 Aug. 1903, 250–58.

31. Van Reenen, *Emily Hobhouse*, 100.

32. Van Rensburg, "Ekonomiese Herstel," 250.

33. Cd. 1551, 14.

34. FSPA, CO 187.4802: Resident Magistrate Bethlehem to Lieutenant Governor, 30 June 1903.

35. Hobhouse, *Boer War Letters*, 21 July 1903, 238.

36. Van Rensburg, "Ekonomiese Herstel," 240; Cd. 1551.

37. NASA, TKP 186, 46.

38. Van Rensburg, "Ekonomiese Herstel," 250–53.

39. Hobhouse, *Boer War Letters*, 21 July 1903, 238.

40. C. J. De Villiers, *Helpers, Healers*, 2:183; Marquard, *Letters*, 10 March, 4 April, and 17 June 1900, 61, 67, 89.

41. Gräbe, "Writing between the Lines," 53.

42. NASA, CJC 685.22; WMBR, 6214/1: De Jager, "Herinneringe," [53]; NASA, CJC 1703.1254; 705.473; 706.530.

43. Ludorf to Green, 5 April 1901, in National Library of Ireland, MS 10.465 (4), quoted by Royle, "St. Helena," 62.

44. Van Niekerk, "Dagboek," 29 May 1900, 66.

45. Alice Stopford Green's Journal, 28 Sept. 1900, quoted in Royle, "St. Helena," 62; Van Niekerk, "Dagboek," 29 May 1900, 66; NASA, SO/POW 71.

46. Farwell, *Great Anglo-Boer War*, 367; Madsen, "Canadian Troops," 50; C. Miller, *Painting the Map Red*, 278–79.

47. Higginson, "Hell in Small Places," 107.

48. F. H. Randal, "A Year in a Boer School," *Canadian Magazine* 12 (1904), 417, quoted by Riedi, "Teaching Empire," 1,340.

49. Lebow, *Politics of Memory*, 26–27.

50. De Reuck, "Politics of Blood," 144.

51. Stanley and Dampier, "Cultural Entrepreneurs," 512.

52. Ibid., 515.

53. W. J. Leyds in a letter to H. C. Bredell, 7 Sept. 1906, quoted in Ken Smith, *Changing Past*, 63.

54. Cf. Hofmeyr, "Building a Nation," 99–105.

55. Breytenbach, *Betekenis*, 69.

56. Van Rensburg, "Ekonomiese Herstel," 189.

57. Thus Steyn; cf. Le May, *British Supremacy,* 136; S. B. Spies, *Methods of Barbarism?* 282.

58. Van den Heever, *General J.B.M. Hertzog,* 148; Steyn quoted in Weber, *Eighteen Months*, 221.

59. Barry, *Ons Japie*, 22 July 1902, 62.

60. WMBR, 1676/4: Correspondence, translated.

61. NASA, CJC 573.49.

62. Schulenburg, *August Carl Schulenburg,* 65, translated.

63. C. Schoeman, *Boer Boy,*166–67. The resident magistrate's comment on his claim for compensation was that it was not certain that he had ever taken up arms; see NASA, CJC 1712.1610.

64. P. Grobbelaar, "Oorlog 1," 62.

65. J. J. Oberholster, *Nederduitse Gereformeerde Kerk,* 119.

66. Richardson, *Selected Correspondence,* 24 Oct. 1902, 57.

67. Hobhouse, *Boer War Letters*, undated, 212.

68. Le May, *British Supremacy,* 213–15.

69. Giliomee, *Afrikaners,* 268; *Acta Synodi*, quoted in J.A.S. Oberholster, *Gereformeerde Kerke,* 275.

70. Lawley to Milner 10 Dec. 1902, in Denoon, *Grand Illusion,* 81.

71. Bouwer, *Memoirs,* 126.

72. Richardson, *Selected Correspondence*, 12 Oct. 1902, 39; *De Fakkel,* 14 May 1903, quoted in G. A. van der Merwe, "Nederduitse Gereformeerde Kerk," 217; A. Grundlingh, *Dynamics of Treason*, 417.

73. DRCA, Notuleboek, Winburg, 2 Aug. 1903, 226–27.

74. NLCT, MSB 317:1 (7).

75. DRCA, Notuleboek, Winburg, 3 Sept. 1904, translated.

76. *Almanak voor de Nederduitsch Gereformeerde Kerk*, 106.

77. DRCA, Notulen Boek, Ventersburg, 28 Feb. 1903, translated.

78. Quoted in G. A. van der Merwe, "Nederduitse Gereformeerde Kerk," 237 and 217.

79. DRCA, Notuleboek, Winburg, 26 Nov. 1904, 189–92.

80. DRCA, Notuleboek, Winburg, 2 Aug. 1903; Ventersburg, 28 Feb. 1903; Senekal, 30 July 1904.

81. Lombard, *Uit die Dagboek,* 160, translated.

82. DRCA, Notulen Boek, Senekal, 6 Aug. 1904, 248, 251.

83. Engelenburg, *General Louis Botha*, 128; Le May, *British Supremacy,* 173–74.

84. Van Rensburg, "Ekonomiese Herstel," 195, 257.

85. A. Grundlingh, *Dynamics of Treason*, 461.

86. Pirow, *James Barry Munnik Hertzog*, 44.

87. Quoted in A. Grundlingh, *Dynamics of Treason*, 462.

88. UW: Bottomley, "Political Resurgence," 20–21.

89. Keegan, "Restructuring," 245–46.

90. Hyam and Henshaw, *The Lion and the Springbok*, 65–70.

91. Ibid., 72.

92. Meintjes, *President Steyn,* 165; Engelenburg, *General Louis Botha*, 215.

93. Swart, "Rebels of 1914," 71.

94. Ibid., 109.

95. Ibid., 97.

96. UG 42–1916, 313, quoted by Bottomley, "Orange Free State and the Rebellion," 32.

97. O'Connor, *The Africander Rebellion, South Africa Today*, 12, quoted in Swart, "Rebels of 1914," 111.

98. Swart, "Rebels of 1914," 46; cf. Giliomee, *Afrikaners,* 382.

99. Holtzhausen, "Nederduitse Gereformeerde Kerk . . . en die Rebellie," 55–67.

100. *De Kerkbode*, 11 Feb. 1915, quoted in Giliomee, *Afrikaners,* 385.

101. Hobhouse, *Boer War Letters,* 30 Sept. 1903, 295.

102. FSPA, CO 74.1818 and FSPA, GRD 6.50, 12 June 1902; CO 74.1874: Resident Magistrate to ORC Colonial Secretary, 20 June 1902.

103. BPL, *Friend,* 20 Oct. 1902.

104. Sheila Rowbotham, *Hidden from History: 300 Years of Women's Oppression and the Fight against It* (London: Pluto Books, 1973). The title of this feminist text seems equally apposite in this context.

105. NASA, CJC 2262.

106. NASA CJC 1910; CO 363.1594/05; CO 3744: List of Civil Claims, 12 Sept. 1902, No. 2217, 2628.

107. FSPA, CS 4796/02, 5 Nov. 1902; Van Rensburg, "Ekonomiese Herstel," 303; Beak, *Aftermath*, 161.

108. FSPA, CO 157.2308: Petition to H. E. the Lieut. Governor, Bloemfontein, received 30 March 1903; CO 115.5141.

109. FSPA, CO 68.1347: Letter from Carl Schwartz, 10 May 1902; Letter from M. C. Terblanche, 14 May 1902.

110. FSPA, CO 68.1347: Report from John Porter to Commissioner of Police, 23 May 1902.

111. FSPA, DLS 29.2105: Letter from George B. Plumptre; DLS 29.2105: Letter from K. P. Apthorp, 21 Oct. 1903; DLS 29.2105: Letter from Secretary, LSB, 16 Jan. 1904.

112. FSPA CO 357.9478/04.

113. Kessler, "Black Concentration Camps," 419; FSPA, CO 74.1818.

114. FSPA, CO 363.1594/05.

115. FSPA, CO 161. 2650.

116. Milner, quoted in Magubane, *Making of a Racist State,* 325.

117. Odendaal, *Vukani Bantu!* 55, 76.

118. "Josiah Tshangana Gumede."

119. Odendaal, *Vukani Bantu!* 156–58, 190; FSPA, CO 559: Minute 933/3, 18 Feb. 1909, 1; CO 559: Minute 993/6, 25 June 1909, 3.

Conclusion

1. Edelstein, "Occupational Hazards," 59.
2. Edelstein, *Occupational Hazards*, 4–7.
3. Richardson, *Selected Correspondence*, 29 Oct. and 9 Nov. 1902, 70, 87.
4. FSPA, 119.1060: Marx, "Vryheidsoorlog Herinneringe," [12–13] and [19–22].
5. Le May, *British Supremacy*, 3.
6. Brits and Spies, "New South Africa," 226.
7. Edelstein, "Occupational Hazards," 59.
8. The Middelburg Proposals, quoted in Kestell and Van Velden, *Vredesonderhandelinge*, 177.
9. Le May, *British Supremacy*, 158.
10. Quoted in Brits and Spies, "New South Africa," 228.
11. Le May, *British Supremacy*, 156.
12. FSPA, DLS 4.532, 12 March 1903.
13. Le Roux, "Grondtoekenning," 17 and 15; UW: Bottomley, "Political Resurgence," 8; BPL, *Friend,* 19 Nov. 1904.
14. Brits and Spies, "New South Africa," 226.
15. ASAI, EM, Adriani, 3 Oct. 1906, Gangel, April 1906, De Jager, 4 June 1906.
16. Bottomley, "Almost Bled to Death," 191.

Sources

Archival Material

NATIONAL ARCHIVES OF SOUTH AFRICA, PRETORIA

Accessions

A 230/2 "'n Vrystater op Kommando: synde die Oorlogservaringe van mnr J. C. Pretorius van Lindley, O.V.S., gedurende die jare 1899–1902"

A 1237 "Herinneringe van mnr Henning Olivier, seun van wyle gnl. J. Olivier" [1940]

A 2030 Research material used by J. Ploeger in writing *Lotgevalle van die Burgerlike Bevolking gedurende die Anglo-Boereoorlog*. Pretoria: Government Printer, 1990

W 19/2 P.H.S. van Zyl Collection: "Herinneringe van mev. Maria van den Heever"

Public Records

Archives of the Central Judicial Commission (CJC)

Archives of the Private Secretary of the Governor (GOV)

Archives of the High Commissioner for South Africa (HC)

Archives of the Military Governor, Pretoria (MGP)

Archives of the Master of the Supreme Court (MHG)

Archives of the Provost Marshal's Office (PMO)

Archives of the Official Concerned with the Recording of Casualties in the Republican Forces and among Civilians (RS)

Archives of the Secretary for Native Affairs (SNA)

Archives of the Staff Officer: Prisoners of War, Cape Town (SO/POW)

Published Records

Transvaal Blue Books (TKP): Vol. 186, Original Report of the Central Judicial Commission

Photocopies of War Office documents in the National Archives, London, and of the Milner Papers in the Bodleian Library, Oxford (FK)

FREE STATE PROVINCIAL ARCHIVES, BLOEMFONTEIN

Accessions

A 69 N. C. Havenga Collection
A 119 Renier Collection
15 Letter from M. H. (Tewie) Wessels, 18 March 1949
52 Letter from M. H. (Tewie) Wessels, 25 June 1949
85 Letter from Piet Beukes, 22 Oct. 1949
89 Letter from Mrs. A. C. Meyer, Bloemfontein, 24 Oct. 1949
418 Letter from H.C.J. Mostert, 28 Nov. 1951
419 D. W. Botha, "'n Geval by Doornberg" [1951]
1056 I. A. Meyer, "Die Ervaringe van 'n Veldkornet in die Engelse Oorlog, 1899–1902"
1060 P. J. Marx, "Vryheidsoorlog Herinneringe"
1099 "Herinneringe van G.J.S. van den Heever," 1 April 1944
1209 "Oorlogsondervindinge van Petrus Jacobus Albrecht Beukes, soos vertel aan H. N. Conradie," March 1961

Public Records

Archives of the Colonial Secretary, Orange River Colony (CO)
Archives of the Director of Land Settlement, Orange River Colony (DLS)
Archives of the Director of the ORC Government Relief Department (GRD)
Archives of the Government Secretary (GS)
Archives of the Master of the Supreme Court (MHG)
Archives of the Adviser of the Native Affairs Branch in the Office of the Colonial Secretary, Orange River Colony (NAB)
Archives of the Chief Superintendent of Refugee Camps (SRC)
Archives of the Volunteer Repatriation Organisation (VRO)

Published Records

ORC 305–307, 309 *Government Gazette of the Orange River Colony*
Pamphlet P730: "Lijst van Stemgerechtigde Burgers voor het District Winburg voor het Jaar 1899," a section of C. Borckenhagen, *Lijst van Stemgerechtigde Burgers OVS 1899*. Bloemfontein, s.a.

NATIONAL ARCHIVES OF THE UNITED KINGDOM, LONDON

War Office (WO) 105, Box 10
CinC 126/144, General Hunter's Despatch, 4 August 1900
CinC 126/163, Major General Bruce Hamilton's Despatch, 29 August 1900.

WAR MUSEUM OF THE BOER REPUBLICS, BLOEMFONTEIN

1676/4 J. C. Pretorius Collection: Correspondence
3465/4 C. R. Swart Collection: Letter from J. J. de Klerk
5107/1 "Herinnering: H. L. Claasen"
5108/1 "Herinnering van mev. H. M. Potgeiter"
5301/5 De Klerk Collection: "Dagboek van J. J. de Klerk"
5583/3 Paulusz Collection: Letter from Gilles van de Wall, 8 May 1903
5591/2 "Die Wel en Wee van die Cilliers Familie, soos vertel deur mev Everdina Cilliers, geb Prinsloo," 25 Nov. 1979
5957/1 "Dagboek van J.P.T. Theron"
6032 "Diary of Elsa Leviseur, 1899–1900"
6166/1 "Herinnering van Wessel Scott se Voorouers, insluitende die Skermutseling van Welgevonden"
6214/1 "Herinneringe van mev. M. A. de Jager" [1943]

ARCHIVES OF THE DUTCH REFORMED CHURCH IN THE FREE STATE, BLOEMFONTEIN

Notulen Boek van den Kerkeraad der N.G. Gemeente te Senekal O.V.S. 27 Nov. 1897 [1897–1911]
Notulen Boek der Ned Geref Gemeente Ventersburg, Boek No. 1 van Des. 1902 tot Nov. 1911
Notuleboek N. G. Kerk [Winburg] vanaf 2 Junie 1888–1 Julie 1911.

BLOEMFONTEIN PUBLIC LIBRARY

Microfilm R7: *Friend,* 2 April 1900 to 31 Dec. 1903; and R8, 10 Nov. 1904 to 31 Jan. 1905

NATIONAL LIBRARY, CAPE TOWN

Marquard Collection MSB 317: 1 (7) Protest against election of M Kritzinger and Jacobus Smith to Church Council, 1903–1904.

UNIVERSITY OF THE FREE STATE, AFRICANA STOCKDALE COLLECTION

"Diary of Betty Wessels, Winburg, 8th May 1900, to Lourenco Marques, 19th October 1900" (1901?); photocopy

UNIVERSITY OF THE WITWATERSRAND, AFRICANA LIBRARY

Bottomley, J. "Political Resurgence in the Orange River Colony and the Brandfort Congress of 1904." Unpublished paper delivered at the History Workshop "The Making of Class," University of the Witwatersrand, Johannesburg, 9–14 Feb. 1987

ARCHIVES OF THE SOUTH AFRICAN INSTITUTE, AMSTERDAM

H. J. Emous Collection, EM 7 and 8

Official Publications

PARLIAMENTARY PAPERS PUBLISHED BY COMMAND OF THE GOVERNMENT

Cd. 261 *Further Correspondence relating to Affairs in South Africa.* (1900)

Cd. 426 *Army Proclamations issued by Field Marshal Lord Roberts in South Africa.* (1900)

Cd. 546 *Letter from Commandant Louis Botha to Lord Kitchener dated 13th February, 1901.* (1901)

Cd. 547 *Further Correspondence relating to Affairs in South Africa.* (1901)

Cd. 582 *Correspondence between the Commander-in-Chief in South Africa and the Boer Commanders so far as it affects the Destruction of Property.* (1901)

Cd. 608 *Return of Numbers of Persons in the Concentration Camps in South Africa, June 1901.* (1901)

Cd. 694 *Further Returns of Numbers of Persons in the Camps of Refuge in South Africa, July 1901.* (1901)

Cd. 819 *Reports, etc., relating to the Working of the Refugee Camps in the Transvaal, Orange River Colony, Cape Colony, and Natal.* (1901)

Cd. 821 *Correspondence relative to the Treatment of Natives by the Boers.* (1901)

Cd. 853 *Further papers relating to the working of the Refugee Camps in the Transvaal, Orange River Colony, Cape Colony and Natal, December 1901.* (1901)

Cd. 893 *Report on the Concentration Camps in South Africa, by the Committee of Ladies appointed by the Secretary of State for War, containing Reports on the Camps in Natal, the Orange River Colony, and the Transvaal.* (1902)

Cd. 903 *Further Correspondence relating to Affairs in South Africa.* (1902)

Cd. 939 *Statistics of the Refugee Camps in South Africa.* (1902)

Cd. 942 *Statistics of the Refugee Camps in South Africa* (in continuation of Cd. 942). (1902)

Cd. 981 *Papers relating to the Administration of Martial Law in South Africa.* (1902)

Cd. 1161 *Statistics of the Refugee Camps in South Africa.* (1902)

Cd. 1551 *Papers relating to the Progress of Administration in the Transvaal and the Orange River Colony.* (1903).

All Other Monographs, Collections, Theses and Dissertations, Articles, and Papers

ADL [A. D. Lückhoff]. *Woman's Endurance.* Edited by F. Pretorius. Pretoria: Protea Book House, 2006 [facsimile reprint of the first edition published by S.A. News Co., 1904].

"Ahmednagarfort, Indië: Herinneringe en Dagboeke," edited by A.W.G. Raath. *Christiaan de Wet-Annale* 9 (1997): 167–72.

Albertse, Willie. "Seun, Hond Byna Gesien." In *Ons Lesers Vertel: Die Lief en Leed soos ná 100 Jaar Onthou,* 1:11–13. Bloemfontein: War Museum [2001].

Allum, J. "Julius Allum's Anglo-Boer War Observations: The Report of a Norwegian Military Attaché," edited by C. de Jong. *African Historical Review* 9, no. 1 (1977): 31–50.

Almanak voor de Nederduitsch Gereformeerde Kerk in Zuid-Afrika voor het Jaar 1907. Cape Town: Dutch Reformed Church Office, 1907.

Armstrong, H. *Camp Diary of Henrietta E. C. Armstrong: Experiences of a Boer Nurse in the Irene Concentration Camp, 6 April–11 October 1901*. Edited by T. van Rensburg. Pretoria: HSRC, 1980.

Avant, D. D. "The Institutional Sources of Military Doctrine: Hegemons in Peripheral Wars." *International Studies Quarterly* 37, no. 4 (1993): 409–30.

Badenhorst, A. *Tant' Alie of Transvaal: Her Diary, 1880–1902. Translated from the Taal by Emily Hobhouse*. London: Allen & Unwin, 1923.

Badenhorst, C.C.J. *Uit den Boeren-Oorlog, 1899–1902: Ervaringen en Aantekeningen*. Amsterdam: Höveker & Wormser, 1903.

Bannerman, S. J. "Manliness and the English Soldier in the Anglo-Boer War, 1899–1902: The More Things Change, the More They Stay the Same." MA diss., University of Lethbridge, Alberta, Canada, 2005.

Barfield, Doreen. "The Royal Wiltshire Yeomanry (Prince of Wales' Own)." *Military History Journal* 2, no. 1 (1971). http://samilitaryhistory.org/vol021db.html. Accessed 18 Feb. 2015.

Barnard, Leo. "Die Afrikaner en die Naweë van die Anglo-Boereoorlog: Oorwonne of Oorwinnaar?" *Joernaal vir Eietydse Geskiedenis* 27, no. 2 (2002): 126–36.

Barry, A. *Ons Japie: Dagboek gehou gedurende die Driejarige Oorlog*. Johannesburg: Afrikaanse Pers-Boekhandel, 1960.

Baumann, G., and E. Bright. *The Lost Republic: The Biography of a Land Surveyor.* London: Faber & Faber, 1940.

Beak, G. B. *The Aftermath of War: An Account of the Repatriation of Boers and Natives in the Orange River Colony, 1902–1904*. London: Edward Arnold, 1906.

Berger, Nathan. *Chapters in South African History, Jewish and General*. Johannesburg: Kayor Publishers, 1982.

Binny, S. "Letters of Lieutenant Steuart Binny." In *The Defence of Ladysmith and Mafeking: Accounts of Two Sieges, 1899 to 1900, Being the South African War Experiences of William Thwaites*, edited by Arthur Davey, 97–102. Johannesburg: Brentwood Press, 1983.

Blake, Albert. *Boereverraaier: Teregstellings tydens die Anglo-Boereoorlog*. Cape Town: Tafelberg, 2010.

Boldingh, Gerrit. *Een Hollandsch Officier in Zuid-Afrika: Nagelaten Geschriften van Luitenant Gerrit Boldingh*. Rotterdam: B van de Watering, 1903.

Bosman, Jan. "Boervrou looi Hensopper toe met Stuk Vleis." In *Ons Lesers Vertel: Die Lief en Leed soos ná 100 Jaar onthou* 1:130–32. Bloemfontein: War Museum [2001].

Bosman, J. P. *Slaan en Vlug* [Pretoria: L. W. Bienedell, 1909].

Bottomley, John. "'Almost Bled to Death': The Effects of the Anglo-Boer War on Societal Transformation in the Orange River Colony." *Historia* 44, no. 1 (1999): 183–209.

———. "The Orange Free State and the Rebellion of 1914: The Influence of Industrialisation, Poverty, and Poor Whiteism." In *White but Poor: Essays on the History of Poor Whites in Southern Africa, 1880–1940,* edited by R. Morrell, 29–39. Pretoria: University of South Africa, 1992.

Bourke, Joanna. *An Intimate History of Killing: Face-to-Face Killing in Twentieth-Century Warfare.* London: Granta, 2000.

Bouwer, B. *Memoirs of General Ben Bouwer as written by P. J. le Riche.* Edited by O.J.O. Ferreira. Pretoria: HSRC, 1980.

Boveri, Margret. *Treason in the Twentieth Century.* London: Macdonald, 1961.

Bradford, Helen. "Gentlemen and Boers: Afrikaner Nationalism, Gender, and Colonial Warfare in the South African War." In *Writing a Wider War: Rethinking Gender, Race, and Identity in the South African War, 1899–1902,* edited by G. Cuthbertson, A. Grundlingh, and M. Suttie, 37–66. Athens: Ohio University Press, 2002.

Breytenbach, J. H. *Die Betekenis van die Tweede Vryheidsoorlog: Vyftig Jaar, 11 Okt. 1899–11 Okt. 1949.* Johannesburg: FAK, 1949.

———. *Die Geskiedenis van die Tweede Vryheidsoorlog.* Vols. 1–6. Pretoria: Government Printer, 1969–1996.

Brink, J. N. *Ceylon en de Bannelingen.* Amsterdam: HAUM, 1904.

Brits, J. P., and S. B. Spies. "A New South Africa in the Making." In *New History of South Africa,* edited by H. Giliomee and B. Mbengu, 224–44. Cape Town: Tafelberg, 2000.

Britz, D. "The Life and Times of Christof Sandrock, Missionary of the Berlin Missionary Society during the Anglo-Boer War (1899–1902) at Springfontein, South Africa." *Studia Historiae Ecclesiasticae* 38, no. 2 (2012): 223–46.

Brohier, R. L. "The Boer Prisoner of War in Ceylon (1900–1902)." *Journal of the Dutch Burgher Union of Ceylon* 36, no. 2 (1946).

Brown, S. M. *With the Royal Canadians.* Toronto: Publishers' Syndicate, 1900.

Burger, M. "Luistervink." In *Ons Lesers Vertel: Die Lief en Leed soos ná 100 Jaar onthou* 1:130–32. Bloemfontein: War Museum of the Boer Republics, [2001].

Campbell, James T. *Songs of Zion: The African Methodist Episcopal Church in the United States and South Africa.* Chapel Hill: University of North Carolina Press, 1998.

"Camps of Refuge." House of Commons Debate, 25 Feb. 1901. *Hansard,* vol. 89, col. 1022. http://hansard.millbanksystems.com/commons/1901/feb/25/camps-of-refuge. Accessed 18 Feb. 2015.

Childers, Erskine. *In the Ranks of the C.I.V.: A Narrative and Diary of Personal Experiences with the C.I.V. Battery (Honourable Artillery Company) in South Africa,* 1900. London: Macmillan, 1900.

Churchill, Winston S. *The Boer War: London to Ladysmith via Pretoria; Ian Hamilton's March.* London: Leo Cooper, 1989.

Cleaver, R. M. *The War Letters of an English Burgher.* Edited by M. De Fenton. Pretoria: Protea Book House, 2000.

Cock, J. *Colonels and Cadres: War and Gender in South Africa.* Cape Town: Oxford University Press, 1991.

Coetzer, Owen. *Fire in the Sky: The Destruction of the Orange Free State, 1899–1902.* Johannesburg: Covos-Day, 2000.

Colvile, H. E. *The Work of the Ninth Division in South Africa in 1900.* London: Arnold, 1901.

Connell, Bob. *Gender and Power: Society, the Person, and Sexual Politics.* Cambridge, UK: Polity Press, 1987.

Creswicke, L. *South Africa and the Transvaal War.* Vols. 1–6. Edinburgh: T. C. & E. C. Jack, 1900–1901.

Davis, Richard H. *With Both Armies in South Africa.* New York: Scribner, 1900.

Davitt, M. *The Boer Fight for Freedom.* New York: Funk & Wagnall, 1902.

De Bruin, J. H. "'n Regshistoriese Studie van die Finale Oorgawe van die Oranje-Vrystaat se Konvensionele Magte gedurende die Anglo-Boereoorlog (1899–1902)." Unpublished D.Legum thesis, University of the Free State, Bloemfontein, 2009.

De Bruin, Jaco, and André Wessels. "Militêre Verhore in die Oranje-Vrystaat tydens die Anglo-Boereoorlog, 1899–1902." *Historia* 56, no. 2 (2011): 73–93.

De Graaf, H. *Boere op St. Helena: Die Oorlogsdagboek van H. de Graaf.* Edited by P. J. Nienaber. Cape Town: Nasionale Boekhandel, 1950.

De Kiewiet, C. W. *A History of South Africa, Social and Economic.* London: Oxford University Press, 1941.

De Kock, W. J. "Pres. Marthinus Theunis Steyn: Die Siel van die Vryheidstryd." In *Gedenkalbum van die Tweede Vreiheidsoorlog,* edited by J. H. Breytenbach, 245–60. Cape Town: Nasionale Pers, 1949.

Delius, P., and S. Trapido. "Inboekselings and Oorlams: The Creation and Transformation of a Servile Class." In *Town and Countryside in the Transvaal: Capitalist Penetration and Popular Response,* edited by Belinda Bozzoli, 53–88. Johannesburg: Ravan, 1983.

Denoon, D.J.N. *A Grand Illusion: The Failure of Imperial Policy in the Transvaal Colony during the Period of Reconstruction, 1900–1905.* London: Longman, 1973.

———. "Participation in the Boer War: People's War, People's Non-War, or Non-People's War." In *War and Society in Africa: Ten Studies,* edited by B. A. Ogot, 109–122. London: F. Cass, [1972].

De Reuck, Jenny. "A Politics of Blood: The 'White Tribe' of Africa and the Recombinant Nationalism of a Colonizing Indigene." *Critical Arts* 10, no. 2 (1996): 139–57.

De Villebois-Mareuil, G. *War Notes: The Diary of Colonel de Villebois-Mareuil from November 24, 1899, to March 7, 1900.* London: Adam & Charles Black, 1901.

De Villiers, C. J. *Helpers, Healers, and Hospitals.* 2 vols. Pretoria: Protea Book House, 2008.

De Villiers, J.A.J. "The Diaries and Recollections of Jacob Abraham Jeremias de Villiers," edited by M.C.E. van Schoor. *Christiaan de Wet-Annale* 8 (Nov. 1990): 5–106.

De Villiers, Marq. *White Tribe Dreaming: Apartheid's Bitter Roots as Witnessed by Eight Generations of an Afrikaner Family.* London: Penguin, 1987.

De Villiers, R. "'Dagboek' van Rocco de Villiers en Bylaes," edited by M.C.E. van Schoor. *Christiaan de Wet-Annale* 3 (1975): 3–103.

De Wet, C. R. *Three Years War (October 1899–June 1902).* Alberton, SA: Galago, 1986 [facsimile of first edition published by Archibald Constable & Co., 1902].

Dubow, Saul. *A Commonwealth of Knowledge: Science, Sensibility, and White South Africa, 1820–2000.* Oxford: Oxford University Press, 2006.

———. "Thoughts on South Africa: Some Preliminary Ideas." In *History Making and Present-Day Politics: The Meaning of Collective Memory in South Africa,* edited by Hans Erik Stolten, 51–72. Uppsala: Nordiska Afrikainstitutet, 2007.

Du Toit, P. J. *Diary of a National Scout, P. J. du Toit, 1900–1902.* Edited by P. J. Brits. Pretoria: HSRC, 1974.

Dyzenhaus, David. "The Puzzle of Martial Law." Unpublished paper. www.law.yale.edu/documents/pdf/intellectual_life/ltw-dyzenhaus.pdf. Accessed 18 Feb. 2015.

Edelstein, D. M. *Occupational Hazards: Success and Failure in Military Occupation.* Ithaca, NY: Cornell University Press, 2008.

———. "Occupational Hazards: Why Military Occupations Succeed or Fail." *International Security* 29, no. 1 (2004): 49–91.

Eloff, C. C. "Vrystaatse Vlugtelinge in Basoetoland tydens die Anglo-Boereooorlog." *Military History Journal* 6, no. 5 (1985). http://samilitaryhistory.org/vol065ce.html. Accessed 10 March 2015.

Engelenburg, F. V. *General Louis Botha.* Pretoria: Van Schaik, 1929.

Farwell, Byron. *The Great Anglo-Boer War.* New York: Norton, 1976.

Fisk, Robert. *The Age of the Warrior: Selected Writings.* London: Harper, 2009.

Fletcher-Vane, F. P. *The War and One Year After: Containing Reports Made by an Imperial Officer to the Colonial Office Respecting Farm Burning, the Arming of Natives, Martial Law Mal-Administration, and a Reprint of the "Contemporary Review" Article Called "The Fruits of the War."* Cape Town: South African Newspaper Company, 1903.

Fraser, J. G. *Episodes in My Life.* Cape Town: Juta, 1922.

Genovese, Eugene D. *Roll, Jordan, Roll: The World the Slaves Made.* New York: Vintage, 1976.

Gibbs, D. F. "A Chaplain in the Boer War." *Military History Journal* 3, no. 2 (1974). http://samilitaryhistory.org/vol032dg.html. Accessed 18 Feb. 2015.

Gibson, G. F. *The Story of the Imperial Light Horse in the South African War, 1899–1902.* London: G. D. & Co., 1937.

Giliomee, Hermann. *The Afrikaners: Biography of a People.* Cape Town: Tafelberg, 2003.

———. "The Beginnings of Afrikaner Ethnic Consciousness, 1850–1914." In *The Creation of Tribalism in South Africa,* edited by Le Roy Vail, 21–54. Oxford: Currey, 1989.

Girouard, Mark. *The Return to Camelot: Chivalry and the English Gentleman.* New Haven, CT: Yale University Press, 1981.

Gräbe, R. C. "Writing between the Lines: Perspectives on the Anglo-Boer War in Letters from Detention Camps." 39–56. http://www.pala.ac.uk/uploads/2/5/1/0/25105678/grabe.pdf. Accessed 18 Feb. 2015.

Grobbelaar, P. W. *Kommandeer! Kommandeer! Volksang uit die Anglo-Boereoorlog*. Pretoria: Van der Walt, 1999.

———. "Oorlog 1." In *Die Vrystaat en sy Mense,* edited by P. W. Grobbelaar, 62–69. Cape Town: Tafelberg, 1980.

Grobler, Jackie. "Haat, Vrees, Afsku—Boerevroue se Houding teenoor Swart Mense soos weerspieël in Dagboeke tydens die Anglo-Boereoorlog, 1899–1902, en die Nalatenskap daarvan." *Joernaal vir Eietydse Geskiedenis* 27, no. 2 (2002): 31–44.

Grobler, M. J. *Met die Vrystaters onder die Wapen: Generaal Prinsloo en die Bethlehem-Kommando*. Bloemfontein: Nasionale Pers, [1937].

Groenewald, Coen. *Bannelinge oor die Oseaan: Boerekrygsgevangenes, 1899–1902*. Pretoria: J. P. van der Walt, 1992.

Grundlingh, Albert. "Collaborators in Boer Society." In *The South African War: The Anglo-Boer War, 1899–1902,* edited by P. Warwick, 258–78. Harlow, Essex: Longman, 1980.

———. *The Dynamics of Treason: Boer Collaboration in the South African War of 1899–1902*. Pretoria: Protea Book House, 2006.

———. "Sosiale Geskiedenis en die Dilemma in Afrikanergeskiedskrywing." *South African Historical Journal* 19 (1987): 31–49.

———. "Die Stigting van Senekal en Ontwikkeling in die Dorp en Wyk Onderwittebergen tot 1899." Unpublished BA Hons. mini-dissertation, University of the Orange Free State, Bloemfontein, 1971.

Grundlingh, L.W.F. Review of *Putting a Plough to the Ground,* edited by W. Beinart, P. Delius, and S. Trapido. *African Affairs* 88, no. 352 (1989): 125–26.

Hales, A. G. *Campaign Pictures of the War in South Africa (1899–1900): Letters from the Front*. London: Cassell, 1901.

Hancock, W. K. *Smuts: The Sanguine Years, 1870–1919*. Cambridge, UK: Cambridge University Press, 1962.

Harris, Verne. "The Archival Sliver: Power, Memory, and Archives in South Africa." *Archival Science* 2, no. 1–2 (2002): 63–86.

Higginson, J. "Hell in Small Places: African Elites and Collective Violence in the Western Transvaal, 1900–1907." *Journal of Social History* 35, no. 1 (2001): 95–124.

Hillegas, Howard C. *With the Boer Forces*. London: Methuen, 1900.

Hintrager, O. "Dagboek van Oskar Hintrager—Saam met Christiaan de Wet, Mei tot September 1900," edited by J. J. Oberholster. *Christiaan de Wet-Annale* 2 (1973): 3–146.

Hirschfeld, G. "Collaboration and Attentism in the Netherlands, 1940–41. *Journal of Contemporary History* 16, no. 3 (1981): 467–86.

History of the War in South Africa, 1899–1902. Compiled by the direction of His Majesty's Government. Vols. 1–4. Edited by F. Maurice and M. H. Grant. London: Hurst & Blackett, 1906–1910.

Hobhouse, Emily. *Boer War Letters*. Edited by Rykie van Reenen. 2nd ed. Cape Town: Human & Rousseau, 1999.
———. *The Brunt of the War and Where it Fell*. London: Methuen, 1902.
———. *War without Glamour: Women's War Experiences Written by Themselves, 1899–1902*. Bloemfontein: Nasionale Pers, [preface 1924].
Hoffmann, Stanley. "Collaborationism in France during World War II." *Journal of Modern History* 40, no. 3 (1968): 375–95.
Hofmeyr, Isabel. "Building a Nation from Words: Afrikaans Language, Literature, and Ethnic Identity." In *The Politics of Race, Class, and Nationalism in Twentieth-Century South Africa*, edited by Shula Marks and Stanley Trapido, 95–123. New York: Longman, 1987.
Hollenbach, C. A. *Briewe uit die Boere-Oorlog/Boer War Letters: Persoonlike en Seldsame Dokumente rondom die Vryheidstryd, 1899–1902*, Florida Park, SA: Driefontein Publikasies, 1999.
Holtzhausen, L. C. "Die Nederduitse Gereformeerde Kerk in die Oranje-Vrystaat en die Rebellie." Unpublished MA diss., University of South Africa, Pretoria, 1950.
Hyam, Ronald, and Peter Henshaw. *The Lion and the Springbok: Britain and South Africa since the Boer War*. Cambridge, UK: Cambridge University Press, 2003.
Izedinova, Sophia. *A Few Months with the Boers: The War Reminiscences of a Russian Nursing Sister*. Edited by C. Moody. Johannesburg: Perskor, 1977.
Jackson, J. M. "Charlotte Makgoma Manye Maxeke: Her Legacy Lives on." *Studia Historiae Ecclesiasticae* 34, Supplement (2008): 75–89.
Jackson, M. C. *A Soldier's Diary: South Africa, 1899–1901*. London: Max Goschen, 1913.
Jackson, Tabitha. *The Boer War*. London: Macmillan, 1999.
Jansen, E. "Ek ook het besluit om van my bittere lydenskelk te vertel: Het Meervoudige (Post)Koloniale Vertoog in Autobiografische Vrouwenteksten over de Zuid-Afrikaanse Oorlog (1899–1902)." *Tydskrif vir Nederlands en Afrikaans* 6, no. 2 (1999): 1–20.
Jansen, Jonathan D. *Knowledge in the Blood: Confronting Race and the Apartheid Past*. Cape Town: University of Cape Town Press, 2009.
Jones, Huw, and M.G.M. Jones. *A Gazetteer of the Second Anglo-Boer War, 1899–1902*. Milton Keynes, UK: Military Press, 1999.
"Josiah Tshangana Gumede." *South African History Online*. http://www.sahistory.org.za/people/josiah-tshangana-gumede. Accessed 6 Feb. 2015.
Kearney, J. A. *Representing Dissension: Riot, Rebellion, and Resistance in the South African English Novel*. Pretoria: University of South Africa Press, 2003.
Keegan, Tim. *Facing the Storm: Portraits of Black Lives in Rural South Africa*. Cape Town: Philip, 1988.
———. "The Restructuring of Agrarian Class Relations in a Colonial Economy: The Orange River Colony, 1902–1910." *Journal of Southern African Studies* 5, no. 2 (1979): 234–54.

———. "Trade, Accumulation, and Impoverishment: Mercantile Capital and the Economic Transformation of Lesotho and the Conquered Territory." *Journal of Southern African Studies* 12, no. 2 (1986): 196–216.

Kessler, Stowell. "The Black and Coloured Concentration Camps of the Anglo-Boer War." In *Scorched Earth*, edited by Fransjohan Pretorius, 132–153. Cape Town: Human & Rousseau, 2001.

——— "The Black Concentration Camps of the South African War, 1899–1902." Unpublished doctoral thesis, University of Cape Town, 2003.

Kestell, J. D. *Met die Boere-Kommando's*. Translated by D.P.M Botes. Pretoria: Protea Book House, 1999.

Kestell, J., and D. van Velden. *Die Vredesonderhandelinge tussen die Regerings van die twee Suid-Afrikaanse Republieke en die Verteenwoordigers van die Britse Regering wat uitgeloop het op die Vrede wat op 31 Mei 1902 op Vereeniging gesluit is*. Cape Town: Human & Rousseau, 1982.

Kirchner, J. G. "Kampdagboek." Photocopy of unpublished transcription of original poem "Showyard Leven" and part of the diary [April 1901 to March 1902] made by Mrs. S. M. Maree of Pretoria.

Krebs, Paula M. *Gender, Race, and the Writing of Empire: Public Discourse and the Boer War*. Cambridge, UK: Cambridge University Press, 1999.

Krikler, Jeremy. *Revolution from Above, Rebellion from Below: The Agrarian Transvaal at the Turn of the Century*. Oxford: Clarendon, 1993.

Kruger, C. J. H. "Militêre Bewind in die Oranje-Vrystaat Maart 1900–Januarie 1901." Unpublished MA diss., University of Pretoria, 1958.

Labuschagne, P. *Ghost Riders of the Anglo-Boer War (1899–1902): The Role and Contribution of Agterryers*. Pretoria: University of South Africa Press, 1999.

Lamprecht, G. J. "Die Ekonomiese Ontwikkeling van die Vrystaat van 1870 tot 1899. Unpublished doctoral thesis, University of Stellenbosch, 1954.

Lebow, R. N., W. Kasteiner, and C. Fugo. *The Politics of Memory in Postwar Europe*. Durham, NC: Duke University Press, 2006.

Lee, Emanoel. *To the Bitter End: A Photographic History of the Boer War, 1899–1902*. Pretoria: Protea Book House, 2002.

Le May, G.H.L. *British Supremacy in South Africa, 1899–1907*. Oxford: Clarendon, 1965.

Le Roux, C.J.P. "Grondtoekenning en Landelike Vestiging in die Oranjerivierkolonie/ Oranje-Vrystaat, 1900–1912. *Contree* 27 (1990): 12–17.

———. "Die Verhouding tussen Blank en Nie-Blank in die Oranjerivierkolonie 1900–1910." *Archives Year Book for South African History* 50, no. 1. Pretoria: Government Printer, 1986.

Leviseur, S. *Sophie Leviseur Memories*. Edited by K. Schoeman. Cape Town: Human & Rousseau, 1982.

Littlejohn, David. *The Patriotic Traitors: A History of Collaboration in German-Occupied Europe, 1940–45*. London: Heinemann, 1972.

Lombard, P. S. *Uit die Dagboek van 'n Wildeboer deur P. S. Lombard,* compiled by A. M. Jackson [s.l.: s.n., 1939].

Low-Beer, D., M. Smallman-Raynor, and A. Cliff. "Disease and Death in the South African War: Changing Disease Patterns from Soldiers to Refugees." *Social History of Medicine* 17, no. 2 (2004): 223–45.

Lowry, D. "The World's No Bigger than a Kraal." In *The Impact of the South African War,* edited by D. Omissi and A. S. Thompson, 268–88. Basingstoke: Palgrave, 2002.

Mack, Andrew. "Why Big Nations Lose Small Wars: The Politics of Asymmetric Conflict." *World Politics* 27, no. 2 (1975): 175–200.

Madsen, Chris. "Canadian Troops and Farm Burning in the South African War." *Canadian Military Journal* (2005): 49–58.

Magubane, B. M. *The Making of a Racist State: British Imperialism and the Union of South Africa, 1875–1910*. Trenton, NJ: Africa World Press, 1996.

Malan, André. *Oorwinning sonder Roem: 'n Fotoalbum van Herinneringe aan die Anglo-Boereoorlog, 1899–1902*. Pretoria: J. P. van der Walt, 1999.

Malan, Jacques. *Die Boere-Offisiere, 1899–1902*. Pretoria: J. P. van der Walt, 1990.

Malan, J. H. *Die Opkoms van 'n Republiek of Die Geskiedenis van die Oranje-Vrystaat tot die Jaar 1863*. Bloemfontein: Nasionale Pers, 1929.

Malan, S. F. "Openbare Onderwys vir Blankes in die Oranje-Vrystaat, 1874–1899." Unpublished doctoral thesis, University of Potchefstroom, 1951.

———. *Politieke Strominge onder die Afrikaners van die Vrystaatse Republiek*. Durban, SA: Butterworth, 1982.

———. "Die Rol van J. Geo Fraser in die Vrystaat, 1863–1927." *Archives Year Book for South African History.* Vol. 37. Pretoria: Government Printer, 1980.

Marais, Pets. *Die Vrou in die Anglo-Boereoorlog, 1899–1902*. Pretoria: J. P. van der Walt, 1999.

Marquard, Margaret. *Letters from a Boer Parsonage: Letters of Margaret Marquard during the Boer War.* Edited by Leo Marquard. Cape Town: Purnell, 1967.

Matsetela, Ted. "The Life Story of Nkgomo Mma Pooe: Aspects of Sharecropping and Proletarianisation in the Northern Orange Free State." In *Industrialisation and Social Change in South Africa: African Class Formation, Culture, and Consciousness, 1870–1930,* edited by Shula Marks and Richard Rathbone, 212–37. Harlow, Essex: Longman, 1982.

McDonald, R. D. *'n Terugblik op my Oorlogsjare*. Bloemfontein: War Museum of the Boer Republics, 1995.

McLeod, A. J. "The Psychological Impact of Guerrilla Warfare on the Boer Forces during the Anglo-Boer War." Unpublished D.Phil thesis, University of Pretoria, 2004.

Meintjes, Johannes. *President Steyn: A Biography.* Cape Town: Nasionale Boekhandel, 1939.

Merriman, J. X. *Selections from the Correspondence of John X. Merriman, 1899–1905*. Vol. 3. Edited by Phyllis Lewsen. Cape Town: Van Riebeeck Society, 1966.

Miller, C. *Painting the Map Red: Canada and the South African War, 1899–1902*. Montreal: Canadian War Museum, 1993.

Miller, S. M "Duty or Crime? Defining Acceptable Behavior in the British Army in South Africa, 1899–1902." *Journal of British Studies* 49, no. 2 (2010): 311–31.

———. *Lord Methuen and the British Army: Failure and Redemption in South Africa.* London: Frank Cass, 1999.

Milner, A. "Letters: Lord Milner to Hamilton John Goold-Adams, 1901–1905," edited by Elizabeth Main and A. Wessels. *Christiaan de Wet-Annale* 5 (1978): 107–56.

———. *The Milner Papers.* Vol. 2, *South Africa, 1899–1905*. Edited by C. Headlam. London: Cassell, 1931.

Mitchell, C. R., and M. Nicholson. "Rational Models and the Ending of Wars." *Journal of Conflict Resolution* 27, no. 3 (1983): 495–520.

Mohlamme, J. S. "African Refugee Camps in the Boer Republics." In *Scorched Earth,* edited by F. Pretorius, 110–131. Cape Town: Human & Rousseau, 2001.

———. "Black People in the Boer Republics during and in the Aftermath of the South African War of 1899–1902." PhD thesis, University of Wisconsin–Madison, 1985. Facsimile. University Microfilms International, Ann Arbor, Michigan, 1986.

Molema, S. M. *The Bantu Past and Present.* Edinburgh: Green, 1920.

Mongalo, B. E., and Kobus du Pisani. "Victims of a White Man's War: Blacks in Concentration Camps during the South African War (1899–1902)." *Historia* 44, no. 1 (1999): 148–82.

Munslow, A. *Deconstructing History.* London: Routledge, 1998.

Nasson, Bill. *Abraham Esau's War: A Black South African War in the Cape, 1899–1902.* Cambridge, UK: Cambridge University Press, 1991.

———. *The South African War, 1899–1902.* London: Arnold, 1999.

———. *Uyadela Wen'osulapho: Black Participation in the Anglo-Boer War.* Randburg, SA: Ravan, 1999.

———. *The War for South Africa: The Anglo-Boer War.* Cape Town: Tafelberg, 2010.

———. "The War for South Africa." In *New History of South Africa,* edited by Hermann Giliomee and Bernard Mbenga, 206–23. Cape Town: Tafelberg, 2007.

Neethling, E. *Should We Forget?* Cape Town: HAUM, [1903].

Ngcongco, L. D. "Problems of Southern African Historiography." In *The Historiography of Southern Africa: Proceedings of the Experts' Meeting held at Gaborone, Botswana, from 7 to 11 March 1977.* 17–24. Paris: UNESCO, 1980.

Oberholster, J.A.S. *Die Gereformeerde Kerke onder die Kruis in Suid-Afrika: Hul Ontstaan en Ontwikkeling.* Cape Town: HAUM, 1956.

Oberholster, J. J. (with M.C.E. van Schoor et al). *Die Nederduitse Gereformeerde Kerk in die Oranje-Vrystaat: Ter Herdenking aan die Honderdjarige Feesviering van die Kerk in Sinodale Verband.* Bloemfontein: N. G. Kerk in die O.V.S., [1963].

Oberholster, J. J., and J. Stemmet. *Senekal se Eerste Honderd Jaar.* Senekal, SA: Town Council, 1977.

Odendaal, A. *The Founders: The Origins of the ANC and the Struggle for Democracy in South Africa.* Johannesburg: Jacana, 2012.

———. *Vukani Bantu! The Beginnings of Black Protest Politics in South Africa to 1912.* Cape Town: Philip, 1984.

Oosterhagen, H. S. *Oorlogsdagboekie van H.S. Oosterhagen Januarie–Julie 1902*. Edited by C. C. Eloff. Pretoria: HSRC, 1976.

Otto, J. C. *Die Konsentrasiekampe*. Cape Town: Nasionale Boekhandel, 1954.

"Ouma se Stories," published by Suzanne van den Bergh. http://samilitaryhistory.org/diaries/oumaww2.html. Accessed 18 Feb. 2015.

Phillips, Christopher. "The Family of an Irish Soldier Settler—Jeremiah Nunan (c 1805–1861) of King William's Town." *Familia* 26, no. 1 (1989): 18–22.

Phillipps, L. March. *With Rimington*. London: Edward Arnold, 1902.

Pienaar, F. F. *Op Kommando met Steyn en De Wet*. Pretoria: Protea Book House, 2000.

Pine-Coffin, J. E. *One Man's Boer War, 1900: The Diary of John Edward Pine-Coffin*. Edited by Susan Pine-Coffin. Bideford, Devon: Edward Gaskell, 1999.

Pirow, O. *James Barry Munnik Hertzog*. Cape Town: Howard Timmins, [1950?].

Plaatje, Solomon. *Mafeking Diary: A Black Man's View of a White Man's Conflict*. Edited by John Comaroff. Johannesburg: Southern, 1989.

———. *Selected Writings*. Edited by Brian Willan. Johannesburg: Witwatersrand University Press, 1997.

Plokhooy, C. *Met den Mauser: Persoonlijke Ervaringen in den Zuid Afrikaansche Oorlog*. Gorinchem, Netherlands: F. Duym, 1901.

Porter, A. N. *The Origins of the South African War: Joseph Chamberlain and the Diplomacy of Imperialism, 1859–99*. Manchester, UK: Manchester University Press, 1980.

Preller, Gustav. *Ons Parool: Dae uit die Dagboek van 'n Krygsgevangene*. Cape Town: Nasionale Pers, 1943.

Pretorius, Fransjohan. "Afrikaner Nationalism and the Burgher on Commando." In *Writing a Wider War: Rethinking Gender, Race, and Identity in the South African War, 1899–1902,* edited by G. Cuthbertson, A. Grundlingh, and M. Suttie, 67–84. Athens: Ohio University Press, 2002.

———. *The Anglo-Boer War, 1899–1902*. 2nd ed. Cape Town: Don Nelson, 2013.

———. "Caught up in the Cross-fire: A British Citizen in the Orange Free State during the Anglo-Boer War, 1899–1900." *Historia* 43, no. 1 (1998): 41–71.

———. "The Fate of the Boer Women and Children." In *Scorched Earth,* edited by Fransjohan Pretorius, 36–59. Cape Town: Human & Rousseau, 2001.

———. *Life on Commando during the Anglo-Boer War, 1899–1902*. Cape Town: Human & Rousseau, 1999.

———. "Waarom het die 'Bittereinders' gedurende die Anglo-Boereoorlog van 1899–1902 op Kommando gebly?" *Historia* 35, no. 1 (1990): 57–71.

Prinsloo, Dione. "Vroue in die Anglo-Boereoorlog: 'Feite en Fiksie'?" In *Die Anglo-Boereoorlog: Herdenkingslesings aan die Randse Afrikaanse Universiteit*. Compiled by Grietjie Verhoef, 53–65. Johannesburg: Rand Afrikaans University, 2005.

Quispel, C., and R. Ross. "Theorie en Mentaliteit in de Historiografie van Zuid-Afrika." https://openaccess.leidenuniv.nl/bitstream/handle/1887/4221/1246876_047.pdf?sequence=1. Accessed 18 Feb. 2015.

Raal, Sarah. *Met die Boere in die Veld*. Cape Town: Nasionale Pers, 1938.

Raath, A.W.G. *The British Concentration Camps of the Anglo-Boer War, 1899–1902: Reports on the Camps*. Bloemfontein: War Museum of the Boer Republics, 1999.

———. *Die Boerevrou, 1899–1902*. Vol. 1, *Moederleed*. Nylstroom, SA: Volkskomitee vir die Herdenking van die Tweede Vryheidsoorlog, 2002.

Riall, M. *Boer War: The Letters, Diaries, and Photographs of Malcolm Riall from the War in South Africa, 1899–1902*. Edited by Nicholas Riall. London: Brassey's, 2000.

Rice, M. *From Dolly Gray to Sarie Marais: The Boer War in Popular Memory*. Cape Town: Fischer Press, 2004.

Richardson, L. *Lawrence Richardson: Selected Correspondence (1902–1903)*. Edited by A. M. Davey. Cape Town: Van Riebeeck Society, 1977.

Riedi, Eliza. "Teaching Empire: British and Dominion Women Teachers in the South African War Concentration Camps." *English Historical Review* 120, no. 489 (2005): 1316–47.

Rijksen-Van Helsdingen, J. *Vrouweleed: Persoonlike Ondervindingen in de Boereoorlog*. Pretoria: J. H. de Bussy, 1918.

Rompel, F. *Uit den Tweeden Vrijheidsoorlog: Schetsen en Portretten*. Amsterdam: Van Holkema & Warendorf, [1903?].

Ross, Robert. "Paternalism, Patriarchy, and Afrikaans." *South African Historical Journal* 32 (May 1995): 34–47.

Rosslyn, Earl of. *Twice Captured: A Record of Adventure during the Boer War*. 3rd ed. Edinburgh: William Blackwood & Sons, 1900.

Royle, Stephen A. "St. Helena as a Boer Prisoner of War Camp, 1900–2: Information from the Alice Stopford Green Papers." *Journal of Historical Geography* 24, no. 1 (1998): 53–68.

Saron, G., and L. Hotz. *The Jews in South Africa: A History*. Cape Town: Oxford University Press, 1955.

Schikkerling, R. W. *Commando Courageous: A Boer's Diary*. Johannesburg: Hugh Keartland, 1964.

Schoeman, Chris. *Boer Boy: Memoirs of an Anglo-Boer War Youth*. Cape Town: Zebra, 2010.

———. *Vegter en Balling: Boereoorlog-ervarings van Veldkornet Charles von Maltitz*. Cape Town: Tafelberg, 2013.

Schoeman, Karel. *Die Laaste Afrikaanse Boek: Outobiografiese Aantekeninge*. Cape Town: Human & Rousseau, 2002.

Scholtz, Anna-Marie. "Brit verewig Meisie in Boek." *Volksblad*, 7 May 1999. 152.111.11.6/argief/berigte/volksblad/1999/05/7/4/3/html. Accessed 18 Feb. 2015.

Scholtz, G. D. *Die Geskiedenis van Ventersburg en sy Omgewing, 1873–1973*. Ventersburg, SA: Sentrale Eeufeeskomitee, [1973].

Scholtz, Leopold. *Generaal Christiaan de Wet as Veldheer*. Pretoria: Protea Book House, 2003.

Schreiner, Olive. *Woman and Labour*. London: Unwin, 1911.

———. *Words in Season: The Public Writings with Her Own Remembrances Collected for the First Time*. London: Penguin, 2005.

Schulenburg, C.A.R. *August Carl Schulenburg: Krygsgevangene, Medikus, Boer*. Pretoria: Van Schaik, 1985.

Schutte, G. J. *De Boerenoorlog na Honderd Jaar: Opstellen over het Veranderende*

Beeld van de Anglo-Boerenoorlog (1899–1902). Amsterdam: Suid-Afrikaanse Instituut, 1997.

Scott, Jan. *Die Scotte van Winburg: Nasate van William Edward Scott*. Pretoria: Jan Scott, 1990.

Searle, Charlotte. *The History of the Development of Nursing in South Africa, 1652–1960 (A Socio-Historical Survey)*. Cape Town: Struik, 1965.

Serfontein, Dot. *Deurloop: Keur uit die Essays van Dot Serfontein*. Compiled by Antjie Krog. Cape Town: Human & Rousseau, 1992.

———. *Keurskrif vir Kroonstad: 'n Kroniek van die Ontstaan, Groei en Vooruitsigte van 'n Vrystaatse Plattelandse Dorp*. Kroonstad: Perskor, 1990.

Setiloane, G. M. "Swart en Bruin Mense: ABO-herdenking te Sensitief vir Swart Deelname." In *Vir Vryheid en vir Reg: Anglo-Boereoorlog Gedenkboek*, edited by M. van Bart and L. Scholtz, 171–72. Cape Town: Tafelberg, 2001.

Siwundhla, H. T. "White Ideologies and Non-European Participation in the Anglo-Boer War, 1899–1902." *Journal of Black Studies* 15, no. 2 (1984): 223–34.

Smith, Iain R. *The Origins of the South African War, 1899–1902*. London: Longman, 1996.

Smith, Ken. *The Changing Past: Trends in South African Historical Writing*. Johannesburg: Southern, 1988.

Smuts, J. C. *Smuts, Memoirs of the Boer War*. Edited by S. B. Spies and Gail Nattrass. Johannesburg: Jonathan Ball, 1966.

Solomon, V. E. "The 'Hands-Uppers.'" *Military History Journal* 3, no. 1 (1974). http://samilitaryhistory.org/vol031vs.html. Accessed 18 Feb. 2015.

Spies, S. B. *Methods of Barbarism? Roberts and Kitchener and Civilians in the Boer Republics January 1900–May 1902*. Cape Town: Human & Rousseau, 1977.

Spies, F. J. du T. "Engelse Gesindhede in die Vrystaatse Republiek." *Hertzog-Annale* 3, no. 7 (1954): 42–64.

———. Review of S. F. Malan, *Politieke Strominge onder die Afrikaners van die Vrystaatse Republiek*. *Kleio* 15, nos. 1/2 (1983): 91.

Stakhovitch, Pavel, and Vasili I. Gurko. "Die Dépeches van die Russiese Attaché, Kol. Stakhovitch en Lt.-Kol. Gurko," edited by M.C.E. van Schoor. *Christiaan de Wet-Annale* 3 (1975): 123–73, 174–201.

Stanley, L. *Mourning Becomes . . . : Post/Memory, Commemoration, and the Concentration Camps of the South African War*. Manchester, UK: Manchester University Press, 2006.

Stanley, L., and H. Dampier. "Aftermaths: Post/Memory, Commemoration, and the Concentration Camps of the South African War." *European Review of History* 12, no. 1 (2005): 91–119.

———. "Cultural Entrepreneurs, Proto-Nationalism, and Women's Testimony Writings: From the South African War to 1940." *Journal of Southern African Studies* 33, no. 3 (2007): 501–13.

———. "Simulacrum Diaries: Time, the 'Moment of Writing,' and the Diaries of Johanna Brandt-Van Warmelo." *Life Writing* 3, no. 2 (2006): 25–52.

St. Leger, Stratford. *Mounted Infantry at War.* Alberton, SA: Galago, 1986.

Stemme uit die Verlede: 'n Versameling van Beëdigde Verklarings van Vroue wat tydens die Tweede Vryheidsoorlog in die Konsentrasiekampe verkeer het. Compiled by M. M. Postma. Johannesburg: Voortrekkerpers, 1939.

Sternberg, Count A. *My Experiences of the Boer War.* London: Longmans, Green & Co, 1901.

Strange, Julie-Marie. "'She cried a very little': Death, Grief, and Mourning in Working-Class Culture." *Social History* 27, no. 2 (2002): 143–61.

Sullivan, P. L. "War Aims and War Outcomes: Why Powerful States Lose Limited Wars." *Journal of Conflict Resolution* 51, no. 3 (2007): 496–524.

Surridge, K. T. "British Civil-Military Relations and the South African War (1899–1902)." PhD thesis, King's College, University of London, 1994.

Swart, S. "The Rebels of 1914: Masculinity, Republicanism, and the Social Forces That Shaped the Boer Rebellion." Unpublished MA diss., University of Natal, Durban, 1997.

Taylor, H. *Doctor to Basuto, Boer, and Briton, 1877–1906: Memoirs of Dr. Henry Taylor.* Edited by Peter Hadley. Cape Town: Philip, 1972.

Theron, Bridget. "Victorian Women, Gender, and Identity." *Kleio* 38, no. 1 (2006): 3–24.

The Times History of the War in South Africa. Vols. 1–7. Edited by L. S. Amery. London: Sampson Low, Marston & Co, 1900–09.

Tosh, J. (with S. Lang). *The Pursuit of History: Aims, Methods, and New Directions in the Study of Modern History.* 4th ed. Harlow: Pearson, 2006.

Townshend, Charles. *The Oxford History of Modern War.* Oxford: Oxford University Press, 2005.

Tuffin, Trooper. "Personal Diaries of Officers and Other Ranks. 1st the Queen's Dragoon Guards." http://www.qdg.org.uk/diaries.php?id=20&dy=30. Accessed 13 March 2014.

Uys, C. J. "Olivier, Jan Hendrik." *Dictionary of South African Biography.* 1:601. Pretoria: National Council for Social Research, 1968.

Van Aswegen, H. J. "Die Posisie van die Nie-Blanke in die Oranje-Vrystaat, 1854–1899." *South African Historical Journal* 5 (1973): 41–93.

———. "Die Verhouding tussen Blank en Nie-Blank in die Oranje-Vrystaat." *Archives Year Book for South African History* 34, no. 1. Pretoria: Government Printer, 1971.

Van den Berg, Karel. *Beste Ouders!: Brieven uit de Transvaal van Karel van den Berg, 1896–1900.* Edited by G. J. Schutte. Amsterdam: Suid-Afrikaanse Instituut, 1999.

Van den Heever, C. M. *General J.B.M. Hertzog.* Johannesburg: A.P.B., 1946.

Van der Bank, D. A. *Burgermonumente van die Anglo-Boereoorlog in die Oranje-Vrystaat.* Bloemfontein: Nasionale Museum, 1995.

Van der Merwe, F.J.G. *Sport en Spel in die Boerekrygsgevangenekampe tydens die Anglo-Boereoorlog, 1899–1902.* Stellenbosch, SA: University of Stellenbosch, 1995.

Van der Merwe, G. A. "Die Nederduitse Gereformeerde Kerk in die Oranje-Vrystaat

tydens die Anglo-Boereoorlog, 1899–1902." Unpublished DTh thesis, University of the Orange Free State, Bloemfontein, 1988.
Van der Merwe, N. J. *Marthinus Theunis Steyn: 'n Lewensbeskrywing*. Vols. 1 and 2. Cape Town: Nasionale Pers, 1921.
Van der Spuy, R.J.R. "Profiel van die Afrika Onafhanklike Kerke onder die Suid-Sotho in die Senekalse Distrik: 'n Empiries-Historiese Studie." Unpublished DD thesis, University of Pretoria, 1995.
Van der Walt, H. S. "Oorlogsdagboek, 1899–1902," edited by H. H. Coetzee. *Christiaan de Wet-Annale* 8 (Nov. 1990): 107–150.
Van Heyningen, E. "British Concentration Camps of the South African War, 1900–1902. Winburg." http://www2.lib.uct.ac.za/mss/bccd/Histories/Winburg. Accessed 18 Feb. 2015.
———. "British Doctors versus Boer Women." In *Scorched Earth,* edited by Fransjohan Pretorius, 178–97. Cape Town: Human & Rousseau, 2001.
———. *The Concentration Camps of the Anglo-Boer War: A Social History.* Johannesburg: Jacana, 2013.
——— "Daily Life in the Concentration Camps." In *The War at Home: Women and Families in the Anglo-Boer War*, edited by Bill Nasson and Albert Grundlingh, 92–119. Cape Town: Tafelberg, 2013.
——— Review of ADL, *Woman's Endurance, Kleio* 38, no. 2 (2006): 214–16.
———. "Women and Gender in the South African War." In *Women in South African History: Basus'iimbokodo Bawel'imilambo,* edited by N. Gasa, 91–124. Pretoria: HSRC, 2007.
Van Jaarsveld, F. A. "Die Veldkornet en sy Aandeel in die Opbou van die Suid-Afrikaanse Republiek tot 1870." *Archives Year Book for South African History* 13, no. 2: 187–354. Pretoria: Government Printer, 1950.
Van Niekerk, H. H. "Dagboek van Hugo H van Niekerk," edited by M.C.E. van Schoor. *Christiaan de Wet-Annale* 1 (1972): 7–207.
Van Oostrum, O. *Bestendige Onbestendigheid: My Suid-Afrikaanse Ervaringe*. Pretoria: Van Schaik, 1943.
Van Reenen, R. *Emily Hobhouse: Heldin uit die Vreemde.* 2nd ed. Cape Town: Tafelberg, 1999.
Van Rensburg, A.P.J. "Die Ekonomiese Herstel van die Afrikaner in die Oranjerivier-Kolonie 1902–1907." *Archives Year Book for South African History* 30, no. 2: 134–340. Pretoria: Government Printer, 1967.
Van Schoor, M.C.E. "Brand, Johannes Henricus." In *Dictionary of South African Biography,* 1:115–16. Pretoria: National Council for Social Research, 1968.
———. *Christiaan Rudolph de Wet: Krygsman en Volksman*. Pretoria: Protea Book House, 2007.
———. "Ons Vrystaat." In *Die Vrystaat en sy Mense,* edited by P. W. Grobbelaar, 1–13. Cape Town: Tafelberg, 1980.
Van Warmelo, D. S. *On Commando*. Johannesburg: Ad Donker, 1977.
Veg en Vlug: Manne en Vroue vertel hul Ware Verhale uit die Anglo-Boereoorlo. Compiled by J. C. Steyn. Cape Town: Tafelberg, 1999.

Venter, W. H. "Die Geskiedenis van Winburg tot 1902." Unpublished MA diss., University of the Orange Free State, Bloemfontein, 1974.

Viljoen, E. H. "Virginia, 1892–1980: Van Spoorweghalte tot Mynboudorp." Unpublished MA diss., University of Pretoria, 1994.

Wade, E., G. Phillips, and A. Bradley. *Constitutional Law: An Outline of the Law and Practice of the Constitution including Central and Local Government, the Citizen and the State, and Administrative Law.* 8th ed. London: Longman, 1970.

Watt, S. A. "The Skirmish at Senekal: The Battle of Biddulphsberg, May 1900." *Military History Journal* 8, no. 6 (1991). www.samilitaryhistory.org/vol086swhtml. Accessed 21 Feb. 2015.

Warwick, Peter. *Black People and the South African War, 1899–1902.* Johannesburg: Ravan, 1983.

Weber, Max. *Eighteen Months under General De la Rey: Being the Diary of the Swiss Geologist Max Weber Who Fought for the Boers in the Western Transvaal during the Anglo-Boer War.* Translated from the German by Juliet Marais Louw. Pretoria: Bienedell, 1999.

Weideman, H.J.S. "Die Geskiedenis van die Ekonomiese Ontwikkeling van die Oranje-Vrystaat met Verwysing na die Ontstaan van die Armblankedom (1830–1870)." Unpublished MA diss., University College of the Orange Free State, Bloemfontein, 1946.

Wessels, André. "Boer Guerrilla and British Counter-Guerrilla Operations in South Africa, 1899 to 1902." *Scientia Militaria* 39, no. 2 (2011): 1–24.

———. *Die Militêre Rol van Swart Mense, Bruin Mense en Indiërs tydens die Anglo-Boereoorlog (1899–1902).* Bloemfontein: War Museum of the Boer Republics, 1998.

Wessels, Jannie. "Ryswater na kleilat-gooiery." www.boerevryheid.co.za/forums/archive/index.php/t-30233.html. Accessed 18 Feb. 2015.

Wessels, S.J.C., and S.F.G Wessels. *Die Nageslag van Johannes (Jan) Wessels.* 2 vols. Stellenbosch: S.F.G. Wessels, 1999.

Wilcox, C. "Australia's Boer War: The War in South Africa, 1899–1902." Adapted extracts in *Wartime: Official Magazine of the Australian War Memorial.* http://www.awm.gov.au/wartime/21/article.asp. Accessed 7 May 2004.

Wilson, A.H.J. "The Railway War: A Study and Assessment of the British Defeat of the Boer Guerillas, South Africa, 1899–1902." MA diss., University of New Brunswick, 1993.

Wilson, Sarah. *South African Memories: Social, Warlike, and Sporting, from Diaries written at the Time.* London: Arnold, 1909.

Witnesses to War: Personal Documents of the Anglo-Boer War from the Collections of the South African Library. Edited by Karel Schoeman. Cape Town: Human & Rousseau, 1998.

Worsfold, W. B. *Lord Milner's Work in South Africa, 1897–1902.* London: Murray, 1906.

Index

JOHN BOJE is a research associate of the Department of Historical and Heritage Studies at the University of Pretoria. His four grandparents lived in the Winburg district and their varied experiences of the war were typical of those recorded here.

The University of Illinois Press
is a founding member of the
Association of American University Presses.

Composed in 9.75/13 Sabon
by Jim Proefrock
at the University of Illinois Press
Manufactured by Sheridan Books, Inc.

University of Illinois Press
1325 South Oak Street
Champaign, IL 61820-6903
www.press.uillinois.edu